# ADORNO AND DEMOCRACY

# ADORNO
### AND
# DEMOCRACY

## THE AMERICAN YEARS

SHANNON L. MARIOTTI

UNIVERSITY PRESS OF KENTUCKY

Scholarly publisher for the Commonwealth,
serving Bellarmine University, Berea College, Centre College of Kentucky, Eastern
Kentucky University, The Filson Historical Society, Georgetown College, Kentucky
Historical Society, Kentucky State University, Morehead State University, Murray State
University, Northern Kentucky University, Transylvania University, University
of Kentucky, University of Louisville, and Western Kentucky University.
All rights reserved.

*Editorial and Sales Offices:* The University Press of Kentucky
663 South Limestone Street, Lexington, Kentucky 40508-4008
www.kentuckypress.com

An earlier version of part of chapter 3 was published as "Damaged Life as Exuberant
Vitality in America: Adorno, Alienation and the Psychic Economy," in *Telos* 149
(Winter 2009). Earlier versions of sections of chapter 4 were published as "Adorno on
the Radio: Democratic Leadership as Democratic Pedagogy," in *Political Theory* 42, no.
4 (2014).

Library of Congress Cataloging-in-Publication Data

Names: Mariotti, Shannon L. (Shannon Lee), author.
Title: Adorno and democracy : the American years / Shannon L. Mariotti.
Description: Lexington, Kentucky : University Press of Kentucky, 2016. |
   Includes bibliographical references and index.
Identifiers: LCCN 2016011183| ISBN 9780813167336 (hardcover : alk. paper) |
   ISBN 9780813167404 (pdf) | ISBN 9780813167398 (epub)
Subjects: LCSH: Adorno, Theodor W., 1903-1969. | Democracy—Philosophy. |
   Democracy—United States.
Classification: LCC B3199.A34 M28 2016 | DDC 320.092—dc23
LC record available at http://lccn.loc.gov/2016011183

This book is printed on acid-free paper meeting the requirements of the American
National Standard for Permanence in Paper for Printed Library Materials.

∞

Manufactured in the United States of America.

Member of the Association of
American University Presses

To David, again and always.

To our son, Walter Robert Rando,
  who came into the world alongside this book.

# Contents

# Preface

A considerable part of the leading German intelligentsia, including Adorno, have taken up residence in the "Grand Hotel Abyss" . . . "a beautiful hotel, equipped with every comfort, on the edge of an abyss, of nothingness, of absurdity. And the daily contemplation of the abyss between excellent meals or artistic entertainments, can only heighten the enjoyment of the subtle comforts offered."
—Georg Lukács, *The Theory of the Novel*

Horkheimer: What view, for example, are we to take of America?
Adorno: We have to believe that things can come out right in the end.
—Theodor Adorno and Max Horkheimer, *Towards a New Manifesto*

Gloomy. Pessimistic. Apolitical. Elitist. Escapist. Withdrawn. An aesthete. A cultural mandarin. Until very recently, any time Theodor W. Adorno was mentioned, one of these descriptions usually accompanied his name. Georg Lukács's now famous characterization of Adorno, noted above, is worth recalling because of how it has captured the various justifications for excluding Adorno from meaningful conversations about politics and democracy, much less political theory and democratic theory. The works that Adorno is most well known for in the Anglophone world, *Dialectic of Enlightenment* and the writings collected as *The Culture Industry,* have been received in ways that paint their author as a relentlessly negative critic of modern society who has nothing productive to say about political action, citizenship, or democracy. After all, what could be positive about a thinker who wrote a book titled *Negative Dialectics*? This impression of pessimism and elitism is only intensified if the United States is brought into the equation. As the story goes, Adorno, a German Jew, was exiled to the "cultural wasteland" of America during World War II, and here he composed *Dialectic of Enlightenment* and the writings on the culture industry, as well as the collection of aphorisms titled *Minima Moralia: Reflections from Damaged Life*. This conventional framing of Adorno, familiar to anyone who studies critical theory, serves to justify dismissing him as a politically relevant thinker, much less as someone who sought to inform the everyday practice of democracy in the United States. How could this gloomy, pessimistic resident of the Grand Hotel Abyss have anything valuable to say about American democracy?

This book will illuminate a very different Adorno, one who is often surprising in both style and substance. My research presents Adorno as not just a social theorist, but a political theorist, and not just a political theorist, but a democratic theorist. *Adorno and Democracy* shows how he puts forward a valuable theory and practice of democracy that advocates for a specific type of democratic leadership in the form of democratic pedagogy. Not only does Adorno argue for this combined practice of critique and pedagogy, but he also enacts it himself to give us an example of a mode of democratic leadership that is uniquely adapted to navigating the dangers, threats, and pathologies of modernity. The Adorno presented in this book not only rejects any kind of apolitical retreat, but also addresses the pathologies of *existing* (so-called) democracy in America to better inform a more meaningful, substantive, and robust *future* practice of democratic citizenship.

The second epigraph quoted above gives us a new picture of Adorno that comes into focus through analyzing a set of largely unexplored texts that he composed originally in English and directed toward an American audience: these are the works that are the focus of this book. The reader may be struck by the thought that the passage I quote does not even sound like the Adorno we have come to know. Indeed, the essays, books, and radio addresses that *Adorno and Democracy* analyzes show us just how partial that conventional image of Adorno was all along. In different ways, this project complicates and completes our picture of him, forcing us to contemplate some tensions between these two Adornos, but mostly allowing us to see overall consistencies throughout the early and late Adorno, the American and German Adorno, the practical and theoretical Adorno, the Adorno who was broadcast on the radio and the Adorno who wrote *Negative Dialectics* in dense, difficult language geared toward the specialist. The portrait of Adorno presented here makes us rethink a figure we think we know. We are at a point where we have resources available to begin to piece together Adorno's own democratic theory and practice. So this book raises the bar for thinking about Adorno's politics, moving beyond the stage of asserting that he *has* one and toward articulating what it looks like in action.

None of the existing scholarship makes the two primary (and linked) assertions this book will prove: first, that Adorno has a political theory that runs through his corpus and finds the most sharply distilled expression in his thoughts on democratic leadership as democratic pedagogy; and, second, that Adorno develops this positive democratic project in his writings on American political culture. There are limits to existing attempts to recuperate the political aspects of Adorno's work, and even the scholarship that is invested in reshaping the traditional image of a gloomy, apolitical Adorno does not go far enough. As the writings I will explore show, Adorno was deeply critical of liberalism and liberal democracy, but not democracy per se. He directed his skepticism toward existing forms of it, but he did not reject democracy in a wholesale way. Indeed, he wanted to encourage the development of the nascent substantive forms of democracy that he recognized in the practice of citizens in the United States.

But the whole of this political theory and this form of democratic practice are illuminated only when we read Adorno's largely neglected writings on American political culture—the English-language compositions that are the focus of this book—against the backdrop of his larger theory of negative dialectics. And because few scholars have analyzed these texts except as social history or a biography of Adorno's time in America, they are valuable missing pieces of the puzzle for understanding this complex thinker. Rethinking Adorno through the lens of this key set of writings helps illuminate the important ways that democracy fits into his work generally. The other Adorno whom this book finds, in English, in America, reframes and reconfigures the conventional image of a critical theorist whose contributions to political theory and to democratic theory and practice we have missed, and perhaps been too quick to dismiss, constrain, and limit. Writing in America, on America, for Americans, Adorno works to turn the pernicious problems of democracy into productive possibilities.

Adorno's thoughts on American culture give us a kind of updated twentieth-century version of Alexis de Tocqueville's *Democracy in America,* published in 1835. My project is not a comparison of Adorno and Tocqueville. I focus on Adorno exclusively. But thinking about how Adorno saw his own work as sympathetic with Tocqueville's investigations roots this member of the Frankfurt School in the American context and also highlights how centrally concerned Adorno became with democracy in America. Indeed, Adorno's own explorations of twentieth-century democracy in America reflect Tocqueville's in terms of substance, perspective, and style. Both Tocqueville and Adorno were European visitors to the United States with the valuable critical distance of outsiders. Both took the pulse of democracy in America primarily by looking not at political institutions but at the everyday lives of citizens, their customs, habits, and daily exercise of popular sovereignty (or lack thereof). Both also examined the elements working to undermine the individual's ability to truly self-govern. Both explored the connections between social psychology and democracy. Both characterized a core problem of democracy in America in similar ways, in terms of what Tocqueville called the "tyranny of the majority."[1]

This is a problem that uniquely pervades American democracy and is upheld in complex ways by political structures, economic conditions, and the mindset of the people. For Tocqueville, this tyranny is a pervasive feature of democracy in America that works on how we think and feel to drive out multiplicity, plurality, individuality, and independence: that which seems to be other or different is eclipsed by conformity with the majority, assimilated into the majority. Adorno's critique of American democracy resonates deeply with Tocqueville's concerns regarding the sociopsychological elements of authoritarianism and how the majority itself can tyrannize. A century later, Adorno finds that the problems Tocqueville identified have only worsened:

> The analysis Tocqueville offered a century ago has in the meantime proved wholly accurate. Under the private culture monopoly it is a fact that 'tyranny leaves the body free and directs its attack at the soul. The ruler no longer says: You must think as I do or die. He says: You are free not to think as I do; your life, your property, everything shall remain yours, but from this day on you are a stranger among us.' Not to conform means to be rendered powerless, economically and therefore spiritually—to be 'self-employed.' When the outsider is excluded from the concern, he can only too easily be accused of incompetence."[2]

But the story of democracy in America didn't end with the tyranny of the majority for Tocqueville, and it doesn't end with the culture industry and authoritarianism for Adorno. Ultimately, for both, there was a possibility of redemption. Both were interested in the small-scale everyday ways that citizens worked against these pernicious aspects of what Adorno would call "pseudo-democracy" in America. Both explored the "substantive forms of democracy"—Adorno's words—that nevertheless existed, in a latent fashion, beneath the authoritarian structures, beneath the tyranny of the majority, that might be drawn out toward the more meaningful practice of democracy.

Thinking of Adorno as a twentieth-century version of Tocqueville, and thinking of how both are deeply critical of democracy in America and at the same time attentive to the existence of redemptive cultural forms, also helps makes sense of the disjuncture scholars have identified between Adorno's various depictions of America. When we move beyond *The Culture Industry* and *Minima Moralia* and read the works on American culture that Adorno wrote in English during his time in the United States, then the jarring quality of Adorno's early and late thoughts on America dissolves and dissipates. In fact, even in his early years in America, Adorno recognized the existence of these substantive forms of democracy and identified important cultural countertendencies that could foster greater democratic enlightenment. Drawing from *Current of Music, The Psychological Technique of Martin Luther Thomas' Radio Addresses,* and even *The Stars Down to Earth,* we can see how Adorno recognizes and tries to mobilize these valuable countertendencies. Thus, the idea that there are two sharply opposed, contradictory, incommensurable, and inexplicable portraits of Adorno's views on American democracy is not really accurate when we consider the full corpus of his writings on the United States. Like Tocqueville, Adorno critiques American democracy to inform a more robust and meaningful practice of it. Ultimately, the portrait of another Adorno that these pages build up, fill in, and flesh out contains lessons we still need to hear today, over a half century later, to help us realize another America.

# Introduction

# Another Adorno

> We want to face the danger of this sea, not for the sake of fleeing to cultural islands, but for better navigation. Any investigator who does not see the dangers of that sea and who simply allows himself to be drugged by its grandeur, and who sees its waves as waves of unbroken progress, is very likely to be drowned.
>
> —Adorno, *Current of Music: Elements of a Radio Theory*

In the early 1940s two distinct images and metaphors seem to have been swirling around in Theodor Adorno's head. One soon became part of Frankfurt School lore, immediately recognizable to anyone who studies this circle of scholars or one of its most famous members. The other was never well known in the first place and has been all but lost to history. The first image is the "message in a bottle," or *Flaschenpost*. There is a history to this metaphor, and given its significance to the present-day understanding of Adorno and the Frankfurt School, one can find similar versions of the same anecdote recounted in the scholarship. According to the story that passed from Hanns Eisler to Leo Lowenthal, soon after the beginning of World War II, in the early 1940s, after Adorno had moved from New York to California, some of the émigré members of the Institute for Social Research were on a beach in Southern California: "During a beach party where much alcohol had been consumed, so the story goes, Adorno is said to have launched the idea of the message in a bottle. Someone asked, 'What's it supposed to say?' Eisler is said to have answered in broad Viennese dialect, 'I feel *so* awful! [*Mir iss' soo mies!*],' and everyone burst out laughing." Horkheimer had also used the language of a message in a bottle to describe his and Adorno's work in a 1940 letter.[1] Some years later, in part 3 of *Minima*

*Moralia*, dated 1946–1947, Adorno also invokes this image. In aphorism 133, translated as "Contribution to Intellectual History," Adorno discusses Nietzsche's misunderstood genius and his attitude toward "ethical culture," having "rightly decided to break off prematurely its communication with the world." As Adorno writes, "Even at that time the hope of leaving behind messages in bottles on the flood of barbarism bursting on Europe was an amiable illusion."[2] This idea of a message that had to be placed in a bottle and sent off to future generations because it could not be heard in its own day and time became a metaphor to describe much of the work of first-generation critical theory, shorthand for Adorno's self-understanding of his own writings.

The second image, presented in the epigraph above, is recorded in *Current of Music: Elements of a Radio Theory*, a study that Adorno composed originally in English between his arrival in New York in 1938 and departure for Los Angeles in 1941. Again, we have the symbols of water and a message, but with some important differences. Here we have an image of the critic not sending a message in a bottle out over the water to the future, but turning and facing the choppy waters, to learn to navigate through them in the immediate present. Emphasizing the political importance of engaging the cultural object of the radio, Adorno writes that the critic must "dispense with the suspicion that we want to save an island of genuine live music against the threatening sea of mechanization and reification."[3] Instead, he says, we should recognize that radio, "especially its shortcomings," contains "indicators of contradictions in our whole art life and ultimately in our whole social life."[4] Critics must engage the productive contradictions that the cultural object of radio encapsulates.[5] In direct opposition to the "message in a bottle" imagery, the epigraph that begins this chapter strikes a different note. Here, instead of rather impotently casting a message on the waters and hoping it may be received in the future, Adorno rejects withdrawal or retreat, choosing instead to actively navigate difficult waters.

The task of this book is to amplify the broadcast of this second transmission. Ironically, Adorno's first message in a bottle *was* ultimately received. But his communication containing this second powerfully orienting symbol was missed and never picked up. The first image sent out over the water is still the predominant image of Adorno: a figure withdrawing from the pathological culture of his own day, especially during his "exile" in America, having lost hope about the possibility of engaging and changing that culture, resorting to sending out missives to the future containing his critical insights.[6] Here we are presented with an Adorno who is apolitical, escapist, elitist, a cultural mandarin engaging in gallows humor and laughing on the beach about the horror of modernity.

But the second image of Adorno, the critic turning and facing the dangerous waters of the present, engaging with the world immediately surrounding him, was circulating at the same time this first message in a bottle was supposedly being cast out. And this second image complicates the conventional image of Adorno. In the writings that are the focus of this book, Adorno turns and faces both the problems and possibilities of democracy in the United States. *Adorno and Democracy* adopts a similar posture, turning and facing the problems and possibilities of reading this difficult thinker as a twentieth-century democratic theorist, not just to discover a message in a bottle, but to help us chart our current position and navigate our future course.

For this second transmission, the medium matters too, not just the message. This book analyzes *Current of Music: Elements of a Radio Theory, The Psychological Technique of Martin Luther Thomas' Radio Addresses, The Stars Down to Earth,* and several essays and addresses composed in English and offered to citizens of this country. These texts represent only a portion of the surprisingly extensive list of works Adorno composed originally in English.[7] The specific compositions I deal with are selected because they represent the moments when he is most engaged in exploring the political landscape of the United States. The English compositions I analyze are unique in that they indicate an attempt, not always successful, to communicate more directly with the American people and to shape the practice of American democracy. I want to emphasize the moments when Adorno speaks to the public in a different register, to try to cultivate a more autonomous, more truly democratic citizen.

Most of the writings that are the focus of this book concern popular media, specific radio programs, addresses by well-known radio demagogues of the day, as well as newspaper items such as the *Los Angeles Times*'s astrology column. Here Adorno's thoughts on democratic leadership as democratic pedagogy are *broadcast,* in several senses of the word. In focusing on radio, for example, Adorno writes about a cultural object that was an important part of the everyday life of many Americans.[8] He speaks more directly to a wider audience of listeners, drawing out the countertendencies that exist in their immediate material world, illuminating the potential of their own latent responses to the radio. He communicates in a more accessible manner, translating his theory of negative dialectics into the language of leadership and education. And, finally, Adorno even tried to transmit his message about the radio over the radio. He made extensive use of the radio himself, both in the United States and in Germany after his return to that country.[9] In his radio addresses he uses the medium to critique the medium, to turn cultural pathologies into tools to strengthen the practice of American democracy.

Despite their richness, however, when the pieces that are the focus of this book have been studied at all, they have largely been analyzed as biography, as a cultural and social history of Adorno's "exile" in America.[10] But these works are significant for more than their historical value.[11] My analysis of these English-language compositions takes place against the backdrop of Adorno's entire corpus and is informed by his broader theory of negative dialectics. Indeed, there is a high degree of consistency between Adorno's concerns and commitments from his early writings, composed under pressure and in exile in America, and the later writings that are of a more explicitly philosophical nature. Adorno's theory and practice of negative dialectics are constantly at work in all his writings, even in nascent form and even when not explicitly named.

I do not, however, focus on these specific English compositions to "claim" Adorno for American readers or to avoid Adorno's German writings. Adorno's time in the United States prompted an overt consideration of American political culture, aimed at fostering a more robust practice of democracy. My focus on these particular texts is motivated by their relevance to my orienting questions about democracy in America: these are the texts in which Adorno seems to be trying to speak in English to Americans *about* the state of their own political culture. I am interested in the American reception of Adorno, but specifically in the English Adorno the *demos* might have received directly, not necessarily the German Adorno who was and is translated for American audiences.[12] I analyze Adorno's own performance of a unique form of democratic leadership as democratic pedagogy, as he translates a nascent form of negative dialectics directly to an American audience to inform them of the problems and possibilities of their own political culture.

## Laying Out Adorno's Argument about Democracy: The Organization of the Book

Ultimately, *Adorno and Democracy* traces the interrelations and connections among a number of key ideas that show up in Adorno's writings, often in different places and in different kinds of texts directed toward different audiences. The constellation of concepts that this book revolves around concerns the material objects of the world; the nonidentical elements that surround us; thinking, feeling, and the capacity for critique; the universal praxis of humans; alienation; negative dialectics; leadership; education and pedagogy; and democracy. Adorno himself writes about all these ideas, though some are more well known and more closely associated with him than others. But he doesn't always draw the connections between them or show how they work together to add up to a theory and practice of democracy. Adorno doesn't tend to write about negative dialectics and democracy in the same place, for example. He doesn't discuss the nonidentical and education in the same text. So this book will connect those dots in a more explicit way.

The chapters of this book build on each other, but the book also operates in a dialectical and not just a progressive, linear, unidirectional fashion. Each chapter is informed by the others in a way that reflects the development of my own understanding of Adorno and democracy in the United States. The parts of the book are laid out in the order that makes the most sense, moving from abstract theory to concrete plan to practice. But, in fact, we can really fully appreciate the democratic commitments of negative dialectics only if we think about it through the lens of an essay like "Democratic Leadership and Mass Manipulation." And we better understand the significance of Adorno's writings on American culture when we read them in terms of his larger theory. So the chapters of the book really enrich and inform each other in multiple directions and bear on each other moving backward and forward.

I have organized the book to present Adorno's argument about democracy in terms of how I see it developing, starting with the problems and pathologies within American democracy to be overcome and moving through each stage of his "solution," from our material experience of the everyday world to the practice of critique, leadership, pedagogy, and his efforts to draw out the "countertendencies" of American culture toward creating more robust and substantive forms of democracy. Given how closely the organization of the book is tied to the overall argument I make, I will lay out my thesis about Adorno and democracy in America at the same time I discuss the structure of the book.

The first chapter, "Seeing the Large-Scale System: The Pathologies of Modern America and Pseudo-Democracy," lays out the problem to be addressed, exploring the pathological elements of (ostensible) democracy in America, as depicted by Adorno in *Current of Music, The Psychological Technique of Martin Luther Thomas' Radio Addresses,* and *The Stars Down to Earth.* It gives us a sense of the problems that motivate Adorno's project of democratic leadership as democratic pedagogy. In this chapter we gain a fuller picture of the aspects of American culture that Adorno's writings both explicate and seek to remedy.

Here Adorno is primarily concerned with what he calls "pseudo-democracy" in America. From his view, the dominant political and economic culture of liberal capitalism in the United States works against its purported values, making citizens passive and obedient and cultivating a sense of infantile helplessness. There are fascistic tendencies in the way this culture exercises an authoritarianism over dependent citizens, but for Adorno, as for Marcuse, this form of totalitarianism, this "unfreedom," is often "comfortable," "smooth," and "reasonable," something that citizens consent to, even if that consent ultimately turns out to be manufactured.[13] But Adorno comes up against the same obstacle that has challenged other critical theorists and democratic theorists. He is deeply critical of existing forms of mass democracy because of how the structures, institutions, and norms of liberal capitalism work to produce obedient, unthinking, and conformist subjects. The goal is to strengthen the everyday practice of democracy on the part of citizens by cultivating their capacity for negative, critical thought that can go against the grain of the given, that can disrupt and then reconfigure the status quo. Adorno wants to fulfill the promise of democracy by fostering the kind of dispositional and intellectual, social and psychic, change on the part of individuals that would allow "the people" to truly wield power and rule, for the *demos* to have *kratos*.

But how to effect change toward a more robust democracy in a way that is itself democratic? How to push and prompt people to become more autonomous critical thinkers and actors in ways that are consistent with the principles of the desired democracy, without just putting into place new masters and new hierarchical authorities for people to obey? How to find a means to the end where the means is also consistent with the end? How to work toward realizing the alternative world that the practice of critique points toward in a way that itself prefigures the society that is trying to be achieved? Adorno does propose a solution to these dilemmas and an answer to the perennial question that follows his kind of critique, the "what is to be done?" question. The next two chapters of the book begin to lay out Adorno's more positive and prescriptive democratic project.

In chapter 2, "Experience as a Precondition for Meaningful Democracy: Sensory Perception, Affect, and Materialism," I analyze the fundamentally important place of experience in Adorno's political theory. He puts forward a theory of democracy that focuses on experience and that sees the promise of democracy—the idea that the people can have power and authority, the idea that the *demos* can have *kratos*—as fulfilled when humans exercise their fundamental capacity and their universal praxis of sensing, perceiving, and becoming attuned to the particular qualities of the material and ideological world that surrounds them. As a materialist, Adorno thinks that the world around us contains qualities that provoke us to both think and *feel* against the given, against the status quo, against what is presented to us as natural, inevitable, and just the way things are. These particular qualities, which he calls the nonidentical, ask us to engage in the critical practices that are vital for democratic citizenship, if only we could learn to listen to their dissonant and disruptive calls, which are more often drowned out by other forces of modernity. So for Adorno, democracy is, at a fundamental and essential level, about trying to experience the world around us differently, trying to see, hear, feel, perceive, and sense in a deeper, more sensitive, and more immediate way. Meaningful democracy is about experience, and the promise of democracy is fulfilled when we can open ourselves up to the nonidentical qualities of the world whose voices and lessons can work to make us more critical but also more compassionate, that can help us think against, but also feel against, the world we are given, that can enlighten us but also make us sensitive, as opposed to hard, cold, or numb.

If we were to draw a flowchart that schematizes the key terms and concepts of Adorno's constellation, the starting point would be a materialist's attention to the objects of the world around us. Adorno's theory begins, like Marx's, by granting "preponderance" to the objects that surround us in our everyday lives. These objects, Adorno says, contain contradictory, dissonant qualities—the nonidentical—that resist being fitted into the dominant systems and logics of modernity. These nonidentical elements, these particular qualities of the surrounding world, call out to us in their resistance to "what is" and their ruptures of the given status quo, but their voices tend to be silenced by the same aspects of modernity that they try to resist: the capitalist logic of abstract exchange, the idealist tendency toward identity thinking, and other trappings of modernity such as the culture industry. Given all this, Adorno's efforts are directed toward trying to cut through these (at best) distracting and (at worst) violent logics, to allow humans to engage in the practice of "thinking."

Thinking for Adorno is a praxis that humans universally share *as* humans, which is based on listening to, attending to, the nonidentical qualities of the material world. Thinking is not necessarily a rarefied intellectual activity for Adorno but, rather, is the ability to perceive and to experience our circumstances in a more direct and immediate way that allows us to see and hear the nonidentical qualities that tell us that things are not as they should be, that tell us something is wrong, that push us to resist the world we are given, and that point toward alternative possibilities. Thinking is something that all humans can do, for Adorno: it defines our humanity. But thinking is not just a capacity that is inside humans. Rather, it is best understood as an openness to hearing what the nonidentical elements of the material world have to teach us. So thinking is a kind of feeling, a kind of experiencing, a kind of perception that defines us as humans. And using this mode of experience then to think against, and to feel against, the world we are given—to negate it—is to engage in the practice of critique. But when we cease to think, we suffer a loss of self: we become alienated. This form of loss under modernity, this numbing inability to think against, can be experienced as a psychically painful loss that we experience as suffering. But, as Adorno discovered during his time in America, alienation might also take the form of a kind of automated, robotic, cheerful normality.

But how does democracy fit into all this? In chapter 3, "Critique and the Practice of Democracy: Negative Dialectics, Autonomy, and Compassion," I build on these arguments about experience to analyze the democratic value of Adorno's practice of critique, to show how his method of negative dialectics is motivated by fundamentally democratic concerns. Adorno says that critique is the essence of democracy, that democracy is defined by the practice of critique. In essence, this means that fulfilling the promise of democracy relies on a certain way of experiencing other bodies, a certain mode of comportment, a certain disposition. To truly think and feel against what we are given as second nature, as inevitable, as just the ways things are—and thereby to engage in the practice of critique, which is the essence of democracy for Adorno—we need to attune ourselves to, open ourselves up to, the nonidentical, the contradictory, the disruptive, the disharmonious. We need to try to experience our world more deeply and directly, without the framing filters of conventions, norms, assumptions. Thus, for Adorno, fulfilling the promise of democracy is fundamentally about learning to think, feel, and experience in a different way.

The next two chapters lay out Adorno's plan for a mode of democratic leadership that works through a democratic form of pedagogical practice. Chapter 4 is titled "Democratic Leadership: Egalitarian Guidance and a Plan for Empowering the People," and chapter 5 is titled "Democratic Pedagogy: Resistance and an Alternative Model for Civic Education." Here I draw from essays and radio addresses in which Adorno discusses the need for specifically democratic modes of leadership and pedagogy. In these pieces we see Adorno speaking in a much more accessible register and translating his theory for a broader audience in surprising ways. A very important part of these two chapters concerns Adorno's short essay, composed in English for an American audience and first published in an edited volume on leadership, titled "Democratic Leadership and Mass Manipulation." This little-known essay provided a great deal of illumination for the project as a whole as I began researching. It works as a linchpin between the theory sections of chapters 2 and 3 and the practice sections of the chapters that follow. In this short essay on democratic leadership, we see Adorno introducing and translating his theory of negative dialectics to a wider audience and outlining a concrete plan for how to put it into practice, a plan that he works to carry out, as I show, in the writings and radio addresses I analyze in chapter 6.

Along with "Democratic Leadership and Mass Manipulation," a set of writings on pedagogy provides the key to understanding the political significance of Adorno's writings on American culture. These essays and addresses on education and teaching were composed primarily after Adorno's return to Germany. Together, they provide the lens through which I analyze the democratic value of *Current of Music, The Psychological Technique of Martin Luther Thomas' Radio Addresses,* and *The Stars Down to Earth.* Though Adorno did not publish *Negative Dialectics* until 1966, after his return to Germany, these earlier studies of American culture exemplify the kind of critique he outlines in his major theoretical statement and help us appreciate how democracy figures into his corpus more broadly.

The final chapter of the book mirrors the first, in that it presents the "solution" to the "problem" as it is laid out in chapter 1. Chapter 6, "Seeing Small-Scale Resistance: Turning Countertendencies into Vaccines to Strengthen Democratic Practice," shows how Adorno attempts to put into practice the theory of democracy and the plan for democratic leadership articulated in the earlier chapters. Returning to the same writings on American culture explored in the first chapter, I draw out the "countertendencies" and "vaccines" that we can identify in *Current of Music, The Psychological Technique of Martin Luther Thomas' Radio Addresses,* and *The Stars Down to Earth.*

In this final chapter, I show how Adorno identifies small-scale, modest, less visible "substantive democratic forms" in the United States that act as countertendencies that might be drawn out as a vaccine against more prevalent fascistic elements of pseudo-democracy in America. In his writings on American culture, we see Adorno employing the same mode of critique that Marx applies to the commodity, but with a different object: Adorno's critique is directed toward an exploration of the radio or the *Los Angeles Times*'s astrology column, for example, as microcosms of the larger modern capitalist culture in the United States. Adorno explores these particular things not just to lambaste and lament American culture as "wrong life." For a long time this was the dominant interpretation of Adorno's writings from the presumed cultural wasteland of California. But Adorno aims to illuminate how even these seemingly insignificant cultural objects actually contain important nonidentical qualities—countertendencies—that protest against and can be used to unsettle the problematic conditions that they otherwise participate in and uphold.

Adorno's writings on democracy in America also exemplify his method of negative dialectics. He focuses on particular material objects that contain elements of the larger modern capitalist culture in microcosm, and—in a mode of critique that is also a form of praxis—draws out the typically unseen qualities that contain a utopian moment in their protest against given conditions. Those who have seen Adorno's writings on America as wholly gloomy and critical miss the unconventional politics that he is performing through his critiques. For these reasons, Adorno's writings on American culture must be read in terms of his theory and practice of negative dialectics for our picture of him to avoid the problematic distortions it has been subjected to in the past. In this way, Adorno sees the potential for change—what might be— arising from the tensions and contradictions—the countertendencies—that exist within a problematic status quo. Thus, even the predominant retrograde qualities of pseudo-democracy can be approached in ways that might cultivate what he calls "democratic enlightenment." And, indeed, this kind of unspectacular, small-scale, everyday recuperation that takes place in and among existing pathologies seems, for Adorno, to represent the best hope for the creation of more meaningful democracy in America.

Through these chapters that lay out Adorno's theory and practice of democracy, we will see how the thinker associated with the idea of the "totally administered world" in fact thought there were ways that U.S. citizens could work against that seeming system. Adorno was never as entirely pessimistic about the possibility of resistance as some of his critics have made him out to be, as a careful understanding of the practice of critique immediately makes clear. Critique and negative dialectics are a kind of praxis, and they even encapsulate a utopian moment of hope that "the way things are" is not the way things have to be, that we could order our worlds in alternative ways. But even if reading Adorno as the gloomy pessimist who draws a portrait of the totally administered world of modernity as an impenetrable system is in fact a flawed and partial interpretation, it is certainly fair to say that at moments he focuses his gaze on the world around him at the level of the system in ways that seem inconsistent with the micro-level countertendencies and small-scale forms of resistance that I discuss in this book.

This is all to show that if Adorno thought that the logic of identity, the capitalist system of abstract exchange, and idealism worked together in the modern era to create what could at times look like an unbroken pattern of domination, he also knew that was only part of the story, only one moment in his critique. He knew the value of shifting his gaze. Adorno is the thinker who is perhaps most closely associated with the idea that modernity is a system, that the culture industry and capitalism, for example, form a net that ensnares every aspect of our lives. And yet even Adorno recognizes that we can always look past the realities of this entangling system of modernity to the small-scale subversions that people enact against it. If we keep our gaze focused on these networks of domination, however, we will fail to see the little ways, micro as opposed to macro, that people operate against the logics that otherwise order their lives. But we can't look up and down simultaneously, and it is difficult to focus on the large and small, macro and micro, abstract and particular, at the same time. So Adorno shifts his gaze.

In the writings on American culture that I analyze here, he looks at the little things people do to throw wrenches in the system, so to speak, even when it is not necessarily their goal to bring down the system. Adorno sees substantive forms of democracy that people practice and enact, despite large-scale pathologies, and he shows how people work against the system even when they are not consciously being critical of the prevailing ideology. In an interesting reversal, Adorno shows how Americans resist the dominant ideology in small ways even when they are not aware that they are resisting. Usually, critical theorists—including Adorno—emphasize the unconscious ways that ideology operates on people, not the unconscious ways they work against it. But this almost instinctual refusal of the given culture industry is actually the kind of subversion Adorno describes in these writings, given what he sees as the deeply rooted democratic inclinations that persist in people's dispositions and modes of comportment. Again, these substantive forms of democracy exist *despite* the overarching ways that citizens are made into dependent objects by the forces of modernity.

Adorno, of course, makes his statements about these countertendencies not naively, but with full knowledge of the power of the forces of modernity. The countertendencies to which these substantive forms of democracy give rise exist in the crevasses of the systematizing logics of modernity—in fractures that run alongside, beneath, and between all the pathologies he also illuminates. The forces of modernity he explores in his work—the culture industry, the logic of capitalism and abstract exchange, identity thinking, and idealism—as well as the pseudo-democracy he identifies in the United States are all *systems* that work without an agent, that work subtly and in complex networks. But they are not totalizing or all-encompassing systems. There are fractures. And in his writings on American culture, Adorno is focused on highlighting these ruptures, these moments when people unknowingly resist the world they are given. Turning these nascent and unconscious counter-tendencies of resistance into actual, conscious, politicized forms of resistance is the goal of Adorno's project of democratic leadership through the form of democratic pedagogy.

Adorno's aim is to illuminate the social, political, and economic forces that undermine autonomy, through an immanent critique *with* people to cultivate their understanding of how existing powers actually work against the democratic ideals they ostensibly support. Then, the hope and the goal are that this new critical consciousness prompts people to act, to build more meaningfully democratic social structures, institutions, and norms in the world around them—all of which truly try to give power to the people. At the same time, these individuals will also be living their own everyday lives in more robustly democratic ways, which demonstrate their own power by their ability to negate and to critique, but also by their ability to do the other things that Adorno sees as vitally important to democracy, such as attending to the suffering and pain of others.

Ultimately, as this book shows, exiled in the United States, writing in English for an American audience, Adorno is engaged in the kind of world-building enterprise that defines the subfield of political theory at its best, turning critique into action and discontent into empowerment. The constellation of concepts this book traces—experience, critique, negative dialectics, pedagogy, leadership, democracy—demonstrates the reparative work that Adorno performed on the practice of American citizenship during his years in the United States, as part of the world-building activity of transforming "what is" to "what should be." Or, at least, "what might be." Adorno walks us through the changes that can be made, at the level of experience and sensation, to realize the alternative possibilities for a better world that exist even within and among the pathologies of the existing world. He gives us plans and programs for how we can work on ourselves, revising our habits to try to get out from under the thumb of the various forces of modernity—the culture industry, identity thinking, the capitalist logic of abstract exchange—and instead, to fall back on the aboriginal human praxis for thinking and feeling against the given that is still always there, but bound, gagged, and blindfolded. Through conversation, through discussion, we can learn to reconnect with this more spontaneous and autonomous mode of perception that is available to us, and we can revise the self to inhabit new ethical positions and more compassionate subjective states. Through an unconventional kind of democratic leadership that operates as democratic pedagogy, we can become more attuned to the nonidentical elements of the world. We can push ourselves to experience life more fully, deeply, and immediately, and then let ourselves be unsettled by the dissonant voices we hear, the disruptive sights we see, the sensations of anxiety and unease we feel. Through the work on the self that enables such encounters with material particularity, and in conversation with others who help cultivate our critical capacities, we can be drawn toward a more meaningful practice of democracy.

## The Contributions of This Book

The rest of this introduction outlines the innovations of *Adorno and Democracy*, while also briefly showing how my argument builds on, but moves beyond, existing scholarship. (Fuller discussions of the relevant secondary literature take place in the individual chapters.) There are many advances in recent scholarship that both make my analysis of Adorno's thoughts on democracy in America possible and create a space for the kinds of questions I explore. But in each of the relevant areas for my particular project, the existing scholarship also contains limitations, shortcomings, and omissions that highlight the need for the further exploration that this particular book undertakes.

The book's first major contribution, of course, concerns a dramatically revised narrative of his relationship to the political. This book stands on the shoulders of all the recent scholarship that has productively complicated the tenacious yet flawed image of Adorno as a resident of the "Grand Hotel Abyss." Recent studies have analyzed the practical, ethical, and political dimensions of Adorno's life and work, exploring his thoughts on critique as praxis and articulating the nature of his unique modes of political engagement.[14] And, though there is much more work to be done in this area, a few scholars have begun to explore how Adorno's work might productively inform current politics.[15]

But much of the scholarship working to unsettle this traditional framing of Adorno is still quite limited in scope. Even the scholarship that is most consistent with my project is generally content to prove the point that Adorno was more engaged in contemporary politics than is commonly appreciated.

Or that Adorno's thought contains politically valuable utopian moments. Or that his aesthetics represent the political promise contained in his concept and practice of critique.[16] Or that Adorno's writings are concerned with ethics, justice, and suffering in politically important ways. Ultimately, even the scholars who seek to recuperate the political value of Adorno's thought are, by and large, still seeking to prove that he wasn't actually quite as apolitical as we thought. His work is still seen as having some major political liabilities, such as his attitude toward "the masses" and mass society, his seemingly wholesale rejection of twentieth-century liberal democracy, and his inaccessible and elitist style of writing. Even among his sympathetic readers, Adorno's writings are thought to have a more or less insurmountable democratic deficit, and his political theory seems best described in terms of utopian moments that point toward an alternative order. Indeed, many people would still assert, as Albrecht Wellmer said in a conversation with Dana Villa, that "Adorno did not have a political theory—he had a dream."[17]

Given how deeply entrenched this traditional image of Adorno has become, scholars often find themselves still working to prove that Adorno was *not* apolitical, that he was *not* wholly gloomy, that he did *not* completely hate America. In contrast, *Adorno and Democracy* will not just argue that Adorno wasn't apolitical, but will illuminate the positive political project that comes through when we read several of his largely neglected English-language compositions on American political culture in conjunction with one another and against the backdrop of this larger theoretical corpus. *Adorno and Democracy* will argue not just that Adorno wasn't wholly gloomy, but that he had a great deal of optimism and hope about what he called the "substantive forms of democracy" that persist as a part of American political culture. This book will not just argue that Adorno wasn't elitist, but will emphasize how his deep commitments to democracy shape both the form and content of these writings composed in America, directed toward U.S. citizens, and communicated in a register more accessible to a wide audience, even on the radio. And, finally, *Adorno and Democracy* will argue not just that Adorno didn't hate America, but that his time in the United States proved formative to his later thinking. The texts that are the focus of this study help us better understand how a concern with the problems and possibilities of democracy shapes the goals for Adorno's larger theory and motivates the practice of negative dialectics. As this book shows, an explicit democratic political program can be identified in Adorno's English-language writings, and once it is illuminated, we can also see how this plan for democratic leadership as democratic pedagogy runs throughout his writings.

The second major contribution of this book concerns the place of America in Adorno's theorizing. Though Adorno is most closely associated with Germany and the Frankfurt School, recent scholars have explored Adorno's complex relationship with America. Forced to flee Germany before World War II because he was Jewish, he wrote some of his most influential texts during the nearly fifteen years he spent in the United States. Researchers have begun to explore how this time in the United States was not something incidental or minor, but shaped his thought in constitutive ways.[18] Given his method of social theorizing, and his unique integration of Marxist and Freudian theory, we should not be surprised to hear that Adorno's writings attended to the conditions of the world around him and bear the imprint of the postwar culture in the United States.

But the vast majority of secondary scholarship on this theme still tends to highlight the distinction between Adorno's early, negative, and more pessimistic interpretations of the United States and his later, positive, more optimistic tone on American democracy.[19] Claus Offe's words reflect this general tendency in the literature: "Adorno offers *two* pictures of America that simply do not go together and are each as unconvincing as the other."[20] In important ways, though, the image we get of Adorno's time in America depends on the writings we read, and—even more important—how we read them and whether we study them against the backdrop of the larger theory of negative dialectics. So it is significant that almost none of this existing literature, with the significant exception of Paul Apostolidis's work, explores the neglected texts studied here. The writings I analyze help us appreciate how Adorno is simply engaged in *different moments* of the same overall critique in a way that allows us to move beyond the sense that his early and late writings on America represent oil and water.

Adorno's English-language texts make the same biting critiques and contain the same critical portrayals of this country that we see in *Minima Moralia,* for example, or *Dialectic of Enlightenment,* both written during his years in the United States. But in the English-language compositions he spends more time and energy drawing out the alternative possibilities that always, for him, exist within the nonidentical qualities of a retrograde liberal capitalist landscape. He illuminates political tools in a pathological landscape. And that is because Adorno is speaking more directly to a new audience, an American audience, and is trying to translate his theory into useful tools for everyday life. This kind of tense relationship between negative and positive, critical and prescriptive, thinking and acting, defines Adorno's method of negative dialectics. In this particular moment of his critique, he just goes further to illuminate the countertendencies of everyday life that run through American culture. In the writings that are the focus of this book, Adorno sees, at once, promising elements in the practice of American democracy as well as pernicious qualities. Indeed, his goal is to work against pseudo-democracy. But we get to this point only by using the program outlined in Adorno's essay on democratic leadership as a map to explore texts such as *Current of Music* and *The Psychological Technique of Martin Luther Thomas' Radio Addresses*. Then we can see how his interpretation of American life combines positive and negative, toward creating vaccines to strengthen the everyday practice of American democracy.

My project draws from, but moves beyond, the existing literature on Adorno in America in another important way. As I have already mentioned, to the extent that his writings on American culture have been explored, they have been read primarily by historians or social biographers, not political theorists. The two deepest treatments to date of Adorno in America, by Thomas Wheatland and David Jenemann, both explicitly distance themselves from his theory. Wheatland emphasizes that he approaches Adorno and the Frankfurt School not as a theorist, but as a historian: as he says, "I am a historian of Critical Theory, not a Critical Theorist."[21] Similarly, Jenemann gives us a social history of the America of Adorno's exile rather than a theoretical analysis of Adorno's writings in and on America. Jenemann notes that he has "tried to avoid getting caught up in the thorny, dialectically intricate arguments of both Adorno and his devotees in favor of rediscovering the America that made Adorno so profoundly suspicious and that, at the same time, he nevertheless genuinely admired."[22] In this way, however, my project aims to fill a (perhaps, for their projects, necessary) lacuna in both Wheatland's and Jenemann's valuable social histories by bringing the theory developed throughout Adorno's corpus specifically to bear on his writings on democracy in America. We do not yet have an analysis of Adorno in America that fully explores how the practice of negative dialectics relates to his writings on American culture. My project aims to bring Adorno's theory and practice of negative dialectics fully to bear on his writings on democracy in America and reads these neglected English-language compositions through the lens of his larger theory.

The third major innovation of this book is implied by what I have already outlined in the two previous sections concerning Adorno's theory and practice of negative dialectics. Reading his writings on America against the backdrop of the theory of negative dialectics helps us appreciate how, in America, Adorno performs a nascent practice of the theory he will not develop in its official form until years later. As later chapters will show, the practice of critique that Adorno develops into a theory of democratic leadership in the form of democratic pedagogy anticipates, in a more popular vernacular, his method of negative dialectics. But if understanding negative dialectics helps us understand the political significance of Adorno's English-language compositions on life in the United States, then these writings also help us better grasp the practical application of negative dialectics and give us a sense of what the theory looks like in action. So this book brings together thought and action, theory and practice, conceptualization and application—as well as the United States and Germany—to give us a more whole and complete version of Adorno, another Adorno.

The fourth innovation of my project, also previously alluded to, concerns the political significance of Adorno's thoughts on experience, specifically, how attending to the material elements of the world around us represents the starting point for his theory and practice of democracy. Previous scholars have analyzed Adorno's concept of experience.[23] But no one has connected it to his thoughts on democracy or appreciated the role that experience plays in stimulating the critical capacities that are necessary for democratic action. In Adorno's view, as we have seen, democracy begins with our ability to perceive, hear, feel, and see the world around us in deeper, more sensitive, and more immediate ways. Democracy begins with a change in disposition, whereby we try to open ourselves up to the dissonant call of the nonidentical material elements of the world around us. If we could learn to experience our material worlds more fully, the nonidentical elements that surround us would teach us lessons to make us more compassionate, but also more critical, better able to think and feel against the world we are given—and better able to engage in the practice of critique that is, for Adorno, the essence of democracy. My book shows how the robust practice of democracy that Adorno practices and advocates can be traced to his writings on experience, materialism, and the nonidentical.

The fifth contribution of *Adorno and Democracy* concerns the democratic nature of his pedagogy, as outlined in his writings on education.[24] My study builds on but moves beyond previous work in this area by specifically emphasizing the political significance of Adorno's writings on education and by also highlighting how they work to complicate and reconfigure our traditional conception of him. First, *Adorno and Democracy* analyzes the democratic nature of his writings on education in a way that ties them to his definition of democracy and explicates how this style of teaching is part and parcel of his project for democratic leadership. I analyze Adorno's essays and lectures on education in a way that is informed by the previous chapters on experience, critique, and the theory and practice of negative dialectics that are laid out there. Second, this book explores the specifically democratic nature of Adorno's own performances of his pedagogical project in the context of his writings on American political culture, whereas postwar Germany is the usual frame of reference for this work. Finally, my exploration of Adorno's democratic form of pedagogy is situated within his larger theory of negative dialectics. Adorno's writings on education are intimately connected to his understanding of democratic practice and, as we will see in the next chapter, his model of democratic leadership. And further, we can see Adorno undertaking this form of democratic leadership as democratic pedagogy in the writings on American political culture that I analyze in later chapters.

The final contribution of this book concerns Adorno's lessons for democratic theory and practice today. *Adorno and Democracy* focuses on articulating the political value of his program for democratic leadership as democratic pedagogy and his practice of drawing out countertendencies to produce useful treatments for pathological conditions. But Adorno's work adds to current theory and practice in other ways that I want to briefly note here at the outset, to color what comes later. First, his writing adds substance and rigor to the concept of democracy, which Wendy Brown thinks has increasingly become an "empty signifier" in the present political landscape. In "We Are All Democrats Now," Brown highlights a peculiar inverse relationship. Today, as various social, political, and economic forces undermine any sense that the *demos* has power or is ruling itself, which leads to what she characterizes as a "crisis of de-democratization," the *rhetoric* of democracy has become strikingly more pervasive and ubiquitous.[25] Given this state, it is especially useful to go back to Adorno. Even if we contest his definitions, his deep interrogation of what democracy means on a normative, theoretical, and practical level pushes us beyond the mere rhetorical celebration of an empty concept. Additionally, Adorno's mode of critique contests the tendencies toward abstraction within some forms of theorizing today. Adopting close cultural analysis—looking at the contemporary cognates of radio and of the rhetorical tools of proselytizing political figures—can help us identify important countertendencies in what otherwise might look like an unbroken pattern of authoritarianism. Adorno's method allows us to find alternative possibilities *within* existing conditions, to excavate latent possibilities even in a retrograde political landscape. This lesson is especially important to remember today, as many critiques of neoliberalism make it seem like a hegemonic system that offers no escapes, no possibilities of resistance. Finally, we might heed Adorno's warning that "the American attack on democracy usually takes place in the name of democracy" to analyze the various arguments that are made in the name of democracy today. Adorno reminds us that democracy is a normative promise that the people might have power and asks us to think more deeply about what modern forces distort that aspiration as well as what might be required to fulfill it.

Until recently, scholars generally thought Adorno's writings were too fraught with dilemmas, too difficult to inform political practice. But, as Russell Berman notes, "By labeling Adorno politically impossible, his critics provide themselves an illusory security in their own political self-understanding. . . . In other words, the image of Adorno, the unpolitical aesthete, is little more than a phantom that haunts a left that cultivates its own self-deceptions about an immediacy of political practice. Because it is convinced that progressive politics must be easy, it demonizes Adorno for pointing out the difficulties."[26] But because democratic theory and practice today are also in a particularly difficult place, we might include Adorno in our conversations for the same reasons he was excluded in the past.

Adorno asks many of the same questions that pervade democratic theory today.[27] What is the true meaning of democracy, apart from its current manifestations? Is there any value left in democracy, or has it been completely co-opted and corrupted by liberal capitalism? How can one argue that liberal capitalism cultivates a passive citizenry and also that it is possible today to foster independent thinking and action? How can we work against liberal capitalist hegemony, or, today, the seeming hegemony of neoliberalism? In the writings I analyze, Adorno explores the democratic horizon and identifies sites in everyday life where the promise of popular sovereignty might develop. An unorthodox Marxian thinker, Adorno is critical of how liberal capitalist institutions cultivate a sense of dependency and manufacture consent, but he is also skeptical of leftist programs that simply promote a new kind of conformity to authority. Adorno's thoughts on democratic leadership and democratic pedagogy begin to outline a strategy for slowly reworking social structures and collective identities. This democratic pedagogy helps people develop the capacity for critical detection of nonidentical elements and encourages the countercultural tendencies of everyday life, to turn pathologies into vaccines against conformity. For all these reasons, and with Adorno's complicated commitments to democracy in mind, we might begin to read him as a twentieth-century democratic theorist and think about how his writings productively inform both our theory and practice.

## The Moods and Moments of Adorno's Critique

Because the tone of Adorno's voice in the writings I analyze is so surprising at times, I want to take a moment to set the proper mood for this book and to say a word about the mood of Adorno scholarship in particular and current democratic theory in general. Robyn Marasco's wonderful recent book, *The Highway of Despair: Critical Theory after Hegel*, helps us think through some of these themes and provides an illuminating foil for this argument of this book. Marasco gives us one of the best recent analyses of Adorno's somber and mournful moods and a compelling portrayal of the political value of the negative moments of critique. She reminds us: we don't want to turn a blind eye to the reality of the rational grounds for Adorno's pessimism, to the value of his negativity, to the depths of his critique. We also don't want to equate this negative critique with an apolitical withdrawal or apathetic retreat. Marasco emphasizes the mood of despair as one way of recentering passion in the discourse of modernity, to recover negative states as valuable political categories, to see despair as social, historical, and political. And I am deeply sympathetic to approaching such negative states not as retreats or withdrawals but as creative, energetic, productive. Marasco sees despair as "a *dialectical passion*," and "passion suggests energy, movement, and the extrarational intensities of desire, but also excess, suffering, and sacrifice."[28]

There is great value in the way that Marasco sees despair and hope, the negative and the positive, the profound pessimism and the persistent possibility, as all tangled up with each other, as constitutive of each other, and as politically valuable. In a somewhat similar way, my first book, *Thoreau's Democratic Withdrawal: Alienation, Participation, and Modernity,* reads the so-called hermit of Walden Pond through the theoretical lens of Adorno to show how the withdrawals and retreats from conventional society that caused generations of scholars to label Thoreau as misanthropic, solipsistic, apathetic, and apolitical are actually part and parcel of an unconventional practice of democratic citizenship within the burgeoning landscape of modernity.[29] I identify deep sympathies between Thoreau and Adorno, on the basis of their critiques of modernity, their hostility toward the mainstream democracies of their day, and their efforts to enact and encourage alternative political practices that, given the force of the collective in modernity, necessarily take place through critical practices of distancing and withdrawal.

Importantly, though, this negativity should not become a reason for labeling them undemocratic or apolitical, but in fact is the basis for the revisioning of citizenship that is based on the practice of critique that they both undertake and that I articulate in *Thoreau's Democratic Withdrawal*. Both thinkers, in my view, are valuable *for* their negativity. They are characterized by a similar disposition, a similar mood: they can both be scathingly sharp in their negativity, in their gloom, in their despair. This is part of why we need them. Both Thoreau and Adorno are the kind of critics who chasten the American tendency to put a smiley face on everything. They remind us how the alienating logics of modern liberal capitalism, early for Thoreau, late for Adorno, force everything to fit into identical molds in dehumanizing ways. Both advance a critique of modernity as an oppressive system, but both also identify small-scale ways that we can subvert it toward unearthing better alternatives. So they are valuable, in my view, because of how their negativity chastens our tendency to avert our eyes from displeasing sights and to close our ears to unwelcome sounds.

But the research that *Adorno and Democracy* comprises goes one step beyond my first book to show that we also need to be able to see the moments when Adorno moves entirely beyond despair. This is where I depart from Marasco. She begins her chapter on Adorno with these words: "Theodor W. Adorno comes to us in various ways—as a philosopher, a cultural critic, a literary theorist, a sociologist—but *always* in despair."[30] Despair is there, yes, but despair is not all that is there and it is not always there. Marasco sets the tone by recalling Martin Jay's discussion of the photograph of Adorno that is used on the cover of his study of this thinker. Jay also, says Marasco, "deciphers despair in the contours of his downcast lips and eyes, in the 'mournful expression of his face.'"[31] The purpose of *Adorno and Democracy* is not wholly to replace the traditional gloomy image of him. This is, after all, another Adorno, not an entirely other Adorno. My goal is not to call into question the depths of Adorno's critiques or undercut the magnitude of the structural problems of liberal capitalism he is best known for laying out in such stark terms. Rather, I want to build on this knowledge to show how his critique also entails other moments when he articulates and acts out a democratic theory, a form of democratic leadership in the shape of democratic pedagogy.

Adorno's dominant mood may be lugubrious, but he is not entirely dour and doleful. Even the most cynical moments of his critique necessarily contain, given his materialist method of negative dialectics, a utopian element of hope and possibility. For Adorno, the negative is always also productive and filled with possibility, however minimal. That is the essence of negative dialectics. His materialist methodology focuses on the contradiction, the latent potential, the utopian moment that is represented in the nonidentical qualities that persist as rebellious features in the overall retrograde landscape of late modern liberal capitalism that he charts so thoroughly, so adeptly. Given all this, it is easy to lose sight of his overall method and forget that his mode of critique means that the latently positive is always encapsulated within the negative. The neglected texts that this book analyzes state the case for another Adorno in clear terms that will make it easier to remember and harder to forget: that there is another Adorno, that there is another moment in the critique that more explicitly focuses on identifying and drawing out those possibilities, and that these more positive moments are also part and parcel of the practice of negative dialectics. The writings that are the focus of this book pause longer in the space of that potential and devote more energy to drawing out the productive moments of the critique.

After reading this book, to the extent that we still close our eyes to another Adorno, we might ask ourselves: What investments do we have in maintaining the traditional image of Adorno? What attraction do we on the left have with the idea that to be critical means to be wholly pessimistic or despairing? To put things another way, why have the writings on which I focus been neglected by scholars? We might be disturbed to think about how the dominant trends of scholarship on Adorno can also refuse to see, drown out, or forget the positive potential that is always also part of critique in a way that, perversely and unintentionally, mirrors how modern liberal capitalism works to silence the dissonant call of the nonidentical. The gloom, pessimism, and despair are there for Adorno, but this book reminds us: that's not all that's there.

But if another Adorno is not entirely gloomy, neither is he glib. This is not a thinker who, in the space of America, relaxes and becomes comfortable with the prospects offered by the micro-level forms of resistance he finds, the latent potential of the substantive forms of democracy he draws out of the culture. Nothing I say in this book contradicts or dispels the depths of his critique of bourgeois liberal capitalism. The Adorno presented here is still a Marxist Adorno, as I show, a materialist Adorno, not an Adorno reconfigured as a poststructuralist theorist now wholly preoccupied with the micro, matters of disposition, character, and a personal ethos. The current "ethical turn" in democratic theory can be seen as too concerned with style and not concerned enough with system and structure. But even as I establish sympathies between Adorno's writings and affect theory, between Adorno's writings and the micro, between Adorno and thinkers like Gibson-Graham, we need to remember that his work on micro-level forms of resistance takes place against the backdrop of a Marxist theory that critiques modern liberal capitalism as systems. He is not just celebrating little things here for their own sake. *Adorno and Democracy* builds on the structural critique we are already familiar with from this theorist—also laid out here in the first chapter, in the English-language texts that are my focus—but layers on top of that a novel sense of how important small acts of subversion and resistance can be as a way of raising the consciousness of citizens to reject bourgeois liberal capitalism and create more enlightened and humane alternatives. With all this in mind, the following chapters lay out the contours and character of this new Adorno, another Adorno.

# 1

# Seeing the Large-Scale System

## The Pathologies of Modern America and Pseudo-Democracy

> The American attack on democracy usually takes place in the name of democracy.
>
> —Adorno, *The Psychological Technique of*
> *Martin Luther Thomas' Radio Addresses*

Scholars have struggled over how best to characterize Adorno's complicated relationship with the United States, an area of research that has gained increased attention in recent years.[1] Adorno is best known for his sharp criticisms of the alienation, reification, monopolization, commodification, and homogenization defining American culture under modern capitalism. After returning to Germany, however, he had more positive things to say about American democracy.[2] Scholars have not yet found a good way to account for these mixed messages. A sense still lingers that Adorno ultimately presents two very different visions of America: one early and one late, one positive and one negative, one developed during his time in the United States and one expressed after the return to Germany.[3] Even when students of Adorno emphasize the dialectical aspects of his time in America and Germany and the interconnected nature of his writings on these two countries, they generally do not explain the relationship between the starkly negative statements he makes about totalitarianism, modernity, and the culture industry in the United States and the surprisingly positive comments he makes about the democratic spirit of everyday customs and substantive democratic forms in this country.[4] As Claus Offe says, "As far as I am aware . . . Adorno never made a single statement casting light on this complete turn-around in his perceptions of America."[5] There may not be one single statement that captures the complexity of Adorno's thoughts on democracy in America. Indeed, it may take a whole book to do that: this one attempts to provide just that kind of broad and deep analysis to help us fully understand his attitude toward and relationship with the United States.

This book situates Adorno's writings on the United States within his (interrelated) thoughts on negative dialectics and democracy and shows how his early and late writings on America represent different moments of the same overall critique. But to see this larger picture, we need to piece together a diverse body of writings that are relevant to democracy and written in America. We can take in the whole picture, in its consistency, only when we parse it out moment by moment. This book, chapter by chapter, undertakes that project, piecing together the constellation of concepts that runs throughout Adorno's writings. Ultimately, as *Adorno and Democracy* illustrates, we see the sympathies between his seemingly diverse writings only when we appreciate them as different moments in his overarching project: a plan for democratic leadership in the form of democratic pedagogy.

This chapter takes up the first moment of Adorno's critique. Here he discusses the de-democratizing forces in World War II–era America that impoverish citizens' practice of autonomy, describing the problems his political project will address and seek to work against. This chapter gives a sense of how Adorno portrayed the landscape of the United States to its own citizens, writing in English in a more accessible register, to explore the forces undermining meaningful democracy in an ostensibly democratic nation. All the writings I focus on here to lay out the forces working *against* American democracy in the postwar era—*Current of Music, The Psychological Technique of Martin Luther Thomas' Radio Addresses,* and *The Stars Down to Earth*—are also analyzed in the final chapter, where I show how Adorno draws from these same texts to illuminate other forces working *for* American democracy. The first and the last chapter of the book, then, operate as bookends to each other: this one draws from Adorno's American texts to lay out the "problem," whereas the final chapter draws from the same texts to describe his "solution."

But here I explore only Adorno's discussions of de-democratizing factors, to set the stage for the later chapters and to give a sense of the particular problems that his project for democratic leadership in the form of democratic pedagogy works to address. Focusing only on the negative parts of Adorno's descriptions of life in America, this chapter presents a portrait of him that is far more familiar than the picture that will be sketched out in the subsequent chapters. The descriptions of American pathologies found here are not novel, but, in most ways, they mirror the portraits of late capitalist modernity that we see in *Minima Moralia: Reflections from Damaged Life* and *Dialectic of Enlightenment,* both of which were also composed during Adorno's years in the United States and meditate on the surrounding culture.

The key difference between the texts analyzed here, though, and works like *Dialectic of Enlightenment* concerns language and audience. The writings I study in this chapter were all composed in English, written in a more accessible style, and seem to be directed toward a broader cross-section of American readers, whereas *Minima Moralia* and *Dialectic of Enlightenment* were composed in German, directed toward a primarily German audience, and written in a more explicitly theoretical and academic register. And though all Adorno's writings quite consistently practice the same method of negative dialectics, sometimes in a nascent form, his English-language compositions are notable because of how they amplify and elaborate on the productive and positive moments of his critique. This is understandable given his audience: Adorno is explicitly seeking to critique and inform the practice of American democracy in a more immediate way.

In each of the three texts I analyze here, Adorno, despite focusing on different cultural objects of analysis, gives the same general diagnosis of the social, political, and economic landscape of the United States. Various aspects of modern life in America, ranging from capitalism to liberalism to the culture industry, combine to make individuals feel small, disempowered, dependent, like passive objects who must adapt and accommodate to existing social molds and forms rather than being active subjects who feel that they have the agency to participate in shaping the patterns of their own lives. Though Adorno's unique conception of democracy will be developed throughout the coming chapters, here it is important to note that he measures its vitality and authenticity in relation to the lived experience of citizens. Democracy, for Adorno, is defined in terms of how robustly ordinary people are willing and able to think and feel against the conditions they are given as natural and inevitable. This change in perception fosters a way of experiencing the world that is more autonomous, critical, and compassionate and—ideally—works toward building alternative forms of collective life that better reflect these values and more truly fulfill the promises of self-government, popular sovereignty, and empowering the people.

Adorno explores the de-democratizing factors of World War II–era America through an analysis of specific cultural objects. He sees the form of radio, the content of radio, and a weekly astrology column as ordinary, everyday objects that, like monads, reflect the larger tendencies of the social whole. So he analyzes these specific things with a microscopic gaze to draw wider conclusions about the patterns and dynamics of everyday life in the United States. But he undertakes this study to draw out the tensions, contradictions, and antagonisms that reside within these particular cultural objects. Fractures in the seemingly smooth surface of the world we are given testify that it contains alternative possibilities that may be amplified through critical analysis. Adorno's method focuses on highlighting these contradictions and drawing out the productively disruptive qualities that can work to unsettle the problematic status quo. As he says, "We do not want to systematize what may be disorderly. We do not want to harmonize what may be discordant. Our set of categories may contain contradictions, but we hold . . . that these contradictions in the categories express contradictions in the subject matter itself and, in the last analysis, contradictions in our society."[6] This method of drawing out tensions and antagonisms that testify to alternative possibilities is part of the practice of negative dialectics. Later chapters will focus more on the productive countertendencies that Adorno identifies within his chosen cultural objects, whereas this chapter centers on painting a portrait of the pathological aspects of what Adorno elsewhere calls "damaged life" and "wrong life," with a particular focus on the obstacles they pose to his ideal of democracy.

## Radio and *Current of Music*

### *"The Radio Generation"*

In his writings on radio, Adorno draws a picture of modern capitalism that emphasizes several familiar critiques. He expresses concern about how commodities and profits outweigh satisfying human wants and needs and how the fruits of production are kept private instead of being made available for common benefit. Standardization, monopolization, and the concentration of capital make the market anything but free. Production forces and capabilities are "fettered" by the profit-oriented relations of production, which create contradictions and "antagonisms" in the economic as well as the cultural sphere, "where they are less easily recognized."[7] Modern capitalism is also characterized by the ever-extending reach of the market. Even something as "ethereal and sublime" as music—which Adorno describes as "a human force"—has become part of the capitalist mode of production: it is commodified, standardized, and "consumed like other consumer goods." Indeed, he notes that "ethereal and sublime" have become "trademarks."[8]

Modern capitalism also forces individuals to adapt to its demands, to become dependent objects rather than autonomous subjects in the various spheres of their lives. Employees must fit themselves into the rhythms and logics of the job. The workplace "no longer permits 'practice' or 'experience' in the old sense," but, rather, a "single path leads from the conveyer belt via the office machine to the 'capturing' of spontaneous intellectual acts through reified, quantified processes."[9] In other words, any nonidentical elements that the individual initially brings to his or her work that don't fit into the mechanics of the workplace are soon tamed anyway, smoothed out, forgotten, left behind.

People must adapt to the workplace but also to their "objects of action," to their "everyday devices."[10] The objects we use, Adorno says, shape how we move through our days, how we operate our bodies, and—given the strong connections between body and mind that Adorno asserts—they also shape how we feel and how we think. Commodities that were created on the basis of a profit motive in the first place come to have a power over us, exert agency, and demand accommodation. We become the tools of our tools, as Thoreau would say, or our commodities become like a fetish, as Marx would say.

But even when we clock out, we don't leave behind this system that forces us to adapt, to fit ourselves into its premade forms. Given the way the culture industry works, the patterns and practices that characterize capitalism also shape leisure pursuits. For example, Adorno characterizes listening to popular music as "a perpetual busman's holiday."[11] A busman's holiday is a vacation that follows the pattern of one's regular job, in which one essentially does the same things one does while one is at work: a bus driver also rides a bus when he or she goes on vacation. Leisure activities, such as listening to popular music, are supposed to be a break from "work." But popular music appeals to the kind of consumer that capitalism has created. It reaches out to individuals who are in a "distracted" and "inattentive" frame of mind, which it then feeds and reinforces. The "whole sphere of cheap commercial entertainment" is "patterned and pre-digested," making people passive consumers instead of active participants in ways that reflect larger political and economic trends, while also providing an "escape from the boredom of mechanized labor."[12] This may just seem like "giving people what they want," but from Adorno's perspective, their very desires are constructed by the dominant mode of production. People are "kneaded" by the same mode of production that inculcates them with a desire for the products that create profits for industry. In this way, music is part of the dominant ideology, "social cement" that adjusts people until they fit into the "mechanisms" of everyday life.[13]

All these tendencies toward standardization, commodification, consumption, adaptation, and reification that characterize modern capitalism generally and are evident in the cultural monad of radio also, of course, shape the development of the self. Indeed, Adorno sees the radio as so strongly reflective of dominant strains of World War II–era culture in the United States that he speaks of "a new type of human being" and dubs it "the radio generation." He is concerned especially with all the ways that this culture issues imperatives for adaptation, adjustment, and accommodation, with the ways people are being made into what Marcuse called "one-dimensional" beings, adjusting to the mold of mainstream culture without even the internal struggle against civilization that Freud assumed (and saw as the root of our neuroses). Adorno worries that people are actually not neurotic *enough* any more, because neuroses are formed through the tensions and antagonisms that are developed through resistance to social imperatives, and that resistance is waning. Instead, as Adorno describes in *Minima Moralia* and as I discuss in greater depth in chapter 3, the unique form of alienation that characterizes postwar America is not experienced in terms of sadness or anxiety, but as a compulsory happiness, a determined cheerful normality. For the radio generation, "happiness consists mostly in integrating, in having the abilities that everyone has and doing what everyone does."[14] The elements of the self that could resist "what is" are weakened from disuse and are in danger of atrophying. The individual of the radio generation does not have direct, immediate experiences of life, but "rather lets the all-powerful, opaque social apparatus dictate all experiences to him, which is precisely what prevents the formation of an ego, even of a 'person' at all."[15]

Society molds the individual directly and even the family fades into the background and no longer operates as a mediating force separating the individual from society. But the "dwindling" of the authority of the family is not figured as progress or liberation. Rather, "the immediately palpable domination of the individual by society, without any intermediary, is so profound that in a deeper layer of its consciousness, the child growing up 'authorityless' is probably even more fearful than it ever was in the good old days of the Oedipus complex."[16] If you don't even recognize an authority as authority, how can you question it? Adorno is worried that members of the radio generation just unblinkingly accept their conditions as reality, just "the way things are," rather than rebelling against them.

These changes in social reality also challenge the assumptions of liberalism. As Adorno notes, liberalism "presupposes the individual as relatively self-enclosed, constant and autonomous in its aims—as the 'ego,' in Freudian terminology."[17] But liberalism's confidence in independence, autonomy, and the ability of people to govern themselves is of course dependent on the kind of ego that is now threatened by modern capitalist society. For the radio generation, the boundaries between self and society are blurred. Autonomy is no longer something that can be automatically assumed, but must be relearned. Given this context, Adorno's task is to rebuild our capacity for more independent critical thinking, but not along the same liberal lines. The goal of his project for democratic leadership as democratic pedagogy is to highlight the contradictory nonidentical elements of everyday life and to bring the nascent countertendencies that still circulate in people, on a subterranean level, to the surface and push us to think through what they mean. Adorno seeks to strengthen the capacity for critical thinking and for autonomy, but not to recover the coldly calculating, atomistic, liberal individual. The goal of Adorno's project is, rather, to push us to truly attend to, perceive, and directly experience the material world around us, to encourage us to respond to the nonidentical elements of our lives, and to cultivate an ability to let our gaze linger on pain and suffering. All this thinking, feeling, and sensing is part of the practice of critique, for Adorno, so these experiences *connect* us with other humans, rather than atomistically individuating us (as we will see in chapter 3). And these forms of critique also aim to prompt action, to move us to rebuild social structures and institutions that foster greater solidarity and agency among humans, that make us subjects, not objects, and that cultivate this relational form of independence rather than dependence.

## *The Physiognomy of Radio and Democracy's Mode of Expression*

Adorno gives us another angle on the pathologies of World War II–era America by turning to the cultural object of radio and analyzing it as a physical entity, as a material thing, by exploring what he calls its "physiognomy," its "face," "voice," mode of expression, and physical features. Physiognomy is the outdated art of judging character or temperament from the features of the human face. Adorno wants to study the physical features of radio to analyze the effects it has on listeners, to draw out the hidden temperament, the hidden character, of radio and the larger society it encapsulates. As he notes, if "a physiognomist tries to establish typical features and expressions of the face not for their own sake but in order to use them as hints for hidden processes behind them as well as for hints at future behavior to be expected on the basis of an analysis of the present expression," in the same way "radio physiognomics deals with the expression of the radio voice" to also draw out hidden processes and possible predictions for the future.[18] Adorno wants to study what he calls the "how" of radio: how it sounds, how it looks, how it expresses itself to listeners, how it communicates.

But Adorno's focus on physiognomy also reveals how he will approach the study of American democracy: he will study the "how" of democracy. Throughout the writings I analyze, Adorno focuses on how democracy is enacted—or not, as the case may be—at the level of everyday life, as opposed to the level of institutions, laws, or public policy. In his writings on American culture, he is most interested in analyzing the lived experience of democracy, in assessing the extent to which "substantive forms of democracy" are enacted by people in arenas removed from the official realms of the political. Whether Adorno is talking about the pathological existing forms of pseudo-democracy, as we explore in this chapter, or the more meaningful forms of democracy that he himself tries to put into practice, he is concerned with how it is communicated to citizens and how they live out the lessons they receive.

He analyzes how pseudo-democracy *feels* to the citizen, the sensations, emotions, and affects that it prompts. He explores how cultural objects like radio—as well as other social institutions and norms that make up the lived experience of democracy in everyday life—can position us as dependent subjects and make us feel weak and powerless. And given this concern with the pathological physiognomy of existing forms of pseudo-democracy, he wants to help create a new mode of expression that prefigures the more robust form of democracy he is trying to cultivate. Accordingly, Adorno's own ideas about democratic leadership and democratic pedagogy are expressed in a different way, to stimulate feelings of empowerment, agency, skepticism, critical thinking, and autonomy that are more consistent with a meaningful lived experience of democracy.

Adorno's concern, throughout his writings on American culture, with the felt experience of democracy is another aspect of his work that anticipates more recent trends in modern democracy theory, such as affect theory. He recognizes, of course, that a society cannot be called democratic just because it has certain kinds of political institutions. In a way that is ahead of his time, he defines democracy as a practice, a lived experience in the everyday life of citizens. But going even more deeply into how we tend to speak of democracy in political theory today, Adorno appreciated, even in the years before World War II, how we could also measure the presence or absence of meaningful democracy in terms of the feelings of citizens. In writing about radio's mode of expression, its physiognomy, and exploring the affective responses that people have to it, Adorno appreciates that emotions shape how people experience their citizenship, ahead of rational or deliberate thought. As he says, "Whenever we switch on our radio the phenomena which are forthcoming bear a kind of expression. Radio speaks to us. . . . It might grimace; it might shock us."[19] But mostly, radio works to intimidate, to make the citizen feel small and insecure. The physiognomy of radio stimulates a fearful affective response and works primarily to cultivate an obedient, dependent citizenry.

Adorno believes we can learn a great deal about American democracy by studying the physiognomy of radio. First, he describes several ways that radio reflects larger social tendencies by giving the appearance of democracy, without producing the feelings of agency and autonomy or the kind of critical consciousness that would be associated with real democracy. For example, radio has the ability to make previously "elite" live performances available on a mass scale, to "make believe that the majority is in the situation of the privileged minority."[20] But this seeming egalitarianism is just an illusion of meaningful democracy, and in fact radio does nothing to overcome class divisions or to cultivate greater equality among listeners.

The radio voice can also seem democratic in tone. It often seems to speak to the listener in an intimate, authentic, and personal voice, as an equal. This illusion of immediacy and closeness "affects our relationship to the radio much more deeply than most people realize," and people tend to think that the sound of the radio is a reflection of reality: "people who are not concentrating attentively forget the unreality of what they are hearing."[21] The immediacy of radio is part of what makes it seem so "real." Indeed, this voice "appears to pour out of the cells of his own most intimate life" and the listener can get "the impression that his own cupboard, his own phonograph, his own bedroom speaks to him in a personal way, devoid of the intermediary stages of the printed word."[22] The authority of the radio voice is all the more hidden "by making it no longer appear to come from outside."[23] But, paradoxically, the fact that the radio speaks in an egalitarian and personal voice is part of what makes it authoritarian rather than truly democratic. Listeners "may be inclined to believe that anything offered by the radio voice is real, because of this illusion of closeness. . . . It has a testimonial value: radio, itself, said it."[24] In this way, the "how" of radio works to quell rather than arouse our critical capacities, dampen rather than sharpen our capacity for negation, and silence rather than incite the tendency to ask questions. All this works against the cause of democracy, despite the conventional wisdom about the medium.

Further, the radio voice is monologic rather than dialogic. Listeners are placed in a subservient position with respect to the radio, able to listen but not to engage: "The very fact that they are confronted by voices without being able to argue with the person who is speaking, or even may feel somewhat in the dark about who is speaking—the machine or the man—may help to establish the authority of the tool."[25] The listener is spoken to but cannot speak back. Indeed, the voice on the radio "appears not to be at all concerned with the listener but to show him, by the disproportion between his huge radio voice and the listener's tiny voice how unimportant the latter is compared with the power which addresses him."[26] Thus, despite the ways it can seem democratic, authentic, egalitarian, and personal, the radio phenomenon is actually another facet of modern life that intensifies the individual's feeling of dependence and impotence.

Adorno also draws attention to how the spatial arrangements of radio listening and the physical location of the object work against meaningful democracy. In postwar America, radio broadcasts went out "into the ether" with the assumption that they would be received by solitary individuals or by several listeners sitting near the radio in the family home. The radio voice speaks to individuals in the private sphere, and this becomes, for Adorno, another source of its authority and another de-democratizing factor. The whole radio phenomenon is structured by this format: "a private person in a private room is privately addressed by a public voice to which he is forced to subordinate himself."[27] Communal listening might help generate conversation and awaken people's tendency to question and think against what they are hearing, which would yield possibilities of resistance to the given narratives of the world. As Adorno notes, "An organized mass of listeners might feel their own strength and even rise to a sort of opposition."[28] But instead, "the authority of radio becomes greater the more it addresses the listener in his privacy," and the "isolated listener definitely feels overwhelmed by the might of the personal voice of an anonymous organization."[29] Instead of creating greater community, the radio voice separates and atomizes listeners.

Finally, radio reflects the pathological tendencies of larger American society in giving the appearance of free choice, independence, and liberty by allowing listeners to turn the dial and make selections according to their own personal tastes and desires. But, as Adorno notes, these seemingly free choices are actually predetermined and standardized in accordance with the logics of the capitalist marketplace outlined earlier:

Radio upholds the illusion of privacy and individual independence in a situation where such privacy and independence do not really exist, which contradicts it. It is evident, however, that this illusion of privacy, immediacy in facing public events, and individual liberty in choosing them, is by no means limited to radio and runs through our entire public life. As people are subjected more and more to public mechanisms of every kind, and as the pressure of those mechanisms upon the individual increases, it is evident that these mechanisms must try all the more to conceal themselves behind the façade of the individual's adaptability, privacy and intimacy, just for the sake of not frightening him so badly that the effect tilts over to the contrary and the individual no longer attempts to escape the inescapable. Here, again, the physiognomics of the "radio voice" fits completely the experience of how modern mass society works in other fields.[30]

Radio is another aspect of modern society that quells discontent by giving the superficial veneer of the freedoms that are impoverished in actual practice. Many of the aspects of radio that give it the semblance of democracy are actually the very elements that undermine it in practice—though, as later chapters will demonstrate, radio—and people's responses to radio—also encompasses other more hidden, less obvious potentialities that are antagonistic to modern mass society.

## The Psychological Technique of Martin Luther Thomas' Radio Addresses

The second text, composed in English and directed toward an American audience, that helps paint a portrait of the American pathologies Adorno seeks to address is his short study of a now-forgotten but once popular and influential radio demagogue. Martin Luther Thomas was a Christian-right radio personality on the air in the 1930s who railed against communism, Jews, foreign policy, the Roosevelt administration, especially its unemployment policies, and bureaucracy, and, in an apocalyptic style, he emphasized many other vaguely outlined indicators of the coming end of the world. Thomas professed to speak to and for the "little guy" who felt increasingly lost and alienated in modern society, simultaneously articulating his fears while giving him a sense of being part of a larger group of like-minded individuals, with Thomas as their leader. Thomas used religion as the basis of his framework, as Adorno notes, "to appeal to people of orthodox and even bigoted religious leanings, mainly Protestant fundamentalists, and to transform their religious zeal into political partisanship and subservience."[31] Thomas's aim, it seems, was to foment a kind of paranoia about the various plots of state officials and bankers, for example, feeding fears with vague details and what Adorno calls the "if you only knew" technique. Thomas's style was strategically irrational, capitalizing on people's psychological fears, their resentment, frustration, and feelings of weakness and discontent in a contradictory and disconnected way, working primarily through a cult of personality, appealing to people's emotions more than their reason.

Most of Adorno's study is concerned with a macro-level and micro-level analysis of the techniques Thomas used to appeal to his audience, also comparing Hitler's use of radio to Thomas's to show how authoritarianism was at work not just in Europe but also on the other side of the Atlantic. Adorno divides these techniques into categories: there is the "lone wolf" tactic, the "emotional release" device, the "persecuted innocence" technique, the "indefatigability" device, the "messenger" tactic, the "great little man" strategy, the "human interest" device, the "listen to your leader" device, the "fait accompli" technique, the "democratic cloak" technique, the "if you only knew" tactic, the "dirty linen" device, the "tingling backbone" device, the "last hour" tactic, the "black hand" device, the "speaking with tongues" trick, the "personal experience" strategy, the "anti-institutions" trick, and the "faith of our fathers" technique.[32] These tactics, with their evocative names, all describe various forms of manipulation that Thomas employed.

In *The Psychological Technique of Martin Luther Thomas' Radio Addresses,* Adorno uses a different cultural object—the content of a specific person's voice on the radio—to draw a portrait of American pseudo-democracy that strikingly parallels the one drawn in *Current of Music.* If *Current of Music* explores the "how" of radio—its voice, face, and mode of expression—*The Psychological Technique* focuses on the "what" of radio, a specific kind of content it produces. Both prove to be pseudo-democratic. In his study of the radio demagogue, Adorno emphasizes how Thomas's speeches *seemed* democratic. Thomas used the rhetoric of democracy, and his style, his voice, his mode of communication, his persona—like the physiognomy of radio itself—gave the illusion of democracy. But the illusion is ultimately hollow, because Thomas's speeches ultimately operated through authoritarian tactics and did not cultivate the feeling of meaningful democracy in his listeners or foster democratic modes of thinking and acting.

Adorno again emphasizes that democracy cannot be defined only in terms of institutions or majority rule. In the United States, however, the will of the majority tends "to become hypostatized . . . as an end in itself rather than as a means," the result being that "certain traits of the population which are due to socially non-democratic processes, and anti-democratic in spirit, may be taken and propagated as the last word in democracy, simply because they are characteristics of the majority."[33] In contrast to the empty formalism of this definition, for Adorno, democracy is defined as an ideal that we work to fulfill by lived practice. But in *The Psychological Technique,* Adorno charts the ways that one radio demagogue appealed to masses of people in an antidemocratic spirit to encourage antidemocratic action, though Thomas cloaked his manipulations in the rhetoric and appearance of its opposite.

American fascism is unique in that it disingenuously roots itself in ideas of freedom and liberty, drawing on the legacy of "the Founders." As Adorno notes, "There is a definite procedure for the perpetration of such distortions, a specific twist by which psychological patterns of democracy are transformed into ideological means of fascism."[34] The fact that "the American tradition is ideologically bound up with democratic ideas and institutions has tended to give some elements of democracy a quasi-magical halo, an irrational weight of their own."[35] In America, democracy is attacked "in the name of democracy" even with an aim to "overthrow democracy in the name of democracy." In the United States, "where, unlike Germany, the idea of democracy has a great tradition and a strong emotional appeal, it would be highly impractical for any fascist leader to attack democracy itself, as the Nazi propagandists freely did."[36] Hitler and his henchmen could "openly attack democracy as such," but the "strength of democratic tradition in America makes this impossible," and every kind of propaganda must advance itself with democratic rhetoric: "The famous saying of Huey Long's, that if there ever should be fascism in America, it would be called antifascism, goes for all of his kin. The American attack on democracy usually takes place in the name of democracy."[37] Thomas constantly referred to the American Constitution and the ideals of the Founders and invoked "democratic personalities" such as Jackson and Lincoln, claiming that his goal was preserving and protecting the values of the Framers and these original liberties. Ultimately, this all "shows that the fascist agitator still has to reckon with democratic ideas as living forces and that he has a chance for success only by perverting them for his own purposes."[38] So, how does this distortion happen?

First, Thomas stimulated fear and anger in his listeners, taking advantage of and reifying their feelings of impotence, dependency, helplessness, futility, loneliness, and isolation. Thomas's speeches only sounded democratic:

they did not feel democratic to listeners, in the sense that they did not feel empowering. Instead, he preyed on people's worst fears. He spoke to listeners who had been rendered impotent and passive in most spheres of their lives, compelled to adjust and accommodate themselves to existing conditions, made into objects rather than subjects by both their work and their leisure activities. Adorno roots the effectiveness of these fascistic techniques in the sense of dependency people feel, because of the economic system, as well as their sense of isolation and loneliness. They are ripe for emotional manipulation because the "social forces to which each individual is subject are so tremendous that he has to yield to them" both economically and psychologically.[39] People feel that they are "somehow at the mercy of society," and no one "but the very rich feels himself as the master of his economic fate any longer but rather as the object of huge blind economic forces working upon him."[40] Adorno thinks that the way the economy is organized "makes life appear to most people as something that happens to them rather than as something which they determine by their own free will. To most people their life actually *is* decided in advance."[41] In contrast, true democracy would cultivate feelings of empowerment, autonomy, reason, critical thinking, hopefulness about the possibility of change, and solidarity.

Second, as we saw in the section on the physiognomy of radio, Thomas used tactics of personalism that gave the illusion of democracy. He appealed to listeners by presenting himself as a normal, average guy, someone just like you, an equal, speaking in a seemingly common, humble, folksy voice. Thomas's style assumed a "veneer of democratic equality": he was "affable," no better than anyone else, aggressively "anti-highbrow," projecting a "carefully calculated image of the common man with sound instincts and little sophistication."[42] He spoke to his audience in an intimate way. Adorno notes that fascist leaders are generally subjective and reach out to listeners in a personal way, in contrast with liberal propagandists, who avoid reference to the private self and remain "objective." But, paradoxically, liberal capitalism itself creates the conditions that make the personalism of the fascist propagandist so appealing. Liberal objectivity "presupposes an intellectual freedom and strength which hardly exists within the masses today"—because of the dependency capitalist conditions cultivate, as Adorno argues at other points—while at the same time "the 'coldness' inherent in objective argumentation intensifies the feeling of despair, isolation, and loneliness under which virtually each individual today suffers—a feeling from which he longs to escape when listening to any kind of public oratory."[43] This personalism is effective because it seems to break down the separations between individuals that liberalism emphasizes: "This situation has been grasped by the fascists. Their talk is personal. Not only does it refer to the most immediate interests of his listeners, but also it encompasses the sphere of privacy of the speaker himself who seems to take his listeners into his confidence and to bridge the gap between person and person."[44] But this personalism is ultimately not aimed at creating true solidarity among people. Just as we saw with respect to the physiognomy of radio, Adorno shows Thomas's style to be authoritarian under the appearance of egalitarianism: "The very immediateness and warmth of his approach, furthered by radio, helps him to get a firmer grip over them."[45]

Third, again as we saw with the physiognomy of radio, the content of Thomas's speeches is in line with American tendencies toward positivism and reifies the status quo of "what is" as real, natural, and inevitable. The spirit of positivism powerfully dominates modernity in the United States and makes people think the status quo is the truth of reality as such, whereas Adorno thinks that "truth" resides in the nonidentical countertendencies that point toward alternative possibilities. By positivism, Adorno means "the widespread tendency of present society to accept and even to adore the existent—that which *is* anyway. . . . In America in particular, the conviction prevails that truth is only that which can be verified [by] referring to facts."[46] The simple fact that "something exists is taken as a proof that it is stronger than that which does not exist, and that therefore it is better."[47] Indeed, "One may go so far as to say that religion largely and unconsciously has been replaced by a very abstract yet tremendously powerful cult of the existent."[48] This tenacious commitment to "what is" persists despite a palpable widespread dissatisfaction with the status quo. Indeed, these discontents are themselves nonidentical moments, but the pervasive attitude of positivism blinds people to these countertendencies. Unrest and unhappiness were the very prerequisites for Thomas's success, yet these energies did not tend to generate a move for greater autonomy but took the form of dependence on a charismatic leader: "Thomas, like all fascists, reckons with followers who are deeply discontented and also even destitute. Their objective situation might possibly convert them into radical revolutionaries. One of the main tasks of the fascist is to prevent this and to divert revolutionary trends into their own line of thought, for their own purposes. In order to achieve this aim, the fascist agitator steals, as it were, the concept of revolution."[49]

The fascist agitator turns people into spectators of the status quo, passive bystanders who don't feel capable of enacting positive change. Thomas "derides any idea of 'Utopia' and enjoys the notion that the world is not only bad, but that it shall remain essentially as bad as it is, and that it is a punishable crime to think that it could be essentially different."[50] This state of affairs "is the agitator's dream, the unification of the horrible and the wonderful, the drunkenness of an annihilation that pretends to be salvation."[51]

Finally, in another parallel to the pseudo-democratic aspects of the physiognomy of radio, Thomas's addresses appealed to listeners by giving the illusion of things that were strikingly absent in practice. Thomas manipulated people by appearing to represent and to offer true democracy, individualism, autonomy, freedom, and independence, while in fact he gained influence only by further undermining these values in practice. The propagandist appeals to people's frustration with a lack of individualism while further eviscerating it. He appeals to people's frustrations with authoritarianism while also re-creating those conditions. He draws on the outrage people feel about their lack of power while also cultivating greater obedience to him. Ultimately, "the more impersonal our order becomes, the more important personality becomes as an ideology. The more the individual is reduced to a mere cog, the more the idea of the uniqueness of the individual, his autonomy and importance, has to be stressed as a compensation for his actual weakness."[52] But to do all these contradictory things, the fascist agitator has to speak to his listeners with "twists and distortions," though he might appear to speak in a rational and logical way.[53] "Thomas is American enough to reckon with the common sense of his listeners, and he therefore upholds the form of rational thinking, corroborating his thesis by examples and apparently making deductions. . . . The logical trick consists of the fact that he always takes for granted that his so-called 'conclusions' are the pre-existing convictions of every true Christian American. While apparently proving something, he actually only wants to corroborate those common prejudices which agree with his plan. Everything is decided before the argument starts. In his confused ideas there is a sort of totalitarian order."[54] Despite his own insistence to the contrary, however, Thomas's radio speeches were actually completely illogical. He assumed his audience to be incapable of rational thought, and, indeed, Adorno notes that the forces of modern society generally work to discourage the practice of thinking. But thinking itself is also a danger Thomas wanted to avoid because it is a power that people hold that stems, in Adorno's view, from the ways the nonidentical conditions of material things speak to us if we listen and can challenge established powers and unsettle the status quo:

> The very fact of consequent, coherent and consistent thinking carries a certain weight of its own, a certain "objectivity," even if it starts

from the most arbitrary presumptions. This objectivity makes theory a problematic tool in the eyes of the fascist, for the reason that thinking *per se* refuses to become completely a tool. Theory as such, the pursuit of autonomous logical processes, offers a certain guarantee to those at whom the fascist wants to strike—it allows them, as it were, to be heard. Hence, theory is essentially taboo to the fascist. His realm is that of unrelated, opaque, isolated facts, or rather, images of facts.[55]

This is why Thomas appealed to the fears, anxieties, and anger of his audience. He capitalized on their reactionary, knee-jerk emotions and feelings to keep them from thinking: for Adorno, thinking itself tends toward critique of the status quo, aims toward change, and represents hope for a better alternative, whereas the fascist agitator wants simultaneously to whip up people's sense of discontent and their dependency, and to solidify their subservience and passivity toward him.

## *The Stars Down to Earth*

The final text that helps map out Adorno's view of the de-democratizing features of the American landscape is *The Stars Down to Earth*. Adorno wrote this analysis of the *Los Angeles Times*'s astrology column during a return visit to the United States from Germany, in 1952 and 1953. The reader is struck by Adorno's deep concern for the way the audience of these columns is being manipulated and deceived, but there is no sense of condescension in his attitude. From the outset, Adorno rejects the idea that the columns are simply benign amusements: "In the functional unity of the whole" he notes, "they may obtain a significance far beyond the harmless and comforting idea which is indicated at first sight."[56] Adorno approaches the astrology columns as another microcosm of broader social tendencies, analyzing "the inner structure of such movements on a small test-tube scale, as it were," before dangerous latent tendencies "manifest themselves so directly and threateningly that there is no time left for objective and detached research."[57] In other words, before it's too late. One has the strong sense throughout his writings on America that Adorno wants to be able to prevent the full flowering of fascism in the United States, to nip it in the bud. The seeds of authoritarianism, nascent or latent, that the *Los Angeles Times*'s astrology column provides mirror the other descriptions of the pathologies of American pseudo-democracy, in four primary ways.

First, the astrology column reinforces the reader's sense of his or her own dependency, passivity, and helplessness. To borrow a term from *Current of Music,* we might say that the physiognomy of the column—its voice, face, and mode of expression—positions the reader as subservient and operates with an assumption of the reader's dependency. The cosmos, the world, our society: all appear as a system on which we are passively dependent. The reader is presented with the world as a fait accompli, as an "unapproachable" and "anonymous" system characterized by "opaqueness," and "inscrutability." [58] The reader is positioned as needing the guidance of the column to navigate his or her fate. As Adorno notes, "This indicates the most important construct of the column—that of readers who are or feel themselves to be basically *dependent,* who find themselves incessantly in situations which they cannot cope with by their own powers and who are beset psychologically by what has come to be known as ego weakness, but is often expressive of weakness in reality."[59] He opens and closes the study on the same note, and dependency is the dominant theme throughout: "Obviously the first concept that comes to mind in this connection is that of social and psychological dependence. Our analysis of the *Los Angeles Times* column has pointed out in detail how dependency needs of the audience are presupposed, fostered and exploited continuously."[60]

Second, the columns dictate accommodation to existing norms and cultivate conformity to the status quo, "helping" the dependent readers navigate their fate by advising them to act in the "right way," in compliance with existing social norms and conventions. They are "incessantly concerned with the addressee's compliance with social norms."[61] The columns are "indeed nothing but messages from the social status quo," and "problems arising out of social conditions and antagonisms are reconciled by the column with social conventionality, and in this aim, threat and help converge."[62] These acts of accommodation and adjustment are not, however, acts of agency, but are just a way of following orders dictated by an anonymous, abstract authority: "While the subject has to follow closely what this agency indicates, he does not really have to act on his own behalf as an autonomous human being, but can content himself with relying on fate. He has to avoid things rather than do them. He is somewhat relieved of his responsibility."[63]

Third, the column reifies existing conditions as real, natural, and inevitable. The American tendency toward positivism that Adorno identifies elsewhere also runs through the astrology column. But this accommodation to conventional norms and reification of "what is" all take place against an illusory backdrop of freedom and choice. This cultivates a sense of helplessness in the reader, a sense of his or her inability to make significant changes to the surrounding world: he or she can only adjust to it. The column promotes "acceptance of the given" and "paralyzes the will to change objective conditions in any respect."[64] The column works to strengthen "the sense of fatality, dependence and obedience" and to "reproduce the status quo within the minds of the people."[65]

Finally, as in the other writings we have explored so far, here too Adorno shows how a kind of authoritarianism operates with the appearance of democratic values that seem to grant agency to the individual. The column's fundamental positivism, as well as its tendency to cultivate dependency, accommodation, and adjustment, is cloaked in the illusion of choice and agency, in ways that seem consistent with democratic values. Readers are told that they do have some agency and power as long as they follow the astrologist's advice and learn to navigate the terrain of their fate. The astrologer is the only one who can help them exercise their power by learning to read the stars correctly. And the reader's agency mostly comes down to timing, pursuing certain actions at a given hour, on given days: "Everything can be solved, so runs the implicit argument, if one only chooses the right time, and if one fails, this is merely due to a lack of understanding of some supposedly cosmic rhythm."[66] The "freedom of the individual amounts to nothing more than making the best of what a given constellation of stars permits."[67] The hollow appearance of free choice is maintained, but this "freedom consists of the individual's taking upon himself voluntarily what is inevitable anyway."[68] In this way, the "empty shell of liberty is solicitously kept intact. If the individual acts according to given injunctions, everything will go right; if he does not, everything will go wrong."[69] And if things go wrong, then you simply haven't played the game according to the correct rules and it is your own fault. Adorno notes how a sense of individualism is maintained primarily through blame: the column constantly pushes readers to find fault with themselves rather than with their conditions.

## Conclusion

As this chapter has shown, there are striking overlaps between the authoritarian features of American pseudo-democracy that Adorno outlines in *Current of Music, The Psychological Technique of Martin Luther Thomas' Radio Addresses,* and *The Stars Down to Earth.* He depicts similar kinds of problems in each of these texts. But it is important to remember that Adorno's goal here is to critique the contemporary landscape toward ultimately strengthening the practice of democracy, to give a sense of the work that needs to be done to address these pathologies. As this book will show, he directs his words in part toward educators—a term he defines broadly—to help them work to cultivate what he elsewhere calls "democratic enlightenment" by facing the realities of what he refers to as the radio generation. Regarding those who would educate, and he includes himself in this category, he says, "Their work is only of use if their reflections take the real changes that have gone on, both in people and in the power of culture, into account without any illusions. It is those reflections to which we are hoping to contribute."[70] He emphasizes that "the nature of this society must form the point of departure for any attempt at change."[71] Accordingly, this chapter has laid out the contours of what Adorno characterizes as a "sick" society that has infected its inhabitants.[72] But in the chapters to come, the attempts at healing will begin and the contours of another Adorno that this book sketches out will become more visible.

# 2

# Experience as a Precondition for Meaningful Democracy

## Sensory Perception, Affect, and Materialism

> Critique . . . is being transformed from the human right and human duty
> of every citizen into a privilege of those who are qualified by virtue of the
> recognized and protected positions they occupy.
>
> —Adorno, "Critique"

In the foreword to a volume on affect theory, Michael Hardt makes a connection between autonomy and receptivity, between our ability to give the law to ourselves and our capacity for responding to other bodies in the world.[1] Tracing a lineage back to Spinoza, Hardt writes that "the mind's power to think corresponds to its receptivity to external bodies; and the body's power to act corresponds to its sensitivity to other bodies"; thus, "the greater our power to be affected . . . the greater our power to act."[2] For Spinoza, Hardt writes, "every increase of the power to act and think corresponds to an increased power to be affected—the increased autonomy of the subject, in other words, always corresponds to its increased receptivity."[3] Furthermore, "each time we consider the mind's power to think, we must try to recognize how the body's power to act corresponds to it."[4] That is, when we expand our capacity to sense, feel, and respond to the world around us, we also expand our capacity to think and to act. When we more fully and deeply experience the material and ideological worlds around us, we are more empowered in intellectual and practical ways as well.

This connection between autonomy and receptivity is helpful in setting the tone for this chapter. Adorno makes similar links between our ability to truly experience the material world around us, to think critically against the conditions we are given as natural and inevitable, and to resist and rebel to create alternative ways of life. In other words, Adorno draws connections between how we experience the world around us, in terms of sensing, feeling, and perception, and our capacities for engaging in the practice of critique, and in turn, our ability to act as truly democratic citizens in our everyday lives. If autonomy is about giving the law (*nomos*) to ourselves (*auto*), this first requires that we be able to experience the world around us more deeply and immediately, distancing ourselves more from the norms, assumptions, conventions, and dominant logics that usually filter everything we perceive. For Adorno, there are multiple forces that frame our experience of everyday life, from the capitalist logic of abstract exchange to the modern dominance of identity thinking to the culture industry. All these forces work in different ways to predigest our experiences for us or to distract us from paying attention to the world around us at all. Given the materialism that structures Adorno's thought, he believes that we miss out on a great deal when we become numb and insulated from the objects that surround us in our everyday lives.

The foundation of Adorno's thought, and the starting point for his theory as a whole, concerns the material objects of the world. For Adorno material objects contain contradictory and disruptive qualities that resist being fit into conventional categories. These rebellious elements, the nonidentical, protest against the status quo and point toward alternative ways of ordering our lives. If we could listen to the world around us and perceive the dissonant qualities of the nonidentical, we would be prompted to think against given conditions and act to order our lives in different ways. Thus, we can trace a line in Adorno's thought from the nonidentical elements of the material world to the promise of democracy that is represented through the practice of critique. Listening to the dissonant calls of the nonidentical can prompt the critical and negating mode of thinking and acting that represents the essence of democracy. But it is just this kind of attentive perception and receptive experience that the forces of modernity work to drown out. Thus, the culture industry, the logic of abstract exchange, and identity thinking are all powers that impoverish our capacity for experience and, at the same time, work against meaningful democracy. Consequently, for Adorno, recovering a more authentic practice of democracy begins with exploring how we experience the world around us. Over the next two chapters, I will trace out this argument as it moves from experience to democracy.

In analyzing the importance of experience in Adorno's thought, and in sensing, feeling, and perceiving, this chapter reworks our conventional image of him as excessively intellectual. Traditionally, Adorno is associated with the mind and not the body, with thinking and not feeling, and with the logical as opposed to the corporeal self. But thinking and feeling are both vitally important to his theory. The connections between the cognitive and the corporeal that affect theory emphasizes are useful in highlighting two primary aspects of Adorno's work. First, affect theory can help us better understand how he can consider critique a praxis and how thinking can also be a form of action. For Adorno, thinking and feeling are not distinct; they rely on each other. Second, this direct relationship between autonomy and receptivity is valuable in understanding why Adorno emphasizes opening ourselves up to the call of the nonidentical. When we attend to that which seems other, different, contradictory, and incommensurable, and when we open ourselves up to the disruptive particularities that can press on both our cognitive and corporeal selves, then our capacity to think against the world we are given is stimulated. Additionally, our tendency toward coldness and hardness, to close our eyes to pain and suffering and to block out discord, is also chastened.

My book departs from the existing scholarship on Adorno and experience by making a particularly political—and democratic—argument about the role that the senses play in his thought.[5] In contrast to other works that explore this theme, *Adorno and Democracy* shows that meaningful democracy depends on a certain kind of perceptive, attentive, mindful experience in which we open our eyes and ears to the nonidentical elements of the world that we would normally ignore or repress.[6] This book highlights the ways that Adorno's writings on democracy map onto his work on experience, showing how both demand a certain mode of comportment, a certain way of sensing and relating to the objects of the world.[7] Thus, Adorno's writings, particularly the ones on American culture that this book analyzes, seek to enliven our capacity for the experience of democracy—the experience of thinking and feeling against what we are given as natural and inevitable—over and against the culture industry, the logic of abstract exchange, and identity thinking. In short, this book analyzes experience as a fundamental part—the base, the starting point, the foundation—for Adorno's larger democratic project.

This chapter begins by laying out Adorno's materialism, by exploring his unique form of Marxism and his critique of idealism, to highlight the important role that our experience of external objects plays in his theory. Second, I explain Adorno's theory of negative dialectics, to show how it takes the form of a specific way of thinking and, importantly, feeling against the world we are given. Third, I explore how affect theory can enrich our understanding of Adorno, as well as how Adorno can also contribute to contemporary theorizing about affect, with a particular focus on how the notion of the affects enriches our understanding of the experience of encountering the nonidentical.

## Materialism and the Nonidentical

### Abstract Exchange and the Logic of Idealism

Adorno's method of analysis stems from his idiosyncratic and unorthodox Marxism.[8] Marx's treatment of the commodity in the first chapter of the first volume of *Capital* serves as an excellent model to trace how this earlier version of materialism influenced Adorno. Marx sees the commodity as an embryonic representation of capitalism, as a microcosm of larger capitalist processes.[9] He begins with an aspect of capitalism that is familiar to the reader and uses this small-scale part of everyday life to interpret and critique the broader social tendencies of capitalism. In a similar way, Adorno's texts such as *Current of Music, The Psychological Technique of Martin Luther Thomas' Radio Addresses,* and *The Stars Down to Earth* also analyze small-scale phenomena in immediate everyday life with the purpose of making broader social critiques.

Marx's critical method, seen vividly in the discussion of the commodity that opens the first volume of *Capital,* aims to highlight how the dynamics of capitalism mask contingent and historical social constructions under the appearance of inevitability. Marx shows how capitalism is a system that, through processes of abstraction, also internalizes—and in so doing, masks and hides—complicated tensions, oppositions, and contradictions to perpetuate and maintain this seemingly harmonious but ultimately illusory system. Thus, capitalism continually, in ways large and small, distorts our perception and tricks our senses, preventing us from seeing things as they actually are. Capitalism mediates our experience so entirely that much of the world that we take in through our senses is based on abstract illusions that have reified and sedimented into forms of knowledge that we simply take for granted as reality. Thus, for both Marx and Adorno, critique is necessary to denaturalize these appearances and help us perceive in a more concrete and particular way.

Marx defines a commodity as an object outside humans that satisfies some kind of desire, but that also has two different aspects to it: a use-value and an exchange-value. Human labor produces both use-values and exchange-values.[10] The production of use-values is a necessary condition of our humanity: humans appropriate materials from nature to satisfy particular wants and needs. The labor that creates use-values is necessary to sustain human life as such: "it is an eternal nature-imposed necessity, without which there can be no material exchanges between man and Nature, and therefore no life."[11]

There are no illusions to be penetrated as long as we are in the realm of use-values. Things are just as they seem. Particular objects are used in particular ways, and thus Marx describes use-value in terms of material qualities, heterogeneity, concreteness, and also clarity. Use-value describes a transparent relationship to the object. We have a human need to fulfill, so we appropriate material from nature to fashion an object that fulfills our need, and then we use it in satisfying ways. We can understand and grasp use-value just by analyzing this immediately apparent relationship.

But all this clarity exists because we have not yet stepped into the realm of capitalism. Use-values exist wherever humans exist, wherever they appropriate materials from nature to meet their needs. Thus, use-values are not a product of capitalism, and they can exist apart from commodities and markets: a "thing can be useful and the product of human labour, without being a commodity."[12] Indeed, use-values cannot be exchanged in the marketplace, given the way they are defined by a direct relationship with satisfying particular human needs. Use-values exist in tension with, in contradiction to, the capitalist market. Use-values resist the logic of the market, whereas exchange-values gain meaning only from the market system itself.

Thus, only when we begin to talk about exchange-values do we enter the marketplace, and then the language of clarity, immediacy, and concreteness disappears. Now we need the practice of critique because mysteries, illusions, appearances, fetishes, and disguises cloak and veil our perception. If use-values are concrete, material, heterogeneous qualities that wear their status as a social relationship between humans and objects clearly on their face, exchange-values are abstract, homogeneous, identifying qualities that develop out of the capitalist marketplace but mask their status as social relations and disguise themselves as essential qualities of objects themselves. Exchange-value makes abstract the particular qualities of the object to assign a value based on monetary price. The exchange principle reduces X and Y to an equal monetary value and holds them to be identical and interchangeable, making particular qualities abstract to establish an illusory equilibrium and identity between highly different and disparate items. As Marx says:

> If we make abstraction from its use-value, we make abstraction at the same time from the material elements and shapes that make the product a use-value; we see in it no longer a table, a house, a yarn, or any other useful thing. Its existence as a material thing is put out of sight. Neither can it any longer be regarded as the product of the labour of the joiner, the mason, the spinner, or any other definite kind of productive labor. Along with the useful qualities of the products themselves, we put out of sight both the useful character of the various kinds of labour embodied in them, and the concrete forms of that labour; there is nothing left but that is common to them all; all are reduced to one and the same sort of labour, human labour in the abstract.[13]

When we make use-value abstract, the immediate, concrete, material elements of the object are "put out of sight" and we can no longer "see" them. All the aspects of the object that our senses could grasp in the most direct way are now made invisible to us. A famous passage describes the nature of this change in perception, as we shift from experiencing an object in terms of its use-value to apprehending it in terms of exchange-value. As Marx says:

> A commodity appears, at first sight, a very trivial thing, and easily understood. Its analysis shows that it is, in reality, a very queer thing, abounding in metaphysical subtleties and theoretical niceties. So far as it is a value in use, there is nothing mysterious about it, whether we see it from the point of view that by its properties it is capable of satisfying human wants, or from the point that those properties are the product of human labor. It is as clear as noon-day, that man, by his industry, changes the forms of the materials furnished by Nature, in such a way as to make them useful to him. The form of wood, for instance, is altered, by making a table out of it. Yet, for all that, the table continues to be that common, everyday thing, wood. But so soon as it steps forth as a commodity, it is changed into something transcendent. It not only stands with its feet on the ground, but, in relation to all other commodities, it stands on its head, and evolves out of its wooden brain grotesque ideas, far more wonderful than "table-turning" ever was.[14]

Exchange-value is not an inherent feature of objects: "So far no chemist has ever discovered exchange-value either in a pearl or a diamond."[15] And yet this ultimately mysterious form of value *appears* to be objective and real: "the social character of man's labour appears . . . as an objective character stamped upon the product of that labour."[16] In other words, the exchange-value that is actually an effect of the capitalist market appears to be an attribute of the object itself. Fetishism makes us think we see things that aren't really there: "There . . . is a definite social relation between men, that assumes, in their eyes, the fantastic form of a relation between things."[17]

Furthermore, the logic of abstract exchange deceives our senses in another way, by convincing us that incommensurable and different objects are actually equal. Under the logic of exchange, "we equate as values our different products, [and] by that very act, we also equate, as human labour, the different kinds of labour expended upon them."[18] This is the violent aspect of the logic of abstract exchange. Objects that have very different histories and very different stories of the labor that is "congealed" within them are imagined to be equal, identical. To find this exchange-value, we must make abstract the particular human story of how an object was made, erase its history, and silence the story about the blood, sweat, and tears that went into making it. When we lose this sense of the conditions under which a commodity was produced, we also lose a sense of the exploitation and injustice that might be written into it. But under the logic of abstract exchange, all those erasures and silences, all those ways that our capacity for experience and perception are impoverished and blinded, happen automatically and unconsciously: "We are not aware of this, nevertheless, we do it."[19]

This change also describes, in microcosmic form, the transformation of experience under capitalism in general. Under the process of "fetishization," our lives and our social relations become less clear, less immediate, less concrete, less based on fulfilling common needs and desires. Life becomes full of disguises, illusions, surface appearances, mysticism, abstraction, and homogenization. Things are no longer accessible, perceptible, understandable on the scale of human needs and human experience. Thus, for Marx, as for Adorno, there are important consequences to the ways that capitalism at once impoverishes and incapacitates our ability to directly and immediately experience the objects around us and, at the same time, seductively convinces us we're seeing things that really aren't there.

But if capitalism works on us at the level of sensory perception, then resisting and rebelling against that system also entails making changes in how we experience the world around us. For Marx, as for Adorno, this revolutionary potential is represented in the contradictions and tensions that can be illuminated when we critically analyze the commodity itself. If capitalism works in various ways on our modes of perception to impoverish our ability to experience the concrete, material, particular aspects of certain objects, this process is not always entirely successful. Something breaks through. The commodity contains a tension between its dual aspects, but that tension is not always perfectly controlled, and the contradictory energies generated between use-value and exchange-value contain a revolutionary potential that is important to Marx and to Adorno as well. Adorno thinks that truth is the "negation of appearance," something transcendent that moves beyond the surface of how things seem. In this process of uncovering, an alternative to "what is" is also revealed: truth contains an emancipatory promise that is illuminated by the practice of critique. Before showing how Adorno expands Marx's concept of use-value into a broader theory of the nonidentical, though, I want to trace a second primary influence on Adorno's thought. Adorno came to his unique form of materialism not just through Marx, but also though a critique of idealists such as Kant.

Like Marx, Adorno was deeply influenced by the same thinkers he ultimately targeted for critique: Kant and Hegel. If Marx started out as a "young Hegelian," we might say that Adorno started out as a very young Kantian, reading Kant with Siegfried Krakauer on the weekends during his teenage years. But for Adorno, Kant's theory ultimately comes to exemplify the problems of the idealist mode of perception, which tries to "strip the world of its uncanny aspect" and create a unified system that organizes knowledge on the basis of the rational subject at its center.[20] Adorno characterizes Kant's "duplication" of the world into two realms, the phenomenal realm and the noumenal realm, as a way of domesticating the world, of making it more familiar to us. For Kant, the phenomenal realm, the world of objects that we immediately experience, is the product of our own subjectivity, created through the forms of time, space, and causality that exist in our minds. The noumenal realm is a kind of shadow world that lies beyond what we can see and experience. This is the realm of the things-in-themselves, of absolute truth, but it is not ultimately a realm we can know, given the way our own perception is skewed by the categories of the mind. For Adorno, Kant's desire to establish security, stability, and certainty, to feel "at-home," is "expressed in the assertion that the world of experience, of things, is my own product: it is my own world."[21]

But there are costs and dangers associated with Kant's theory, even if it is motivated by a desire to create stability and familiarity. As Adorno says, "By making the experienced world, the immanent world, the world of this-ness, commensurate with us, by turning it into our world, so to speak, something like a radical metaphysical alienation is achieved simultaneously."[22] We dismiss our experience of phenomena by marking them as uncertain, transitory, mere appearances, ephemeral, casting the world around us as a projection of our own mind. For Adorno, Kant's idealism "asserts that truth is whatever remains once everything sensory, everything ephemeral, and hence deceptive has been subtracted."[23] The particular objects of the world around us are "left to one side" and dismissed in favor of a more absolute, if distant and unreachable, truth. But this logic also violates particularity, identifying any quality of life that seems different, unique, other, or new with existing categories, forcing everything into the unitary logic of the system: "There is a reifying quality in the very attempt to relate all phenomena, everything we encounter, to a unified reference point and to subsume it under a self-identical, rigid unity, thus removing it from its dynamic context."[24] The idealist mode of perception can alienate us from experiencing the world around us. Here again, the world we know through our senses is denigrated, as under the capitalist system of abstract exchange. The concrete, particular, material world that we can perceive and experience in a more dynamic, direct, and immediate way is deemed less important than abstract forms of knowledge that are not actually available to our senses.

But, for Adorno, despite efforts to construct systems, there are always remainders, particular aspects of life and experience that resist being identified, that refuse to be fitted into categories, that elude any attempt at reconciliation. There are persistent features of objective reality that illuminate the falseness, as well as the dangers, of the logic of idealism. Despite his own desire for "system, unity, reason," even Kant could not fully ignore the disruptive existence of these particular elements. Kant desires to create a system, but as Adorno notes:

> On the other hand, he always has the consciousness . . . the consciousness of a "block." By this I mean the awareness that even though there is no unity other than the one I have already told you about, namely the unity that lies in the concept of reason itself—this is not the whole story and we always come up against some outer limit. We might even say that in a sense the vital nerve of Kant's philosophy as a whole lies in the conflict between these two aspects, the impulse towards system, unity and reason, and, on the other hand, consciousness of the heterogeneous, the block, the limit.[25]

There is something that resists the idealist logic of what Adorno calls "identity thinking" that works to "identify" what is different with what is already known, that attempts to fit everything into existing categories, that tries to create systems. These rebellious elements that block and limit this attempt to create an abstract system are the nonidentical: despite Kant's attempts to dispel it, "the element of non-identity makes its appearance in his thought."[26] Adorno emphasizes how the logics of idealism and abstract exchange break down under closer scrutiny, under what he calls (borrowing from Walter Benjamin) a "microscopic gaze." In contrast to most philosophical thinking after Plato, which finds the absolute and truth in eternal, unchanging transcendental forms and ideals, Adorno places value on the fragmentary, heterogeneous, transitory particulars of the material world, finding truth in what is phenomenal as opposed to noumenal. In this way he aligns himself with a materialism that is also critical of idealism. Adorno's practice of negative dialectics works to highlight this nonidentical element and draw out its possibility and potential. This is important because, for Adorno, if our ability to experience the nonidentical is threatened or obstructed, we are only living what he calls "wrong life" or "damaged life," a pale, numb, mechanical version of the dynamic life humans are capable of living.

## *The Nonidentical*

Adorno transforms Marx's idea of use-value into the larger idea of the non-identical. Marx saw use-value as an antagonistic, contradictory aspect of the commodity that was precapitalist—and potentially anticapitalist—and whose particular, concrete qualities of usefulness were readily accessible to human senses in a clear way that contrasts with the abstract cipher of exchange-value. Adorno expands this into a conception of the nonidentical that holds utopian promise for truth, change, and an alternative to late modern liberal capitalism.[27] For Adorno, the material and ideological world contains these disruptive, contradictory, and antagonistic qualities that push on our senses to negate the fixity of the conditions we are given.

Nonidentical qualities surround us: the history of a commodity is never fully captured or defined by its price on the market, concepts and categories can never totally encompass the things they try to contain, and individuals protest (often by contrary desires and restlessness, but even by illness and pathology) the norms of a modern society that tries to subsume and integrate. But there are also strong powers in modernity that work to veil these disruptive particulars in the interest of maintaining a (false) illusion of harmony in the world as it is, trying to convince us that this world we are given is natural, inevitable, just "the way things are." Because of the value

he places on disruptive particularity, and because it is silenced in modernity (for example, by the idealist mode of perception and by the capitalist
logic of abstract exchange), Adorno's critical theory and practice emphasize
dissonance, negating and breaking apart these attempts at a false and violent reconciliation. Negative dialectics is an "anti-system" that shines light on
the particular qualities that idealist philosophies especially have dismissed
as "transitory and insignificant."[28] Negative dialectics highlights breakages in
what appears whole, interruptions in what seems to be continuous, antagonisms in what sounds harmonious, scars in what feels smooth, cracks in what
looks unified.[29]

This negative mode of critique is all in service of highlighting the alternative possibility that the nonidentical points toward: there is a "utopian
impulse in thinking."[30] For Adorno, the nonidentical contains elements of
truth and utopianism in the way it protests against "what is" and points
toward alternative possibilities, but also because it highlights the violence
that goes into preserving the status quo. Through these fissures an "uninten-
tional truth" could shine out. As Susan Buck-Morss notes, "The bourgeois
thinker expresses the truth in spite of himself; or, rather, like Freudian slips
of the tongue, truth resurfaces in the inconsistencies of his theory."[31] Or as
Espen Hammer puts it, "The moment of truth occurs when a crack shows up
in the otherwise seamless web of illusion that, on the most general level . . .
is linked to the notion of abstraction (economic, psychic, social, and philosophical), yet which in a more determinate sense leads on to a constellation of other critical concepts: 'fate,' 'myth,' 'phantasmagoria,' 'second nature,'
and 'identitarian reason.'"[32] So Adorno's method is always about looking for
breakages, moments of unease and discord in anything that seems harmonious and inevitable.

But ultimately, the nonidentical calls out to us to experience the world
differently, apart from the processes of abstraction, universalization, and sys-
tematization that characterize modernity generally. And Adorno's method
of negative dialectics works to foster and prompt these encounters with the
nonidentical, cultivating an alternative mode of perception. He thinks that if
we can open ourselves to a way of experiencing the world that penetrates the
illusions and abstractions that characterize modernity, we would be shocked
by the lively disruptions and insights generated by the nonidentical. Again,
sense figures in prominently here for Adorno, as it did for Marx. For Adorno,
"If the thought really yielded to the object, if its attention were on the object,
not on its category, the very objects would start talking under the lingering
eye."[33] If we could see and hear differently, if we could experience the world

around us through our own senses instead of through abstract categories, norms, assumptions, and so on, then we could encounter and engage with the dissonant elements of the world that push us to think and feel against what we are given. When we pay attention to particular things, we can see how flashes of the nonidentical—these elements that resist being synthesized—inevitably disrupt the idealist system, forcing at least a momentary recognition that calls the whole into question.

### The Praxis of Thinking and Feeling against the Given

If labor is our common human life activity for Marx and our shared praxis, a critical consciousness fulfills this same role for Adorno: "this is what thought has inherited from its archetype, the relation between labor and material."[34] Negating is part of our "consciousness" as "living subjects," and "no exorcism will expel this from the concept's meaning."[35] Humans are defined in this minimally essential way through acts of resistance to the world we are given: "Thought as such, before all particular contents, is an act of negation, of resistance to that which is forced upon it . . . a revolt against being importuned to bow to every immediate thing."[36] Humans have "the habit to ask what all this may be, and to what end."[37] They are defined by this tendency toward "insistence on the reality of [an] asserted meaning, or on the legitimacy of that meaning."[38] And these critical impulses can also come from our feelings, from pain and suffering, both bodily and mental. As Adorno writes in *Negative Dialectics,* the sense of suffering tells us that something is wrong with the world around us: "The physical moment tells our knowledge that suffering ought not to be, that things should be different. 'Woe speaks: "Go."'"[39]

And if for Marx we become alienated when we lose this ability to engage in free, spontaneous, creative labor, for Adorno we become alienated when we cease to genuinely think and feel against our world. This alienation is depicted as a loss of life itself. All of Adorno's descriptions of alienation revolve around images of "damaged life," "wrong life," and death. In contrast, "life" is represented in terms of the lively, shocking, stimulating, and disruptive encounters with the nonidentical that open up our senses and allow us to really experience the world as conscious, sensing, feeling humans (as opposed to cheerful automatons, hardened, cold machines, or numb drone-like individuals, other depictions of alienation that figure into Adorno's work). As Adorno notes, the habit of being receptive to the nonidentical can be "broken" or "enfeebled" as people yield to "cultural bustle" and find more and more things "self-evident."[40] And "when men are forbidden to think, their thinking sanctions what simply exists. The genuinely critical need of thought to awaken from the cultural phantasmagoria is trapped, channeled, steered into the wrong consciousness."[41]

When we understand how Adorno understands critique as a praxis that we are asked to undertake by the nonidentical qualities of the objective world itself, we see how thinking for him is not necessarily an elitist, rarefied activity limited to the few. Rather, this kind of resistance against given conditions can and should be undertaken by anyone and everyone. At the most fundamental level, the very conditions that push us to think are features of the material world itself, and negative critique is a universal praxis that should define our humanity. Despite the charges of elitism that have been made against him, Adorno expresses concern with how negating and criticism have become "departmentalized" and restricted to intellectuals like professors. The problem is that these ways of thinking and feeling against the conditions we are given are "being transformed from the human right and human duty of every citizen into a privilege of those who are qualified by virtue of the recognized and protected positions they occupy."[42] The authority to engage in negative thinking and critique should not be based on academic privilege and educational credentials, but, rather, the "truth content of critique alone should be that authority."[43] Adorno cites problematic cases "in recent years" in which people "outside the hierarchy" practiced critique, "for instance, criticizing the juridical practices in a certain city" and were "immediately rebuffed as grumblers."[44] The capacity, and the ability, to think and feel against the given—to negate, to critique—is not something you earn by taking examinations, an authority gained by virtue of your career, or a privilege earned by education. Anyone who can access the truth of the nonidentical and experience the disruptive and unsettling shock of that encounter in a way that prompts him or her to critique the inevitability and desirability of modern liberal capitalism has gained all the authority he or she needs.

But Adorno's purported elitism is challenged on an even deeper level when we recognize how his understanding of resistance is not wholly cognitive and mental, but also corporeal, embodied, and sensory. Attending to the nonidentical involves not just the mind, not just the body, but *experience* generally, in ways that relate to the whole self. As J. M. Bernstein notes, Adorno seeks to "expand the scope and character of cognitive life, of knowing" to include responses that derive from sensuous particularity, that are "determined by the sight of the disenchanted body as suffering that disenchantment."[45] Combining sensual experience with the cognitive process of thinking means that philosophy must give itself over to experiencing "the diversity of objects that impinge upon it."[46]

## Adorno and the Affects

Much has been made in recent years of the "affective turn" in social and cultural theory. Interdisciplinary work on the affects has become increasingly popular in the past decade or so, though it traces a lineage that goes back much farther and cites influences from earlier generations. Scholars write of the "affective turn," but what is happening is not so much a revolutionary turn so much as a further elaboration and development of certain strains that were already in existence in earlier theories, perhaps just in nascent forms that needed amplification.[47] As one scholar put it, contemporary affect theory unfolds by "returning to and reactivating work that had been taking place well before and alongside the linguistic turn and its attendant social constructivisms."[48] Notable influences cited in the literature include, at the earliest, Spinoza, but more recently thinkers such as Walter Benjamin, Gilles Deleuze and Félix Guattari, Georg Simmel, and Frantz Fanon, for example. Adorno, however, is notably absent from histories of contemporary affect theory, a forgotten figure when today's scholars recount the earlier generations of influence on their own work. This is striking only because of the sympathies and resonances between his work on the nonidentical and modern theorizing on the affects. These missed conversations are worrisome and impoverishing especially when we appreciate how Adorno anticipates many of the moves of current affect theory, as well as how thinking about the affects enriches our understanding of him. Ultimately, there are valuable parallels between Adorno's work and affect theory, in terms of both substance and style. By charting these overlapping conversations, we rediscover an unacknowledged line of influence on contemporary thought, while also learning how a thinker from an earlier generation actually anticipated some ideas that are presented as novel. The new becomes familiar and the familiar becomes new again: Adorno scholars gain a useful map tracing a line from his work into some important current debates, and affect theorists also gain another model for their own work.

Analyzing Adorno's own stylistic innovations from an earlier era, studying how he had to break some of the conventions of writing and theorizing to grasp his new subject matter, might prove especially useful to today's affect theorists who worry over how to write about a subject matter that seems to strain against the disciplinary conventions of the academy. Many affect theorists experiment with stylistic innovations and speak of a need to break out of established patterns and conventions of writing and research, to engage in creative writing or "critical memoirs" or undertake a "descriptive turn" to capture this new form of social theorizing about the affects and the everyday.[49] Scholars explain how they have to rework what "counts" as political to take in the affects, as well as having to work at the edges of accepted norms of scholarship and research. This language can seem a bit overblown. But given the concerns many scholars express about finding the right fit between their cultural objects and their style of theorizing, it seems especially worrisome that Adorno has been left out of these conversations. After all, he was engaging in stylistic innovations to analyze new cultural objects, and thus his work could potentially provide a useful and reassuring model for framing research in this area. In *Minima Moralia: Reflections from Damaged Life,* for example, Adorno describes the felt experience of life under late modern liberal capitalism, undertaking a cultural critique of both positive and negative affects. He writes in a fragmented, aphoristic, and often personal style that analyzes specific cultural objects of the day, ranging from high to low culture. But throughout his corpus, his style of writing is shaped by his unconventional subject matter and his aims. For all these reasons, putting Adorno in a conversation with affect theory is productive in both directions. In the following section, I begin by elaborating on what the affects are and what they are good for before turning to trace six important lines of connection between Adorno and present-day thinkers working in this area.

## What Are the Affects and What Is Affect Theory?

In contrast to the way traditional philosophy has understood the "mind-body problem," affect theory turns away from the Cartesian split and emphasizes the simultaneity between mind and body, between reason and passion, between the cognitive and the corporeal. Affect theory also breaks down traditional binaries, dichotomies, or dualisms, such as self/other, subject/object, inside/outside, and human/nonhuman. *Affects* is the name given to forces and intensities that we constantly engage and encounter: precognitive impulses, feelings, and desires. Most scholars talk about them as distinct from emotions. *Affect* "signals precognitive sensory experience and relations to surroundings," whereas *emotion* describes "cultural constructs and conscious processes that emerge from them, such as anger, fear, or joy."[50] These powers and resonances pass from body to body, where "bodies" might include material objects or human bodies. Affect describes a body's ability to move and be moved. As Bruno Latour puts it, "to have a body is to learn to be affected, meaning 'effectuated,' moved, put into motion by other entities, humans or nonhumans."[51] Affect is neither wholly corporeal nor wholly cognitive, but straddles both at once. In other words, "affect and cognition are never fully separable—if for no other reason than that thought is itself a body, embodied. . . . With affect, a body is as much outside itself as in itself— webbed in its relations—until ultimately such firm distinctions cease to matter."[52] In other words, affect "is the name we give those forces—visceral forces beneath, alongside, or generally *other than* conscious knowing, vital forces insisting beyond emotion" that stimulate our action or, as the case may be, our inaction.[53]

The affects complicate the boundaries between mind and body, between bodies and other bodies or objects, but also between inside and outside. Those who explore affects may study the "atmosphere" of a room and how that can be transferred to individuals. Some rooms may have a good atmosphere, others a bad one, but in both cases the atmosphere "out there" in the room can come inside us, shaping our mood, our own internal weather.[54] Additionally, the atmosphere inside us, our own moods, feelings, anxieties, frustrations, can also affect our reading of that room, of that external atmosphere. As Ann Cvetkovich notes, affect theory is "a sensational story of a different kind, literally sensational because it's about the impact of the world around us on our senses—which include our bodies, our feelings, and our minds. It can be hard to tell the difference between inside and outside—between what's inside your body and what's out there, between what's inside the house and what's outside in the neighborhood or on the other side of town, between your heartbreak and the misery in the world beyond."[55] As this all shows, affects are moments that defy many of the categories that social theorists use to analyze and understand our collective life together. This is part of their value.

Greil Marcus notes how Henri Lefebvre "argued that social theorists had to examine not just institutions but moments—moments of love, poetry, justice, resignation, hate, desire" and look not just at the realm of everyday life that included one's job, but "one's life as a commuter to one's job" or "one's life as a daydreamer during the commute."[56] Or, as Cvetkovich notes, "As we have learned to think both more modestly and more widely about what counts as politics so that it includes, for example, cultural activism, academic institutions, and everyday and domestic life, it has become important to take seriously the institutions where we live (as opposed to always feeling like politics is somewhere else out there)."[57] So affect theorists tend to focus on the local and the everyday, much in the way Adorno does in the writings this book analyzes, as well as in *Minima Moralia*.

## Adorno and Affect

Adorno's work anticipates the direction of three recent books in the field of affect theory in particular, all of which explore the larger social and political significance of feelings such as depression, optimism, and happiness. Sara Ahmed's *The Promise of Happiness,* Lauren Berlant's *Cruel Optimism,* and Ann Cvetkovich's *Depression: A Public Feeling* all explore the larger significance and potential of these kinds of feelings as public social and cultural phenomena, not—it should go without saying—merely medical and biological ones.[58] All these studies get out from under the thumb of examining feelings and affect in terms of the biological materialism that characterizes the so-called age of the brain, in much the same way that Adorno examined the psychological realm outside the narrow parameters of the psychoanalytic models of his own day, as we will see in the next chapter's case study from *Minima Moralia*. But beyond this idea of taking feelings seriously and of ascribing political significance to them, there are also other ways that Adorno anticipates key moves in current affect theory.

First, nonidentical countertendencies can take the form of affective responses. Countertendencies *are* affective: they are reactions that involve both the body and the mind, and they straddle the cognitive and the corporeal. Adorno writes a lot about the importance of thinking against the world we are given. But his emphasis on the intellectual and cognitive significance of critique, alongside his own reputation for elitism and a difficult writing style, makes it easy for us to associate Adorno too entirely with the head and lose sight of how feelings, affect, and the body fit into his work. But, in fact, critique is also about processing our own affective responses and trying to recognize that feelings can be valuable indicators of larger social problems. The nonidentical is an experience that can straddle the cognitive and the corporeal: Adorno sometimes describes this feeling of disruption when we confront the contradictory elements of the world around us as a "shock." Like affect theorists, Adorno also wants to stay with these momentary pauses—the nonidentical, or what he calls countertendencies in his American writings—these feelings, forces, intensities, and twinges that are experienced as disruptions, intervals, switches, and that represent a kind of modest, minor, and easily missed form of resistance against the status quo, against the dominant hegemonic forms.

Second, like affect theorists, Adorno demonstrates a desire to move beyond a kind of ideological critique that highlights the contours of hegemonic power, that goes further than exposing social constructions and revealing the structural "realities" behind the superstructural illusions. Adorno wants to focus on the small-scale aspects of everyday life, where things are happening that don't take the more clear-cut forms of either resistance or co-optation. Especially in the writings this book analyzes, Adorno explores moments of possibility that represent interruptions of hegemonic powers. These intervals are not yet fully formed but have the potential to be drawn out into something new, something next. Adorno, like Ahmed, Berlant, and Cvetkovich, for example, moves beyond ideological critique to identify forms of agency that hold the possibility for broader productive change. As Cvetkovich writes, "For some time now, there have been calls to think beyond the well-worn grooves of the search for forms of cultural management and hegemony, on the one hand, and modes of resistance and subversion, on the other," to move beyond "exposing the putative realities of underlying structures."[59] Instead, the collaborative known as the "Public Feelings Project" calls for "following the surfaces and textures of everyday life" to notice and describe "the places where it feels like there is something else happening."[60] In a similar kind of way, Adorno's project is not just to illuminate the contours of hegemonic power and highlight the ways that surface illusions are contradicted by underlying structural realities. His critique moves beyond this to also draw out what Berlant, speaking in a slightly different context, calls a form of "interruptive agency." In everyday life, for Adorno, there are moments when we experience nonidentical countertendencies. These are moments when we pause, when we experience a twinge, a feeling of nascent resistance, a sense of unease with the status quo, even as we are largely still caught up in the working of hegemonic powers. These are moments when our own human urge, our human praxis, to think and feel against the world we are given makes itself felt and known as a kind of agency that makes us stop and pause, even if only temporarily. In the writings I analyze here, Adorno spends more time exploring the potentials that are represented by these nonidentical countertendencies, getting a sense of how these minor, modest, and easily missed aspects of everyday life actually contain possibilities for change.

Third, for Adorno, nonidentical countertendencies often take the form of feelings and emotions—from alienation to anxiety to exuberant happiness—that he sees as politically significant. Feelings become critically valuable indicators of larger social trends and problems. Just as the Public Feelings Project explores what capitalism feels like and sees both depression and optimism as richly significant indicators of life lived under neoliberal capitalism, Adorno bridges the psychic and the social in an earlier era to explore the felt experience of "damaged life" under late modernity. In general, Adorno's work combines Freud and Marx, the psychic and the social, in ways that recognize how feelings—whether of exuberant happiness or deadening depression—are critically valuable indicators of larger social and political problems. For Adorno, the call of the nonidentical can come in the form of psychic suffering, such as depression, neuroses, or feelings of alienation and estrangement: these can represent nonidentical elements that protest against the larger identifying, abstracting, systematizing logics of modernity. Adorno's work anticipates the recent strain of affect theory that studies emotions such as happiness, depression, or optimism as feelings that are not subjective or wholly interior, but reflect the experience of living under, with, and in certain social, economic, and political configurations. This is a sympathy I will return to and explore in more depth in the final section of chapter 3, where I work through Adorno's theory and practice by analyzing the specific case of psychic illness as it plays out in *Minima Moralia*.

Fourth, as the above discussion also implies, like much of the queer theory that is part of affect theory, Adorno identifies critically productive value in "negative affects," in feelings of unease such as angst, alienation, and anxiety. Queer theory focuses on nonnormative feelings of shame, melancholy, failure, and depression, but it sees these negative affects as potential jumping-off points for political action and as intertwined with utopia and hope.[61] In a way that is both similar and different, negative feelings are also valuable for Adorno as nonidentical moments that contain utopian possibilities, given how they alert us to the "wrong life" of the status quo and indicate that things should be different, opening a pathway for critical thinking and political action. Even negative affective responses are seen as avenues toward new forms of agency and valuable resources for political action: "Rather than seeing negative feelings of failure, mourning, despair, and shame as getting in the way of politics or needing to be converted to something more active in order to become politics, such work attends to felt experience as not only already political but as transforming our understandings of what counts as politics."[62]

Fifth, if the affects can be described as moments of potential that point toward a different future, Adorno also describes confrontations with the nonidentical in similar terms. These moments of promise can seem to "yield an actualized next or new that is somehow better than 'now.'"[63] This is a particular goal of the Public Feelings Project, which aims "to generate the affective foundation of hope that is necessary for political action; hence the turn to utopia in much recent work related to its projects, but a utopia . . . that is grounded in the here and now, in the recognition of the possibilities and powers that we have at our immediate disposal."[64] Small-scale, local aspects of everyday life may also reveal reasons for hope and optimism and be "less predictably foregone in their conclusions about our dire situation."[65]

But despite their potential, neither affective moments nor the nonidentical inherently or automatically stimulates or motivates change. As much as we would want to believe affect inherently provides the basis for "a better tomorrow" or "a progressive or liberatory politics," these moments instead bear "an intense and thoroughly immanent neutrality" that must be nurtured to fully bloom.[66] Lauren Berlant's *Cruel Optimism* explores the possibility contained within optimism, which she describes as a relationship of attachment to a particular object that signals a bonding to a certain vision of the good life. Optimism, for her, is not a feeling but "a social relation involving attachments that organize the present. It is an orientation toward the pleasure that is bound up in the activity of world-making, which may be hooked on futures, or not."[67] We attach to objects because of the positive vision of the world they signal to us. So there is valuable potential in these attachments and a kind of utopian possibility that is pointed toward in these visions of the good life. But, in her book's only citation of Adorno, she notes this is usually just an unfulfilled moment of possibility, "what Adorno calls the 'it could have been otherwise.'"[68] As Berlant says, "The texts we have looked at stage moments when life could have become otherwise, in the good sense. A substantive change of heart, a sensorial shift, intersubjectivity or transference with a new promising object does not generate on its own the better good life, though, and never without an equally threatening experience of loss."[69] So affective intervals, like the nonidentical, point toward only the possibility of change, not its automatic realization or fulfillment. The meaning and significance of both must be drawn out and cultivated through a critical process.

There is one final overlap between the work of recent affect theorists and the writings I analyze in this book. Given how Adorno was also a materialist, it is not surprising that his work finds some sympathies with the "new materialist" strain of current scholarship. If affect theory studies how forces and intensities can travel from body to body, the new materialisms analyze how these encounters take place with respect to material objects that might initially seem inert. Complicating conventional notions about "dead" matter, scholars are working to show how matter is not simply inert, but has lively, vital qualities that reach out to us and move us. Similarly, Adorno studies the materiality of the radio itself as an affective force, apart from its content or programming. He shows how the seemingly inert material object of the radio actually is quite lively: his work on radio focuses on what he calls the "physiognomy" of this material object, its "face," voice, and mode of expression. And he traces the wide variety of encounters the listeners have with this face, with this voice, as its speakers speak to them.

What does this have to do with democracy, though? Putting Adorno into conversation with affect theory helps us better appreciate how the experience of meaningful democracy is about becoming attuned to the intensities and forces that radiate from other bodies. For the promise of democracy to be realized, for Adorno, we have to learn to both think against and feel against what we are given as second nature. And this requires that we learn to experience the world around us more fully, listen more carefully to the voice of the nonidentical, and try to realize the potential of this productive interval and interruption, turning these moments into opportunities for real change. But this is not to say that attending to a wider range of experience is valuable for democracy because it prompts more conventional forms of political action. Rather, attentive, perceptive, and mindful experience is *itself* part of the practice of meaningful democracy. For Adorno the promise of democracy cannot be fulfilled if people are numb, cold, hardened, or mechanical. If people are to have power and authority, if the *demos* are to have *kratos,* then it is important that people are also empowered to experience the full range of their own humanity. Then they can listen to what their senses tell them and fully take in and process the material and ideological conditions of the surrounding world—the feelings, forces, and intensities—that activate their abilities to think and feel against what they are given as natural, inevitable, just the way things are. In the next chapter I trace the relationship between this mode of experience and democracy more fully.

# 3

# Critique and the Practice of Democracy

## Negative Dialectics, Autonomy, and Compassion

> Critique is essential to all democracy. Not only does democracy require
> the freedom to criticize and need critical impulses. Democracy is
> nothing less than defined by critique. . . . Critique and the prerequisite of
> democracy, political maturity, belong together. Politically mature is the
> person who speaks for himself, because he has thought for himself and is
> not merely repeating someone else; he stands free of any guardian. This is
> demonstrated in the power to resist established opinions and, one and the
> same, also to resist existing institutions, to resist everything that is merely
> posited, that justifies itself with its existence. Such resistance, as the ability
> to distinguish between what is known and what is accepted merely by
> convention or under the constraint of authority, is one with critique. . . .
> He who equated the modern concept of reason with critique is scarcely
> exaggerating.
>
> —Adorno, "Critique"

Recent studies have analyzed the practical, ethical, and political dimensions
of Adorno's life and work, exploring his thoughts on critique as praxis and
articulating the nature of his unique modes of political engagement. Additionally, several biographies of Adorno emphasize the political aspects of his
life and work.[1] Adorno's politics has also been receiving deeper treatment in
volumes intended to introduce new readers to his work.[2] Most significantly
for my purposes, there is also a growing body of literature that foregrounds

Adorno's political commitments in deeper, sustained, and explicit ways. J. M. Bernstein, Espen Hammer, and Russell Berman, for example, emphasize how key political themes such as resistance, ethics, and justice figure into Adorno's work. These thinkers highlight Adorno's hesitancy regarding conventional forms of direct action, while illuminating his political commitments and his efforts to build critical foundations for alternative ways of thinking, acting, and experiencing. In chapter 6, when focusing on countertendencies, I discuss another category of scholars who seek to use Adorno's thought to inform current politics in a direct, immediate, and explicit way. These scholars have a more practical take on Adorno's politics that is in sympathy with the argument I make later in the book. But Adorno's practice of critique is also an important part of his politics and a vital starting point for understanding how a concern for and commitment to democracy fit into his writings, and that is the group of scholars I turn to now.

The most significant thinkers in this category all emphasize the politics of Adorno's theory, his understanding of nonidentity, his mode of critique, and his aesthetics. In different ways, they argue that Adorno gives us a new critical framework for resistance and a new mode of experience that can prompt a novel form of political action. But for all these scholars, Adorno is working primarily at the level of introducing a prolegomena to a new kind of politics. Russell Berman thinks that Adorno's theory can help develop a praxis to work against domination and resistance.[3] Martin Morris sees Adorno's "mimetic shudder" as the starting point for a new politics and a new mode of political being.[4] J. M. Bernstein speaks of Adorno's "fugitive ethical experiences" and sees him building a "microfoundation" for a "new negative politics."[5] Similarly, Espen Hammer describes Adorno's "placeholder politics," his "micro-interruptive operations" to an alternative politics.[6] But the writings I explore in this book open the door to something more fully developed, something that builds and grows beyond beginnings and starting points. Adorno's writings on democracy in the United States and on American political culture show him producing a political theory regarding democratic leadership as democratic pedagogy that is consistent with his method of negative dialectics, as well as attempting to put that theory into practice. So my project builds on this valuable work by Berman and especially Bernstein and Hammer, but it also shows how reading this neglected set of Adorno's writings allows us to push his thinking on politics past the stage of prolegomena.

This chapter outlines how democracy fits into Adorno's broader theoretical corpus. Drawing from his more abstract theoretical writings as well as several important essays and addresses in which he explicitly discusses his thoughts on democracy, the first section highlights the close connections he draws between meaningful democracy and the practice of critique. Then I pull together the lessons from the previous chapter to highlight the structure and significance of Adorno's practice of negative dialectics by exploring a case study drawn from *Minima Moralia: Reflections from Damaged Life*. The second section of the chapter demonstrates how and why experience matters for Adorno by analyzing his writings on psychic illness, mental unease, and the therapeutic revolution in psychiatry in the postwar era. Here we can see why Adorno thinks attending to and perceiving one example of the nonidentical—represented in psychic distress—matters so much for our meaningful experience of the world, our ability to engage in the practice of critique, and democracy generally. But in these sections from *Minima Moralia*, Adorno also demonstrates how modern forces attempt to silence the dissonant call of the nonidentical: here these powers take the form of a normalizing and conventional brand of psychiatry.

As the following analysis of Adorno's critique of psychiatry shows, being able to truly experience the world around us and truly live life—as well as our related ability to engage in the practice of critique and fulfill the promise of democracy—all hinges on our ability to perceive and attend to the nonidentical elements of our world. Thus, the importance of Adorno's method of negative dialectics is clear. Through it he engages in a critique of the dominant logics that numb and alienate us, but at the same time he pushes us to attend to the nonidentical, to sense, perceive, and experience our material and ideological world more deeply, in ways that further his larger political goals. To help flesh out the basic outline he gives us, in the final section of this chapter I turn to two sources who will seem unusual at first glance: the novelist-philosophers Marilynne Robinson and David Foster Wallace.

Robinson is the author of nonfiction and fiction works but is perhaps best known for her first novel, *Housekeeping,* and her *Gilead* trilogy. She teaches creative writing at the Iowa Writers Workshop. As a testament to how richly her writing, especially her fiction, explores philosophical and political themes, Robinson is the subject of a volume I am coediting that brings political theorists together to analyze her work. *A Political Companion to Marilynne Robinson* shows how her fiction helps us think through questions related to living in a democratic community, as we struggle with racial injustice, disability, aging, environmental degradation, and the tensions between religious faith and modern secularism.[7] David Foster Wallace is also aptly categorized as a novelist-philosopher for the many ways his fiction opens itself up to the analysis of our modern condition. He is primarily known as the author of

*Infinite Jest,* a massive novel that meditates on the problems of pleasure and addiction in American culture with near-encyclopedic breadth. My discussion of Wallace, however, focuses on a now-famous commencement address he gave in 2005 at Kenyon College. Before his death, in 2008, Wallace taught creative writing at Pomona College. As we will see later in this chapter, in different ways, both Robinson and Wallace help us better understand the kind of experience, the kind of thinking, that true democracy requires in ways that are deeply sympathetic to Adorno's own vision.

## Negative Dialectics and Critique: The Experience of Meaningful Democracy

For Adorno, when people become alienated from themselves, they become alienated from democracy. To tie this in to the discussions from the previous chapter, if people cannot sense and perceive in a way that is open to the nonidentical, then they are not pushed to negate and they lose the capacity for thinking and feeling against the given conditions of the world. Consequently, when this capacity is impoverished, obstructed, or lost, humans become alienated from themselves. But because this ability to think against, and to be empowered to act against, what seems natural and inevitable is also a vital part of democracy, the inability to truly experience the world around us also alienates us from democracy. As Adorno puts it, "Using the language of philosophy, one indeed could say that the people's alienation from democracy reflects the self-alienation of society."[8]

Democracy requires that people possess a feeling of empowerment: "Democracy, according to its very idea, promises people that they themselves would make decisions about their world."[9] But to be able to exercise these powers, people need the "critical impulses" that they gain from encounters with the nonidentical. As Adorno notes, "Critique is essential to all democracy. Not only does democracy require the freedom to criticize and need critical impulses. Democracy is nothing less than defined by critique."[10] The qualities that democracy requires are the powers "to resist established opinions and, one and the same, also to resist existing institutions, to resist everything that is merely posited, that justifies itself with its existence," to be able to "distinguish between what is known and what is accepted merely by convention or under the constraint of authority."[11] In other words, democracy requires that we have the capacity to think and feel against the given world.

A perceptive, attentive, attuned mode of experience is the prerequisite for all these capacities. Thus, the work of politics is also the work of penetrating the forces that distract and delude us to foster the encounters with the non-identical that stimulate our critical consciousness and prompt the practice of critique. Adorno asserts that politics "is not a self-enclosed, isolated sphere, as it manifests itself in political institutions, processes, and procedural rules, but rather can be conceived only in its relationship to the societal play of forces making up the substance of everything political and veiled by political surface phenomena."[12] Politics is about the dynamic interaction between humans and the nonidentical elements of the world that prompt people to think and feel against, and to resist, to rebel.[13] Thus, uncovering the nonidentical and fostering these encounters becomes the work of theory, the work of critique, which is also the work of politics that moves us closer to the democratic ideal.

Adorno is concerned that people will give up on the ideal of democracy, because of the many ways that ostensibly democratic states, such as the United States, instead foster a sense of dependency, a sense of impotence and futility, and work against "this 'deciding for oneself about the world.'"[14] As Adorno notes, the prevailing economic order renders the vast majority of Americans dependent: "If they want to live, then no other avenue remains but to adapt, submit themselves to the given conditions; they must negate precisely that autonomous subjectivity to which the idea of democracy appeals; they can preserve themselves only if they renounce their self. To see through the nexus of deception, they would need to make precisely that painful intellectual effort that the organization of everyday life, and not least of all the culture industry inflated to the point of totality, prevents."[15]

Because of the forces that work to veil, cloak, and hide the nonidentical and impoverish our capacity for autonomous experience, people are made into obedient, dependent, and adapting subjects. Ultimately, then, the problems that Adorno is concerned with throughout his writings—the culture industry, idealism, capitalism, alienation—are central problems for democracy because of the ways that they "deceive" us, blinding our eyes and stopping our ears. But his goal is also to help us learn to make the "painful intellectual effort" to see through this deception, to foster the practices of critique and negation that help fulfill the promise of democracy.

In the above passage, as in other places, Adorno uses the language of "autonomy" in relation to democracy, a term that is worth analyzing further. Adorno's notion of autonomy and his definition of democracy do not lament the loss of or try to re-create the atomistic, private, sovereign, ideal liberal subject, a subject that we know to be mythical and illusory as well as problematically raced, gendered, and classed. In fact, Adorno is especially critical of conventional notions of liberal autonomy from a Marxist perspective. So even though he uses the language of autonomy, it also becomes clear that his understanding of this concept is unusual in two ways.

First, as a materialist, Adorno thinks that it is the objects of the world around us that stimulate and motivate us, if we listen, to exercise the capacity for critique that he sees as a human praxis. So autonomous thinking, for Adorno, is not self-originating but stems from openness to the nonidentical. As we saw at the start of the last chapter, with Michael Hardt's reference to Spinoza, autonomy can be connected to receptivity: being sensitive to other bodies—sensing and feeling—can lead to an increased capacity for thinking and acting, and vice versa. Becoming more receptive can make us more autonomous, better able to more authentically give the law to ourselves rather than obey conventional authorities. So autonomy, for Adorno, finds its source in the nonidentical qualities of the world around us. If we can learn to become more open to the dissonant calls of these rebellious qualities, we can become more autonomous, as well as more critical and more democratic, as we have seen.

Second, for Adorno, autonomy is ultimately also about collective world building. His understanding of autonomy is about deciding for ourselves what world we want, but as his writings on leadership and pedagogy indicate, this is a collective as opposed to an individual endeavor. Adorno is critical of the ways that liberal capitalism cultivates a sense of dependency through making people feel lonely, apart, powerless, separate. And so his understanding of autonomy, in contrast to liberal autonomy, aims to foster the sense of solidarity that can motivate people to create new social structures that support both critical thinking *and* collectivity. Adorno's critique of existing conditions is oriented toward making new possibilities visible, bringing new worlds into sight, so more people can do the democratic work—in an egalitarian, horizontal way—of making them real.

In this way, Adorno's constellation of related concepts—critique, autonomy, and democracy—exist *between* the nonidentical elements of the material conditions of the world and collective world-building endeavors. Critique is the seed from which true democracy grows, in his view, but it is still only the seed as opposed to the full flowering. Democracy is defined by critique for Adorno because the creation of truly democratic social structures, institutions, and norms begins in these modes of being where we are open, receptive, and attuned to the dissonant call of the nonidentical. If we listen to the particular objects of the world around us, we are prompted to engage in the universal praxis of thinking. This praxis of thinking and critique is an essential element of democracy—indeed, Adorno says it defines the essence of democracy, because truly democratic social structures cannot exist without this kind of critical thinking. But democracy, for Adorno, does not end with critique. For democracy to fully flower and for its normative promise to be realized, the seed of critique must be allowed to bloom into a collective world building and reworking of structures and institutions. Critique should foster the reworking of social structures and institutions to encourage solidarity, in ways that try to fulfill the dual promises of democracy: critical thinking *and* collectivity, together.

This prompts us to consider the spaces and places of these moments of thinking and the relationship between critique and collectivity. In other words, is thinking necessarily solitary for Adorno, or can we think together? Is the essence of democracy that is critique an individual pursuit, or is it an exercise of humans in common? Adorno's writings on thinking move back and forth between what is necessarily individual and what is shared. He sees the capacity for thinking as an element of our shared humanity, a praxis that we collectively share as humans. Further, there are ways that we can work together in common to learn to listen to these nonidentical elements and to tune our ears to the dissonant call of the particular objects of the world. Teaching us to cultivate this receptivity and attunement is what democratic leadership as democratic pedagogy means. And finally, the lessons we learn as a result of the practice of critique then prompt us into the collective world-building endeavors that can realize the promise of democracy.

Ultimately, though, Adorno's thought reflects his fear of the force of the collective that is a legacy of his experience under Nazi Germany, and so there is also a necessary individualism to the practice of thinking: we all still have to go through the process of encountering the nonidentical on our own, and we have to work through the critique in our own heads. We can have conversations in common and engage in kinds of collective action, both *before* the process of thinking and *after* it—to learn to cultivate attunement and to parse out the lessons of these encounters with the nonidentical—but no one else can think our thoughts for us, and there is an importantly individual element to this praxis. The whole idea of democratic leadership as democratic pedagogy is about providing the right balance for both the necessarily individual moments of democracy and its more collective moments, to protect the individual space of thinking while also providing the collective space for conversation, to allow the thinking that happens in our own heads to develop into the action that transforms our shared world.

Adorno is famously skeptical regarding mass movements because he thinks they are unlikely to foster the capacity for the critical resistance that he sees as an important prerequisite for meaningful action. This skepticism has been the primary justification for calling him apolitical, and yet his thoughts on democracy might be seen as radical in that he wants to root out the problematic ways of thinking—idealism, identity thinking, and the logic of abstract exchange—that pervade the (so-called) democratic institutions and practices of modernity. Meaningful democracy is defined by critique for Adorno because the creation of truly democratic social structures, institutions, and norms begins in these modes of being in which we are open, receptive, and attuned to the dissonant call of the nonidentical.

This receptive attunement is important not just for developing our capacities to authentically and autonomously think and feel for ourselves, but also for realizing the promise of democracy. We must be open to experiencing the world in more direct and immediate ways to appreciate how deeply our modes of experience are usually framed and preformed by conventional norms. We habitually experience life in a way that is largely filtered. But if we can try both to learn to see the outlines of these mediating conventions and to perceive our world more directly, we can better appreciate the forces that take power away from us by obstructing our ability to think and feel for ourselves, and we can work to reclaim that power over our own experience. Paradoxically, then, we must be receptive in order to negate; we must be open and accepting in order to learn to think against. Instead of trying to fit our experiences into premade categories, we could attend to the nonidentical feelings and thoughts that tell us something isn't right, that urge us to resist defining, identifying, adapting. We could, instead, hone our capacities for more direct perception through an abiding attentiveness that eschews fundamentalisms and certainties and just tries to see, listen, feel, think, and learn. So critique, for Adorno, is also about adopting a certain disposition, a style of comportment. Critique is also about holding ourselves in a certain way, meeting the world with a certain attitude that is at once more attentive, perceptive, and mindful and that combines critical thinking with compassionate feelings. That is the experience of meaningful democracy for Adorno.

## A Case Study from *Minima Moralia:* The Political Stakes of Experiencing the Nonidentical

Through a case study of one particular theme that is recurringly woven through the aphorisms of Adorno's *Minima Moralia: Reflections from Damaged Life,* I want to give a sense of what the method of negative dialectics looks like in action, when applied to a particular kind of nonidentical experienced in terms of psychological illness. Here the nonidentical is experienced in terms of feelings of angst, anxiety, and other forms of mental unease that can work as indicators of larger social, political, and economic problems. Yet other forces in modernity, here represented in terms of the abstracting, identifying, categorizing logics of conventional psychology, work to silence the dissonant call of these encounters with the nonidentical. The normalizing tendencies of conventional psychoanalysis, as Adorno shows, work to numb people to the critically illuminating experience of psychic illness and unease, cultivating a unique experience of alienation. Here, too, Adorno is fundamentally concerned with our ability to experience the nonidentical and to critique the forces that deaden us to this heightened mode of perception. But here Adorno applies the practice of negative dialectics to a specific cultural object in ways that allow us to see his thought in action. We can begin to see the larger political stakes of his thoughts on experience, which will be more fully developed in the next chapter.

For Adorno, feelings and emotions—especially of angst, anxiety, and alienating loss—are rich indicators of larger social problems. Through these feelings we confront the nonidentical that tells us "life does not live." In *Minima Moralia* Adorno is especially attuned to the unique experience of alienation that came along with the postwar therapeutic revolution in the United States. This was a time when psychoanalysis went mainstream, and both therapists and pharmacists were promising to lift the burden of various forms of psychic unease, anxieties, depressions, and neuroses. But the "cure," from Adorno's perspective, worked to fit everyone into the same mold of what he calls the "regular guy" and the "popular girl," normalizing, disciplining, and standardizing people into conventional forms. People with complex and diverse forms of dissatisfaction were "diagnosed" with general complexes and promised "ready made enlightenment."[16] Furthermore, the promise was not just relief from suffering, but "exuberant vitality" and "champagne jollity."[17]

Adorno reads the larger social and political landscape of post–World War II America through the cultural injunction to be happy. He was concerned with how the dominant psychoanalytic tendencies of the day sought to categorize any feeling other than happiness as pathological and treat it through normalizing therapies. The postwar therapeutic revolution in America tended to domesticate and tame these disruptive but illuminating feelings—these calls of the nonidentical—classifying them into abstract categories and concepts, with no reference to the individual's larger social, political, or economic context. It is no accident that the *Diagnostic and Statistical Manual of Mental Disorders* was first published in 1952. These tendencies are so worrisome to Adorno because he argues that things like anxiety or various types of "psychic wounds" actually hold valuable critical potential as feelings that protest against the sterile, homogeneous, mechanized form of normality that he calls "damaged life."[18] Particularly in *Minima Moralia,* Adorno engages in a quite deep and substantive critique of the ways that being able to actually *feel* our feelings and try to interpret them in terms of our larger context really matters in terms of the overall health of American democracy.

The happiness imperative that Adorno identifies in America—the tendency to repress, deny, or medicate any feelings of psychic unease—alienates us from ourselves, making us into merry automatons, perhaps, but not truly democratic citizens. Democracy demands that we feel, that we think, that we listen to the critical impulses that course through us as we live our daily lives. So anything that numbs these tendencies, whether we are talking about pernicious, overt repression or seemingly beneficial therapeutic medication, can have an alienating effect, for Adorno. This is just one example of how he sees affective responses, feelings, and emotions as politically significant.

As we have seen, at the level of everyday life the abstracting logic of identity (reflecting the logic of capitalist commodity exchange) pushes humans into conformity with conventions and fits both thought and action into established social norms and categories in ways that leave no room for the impulsive, the extraneous. Life is dominated by the logic of identity and the idealist dialectic that serves conservative interests of power, reconciling contradictions and abstracting particular differences to maintain the illusory appearance of equilibrium and harmony. Raging against all that is different, other, irreconcilable, and particular; the logic of identity eviscerates the "qualitative variety of experience" and imposes an "abstract monotony" on the "administered world."[19] Such a life can barely be called living.[20] For Adorno, it is a dull, lifeless, formulaic, alienated mode of experience: "our perspective of life has passed into an ideology which conceals the fact that there is life no longer."[21] Adorno consistently uses expressions such as "not living" and "death" to describe the personal, psychological, and social effects of modernity characterized by the urge to identify, to classify and categorize that which is other, particular, unique, different. In contrast, "life" is represented by the qualities that resist the logic of identity and refuse to be folded into the system. By paying attention to the disruptive qualities of particular things, letting an object "speak," and granting "preponderance to the object," the practice of negative dialectics works to break apart the false harmonies built up by the logic of

identity and the idealist dialectic.[22] Given the dominance of the systematizing logic of late modernity, negative dialectics becomes a politically valuable
practice of working against power and unsettling the status quo.

From Adorno's perspective, postwar psychoanalysis dangerously tamed
the critical power of psychic wounds in several ways: by abstracting particular experiences into universalizable general phenomena, by conventionaliz-
ing illnesses into predetermined categories, which lifts the burden of critical
thought from the individual, and by redirecting the cause of the problem
away from society toward a politically innocuous mechanism or complex.
Illnesses were domesticated, rendered harmless; their critical and political
potential was erased and they were seen as commonplace, even normal, not
a cause for concern or worry.

Adorno criticized how this process of standardization separated the
individual from his or her complexes and disorders, which were objectified
into things, unrelated to the sufferer's life experiences. Anxiety, for example, was seen as a symptom that could be defined in general and abstract
terms, manifesting itself in the same ways, regardless of personal or social
context: "Terror before the abyss of the self is removed by the consciousness
of being concerned with nothing so very different from arthritis or sinus
trouble. . . . They are accepted, but by no means cured, being merely fitted as
an unavoidable component into the surface of standardized life."[23]

The organization of psychoanalysis redirects people's energies toward fig-
uring out which complex they have: "initiates become adept at subsuming
all instinctual conflicts under such concepts as inferiority complex, mother-
fixation, extroversion and introversion."[24] This process of naming, categorizing, and diagnosing has the effect of making the individual's intensely
singular experience just another iteration of a generalized phenomenon:
"Ready-made enlightenment turns not only spontaneous reflection but also
analytical insights—whose power equals the energy and suffering that it cost
to gain them—into mass-produced articles, and the painful secrets of the
individual history, which the orthodox method is already inclined to reduce
to formulae, into commonplace conventions."[25]

Hard-won critical insights into one's condition vanish under the impri-
matur of socially authorized categories. In being officially recognized, individuals find comfort, even pleasure in being like everyone else, a specimen of
the majority, even in their weakness, even in their defects. "Catharsis, unsure
of success in any case, is supplanted by pleasure at being, in one's own weakness, a specimen of the majority. . . . One proves on the strength of one's
very defects that one belongs, thereby transferring to oneself the power and

vastness of the collective. . . . The individual is now scarcely capable of any impulse that he could not classify as an example of this or that publicly recognized constellation."[26]

As part of this standardization, conventionalization, and rationalization, a kind of quasi-Hobbesian subject is created, a mechanistic assemblage of moving parts. The individual is imagined as an apparatus composed of objectified instincts, psychological mechanisms, biological impulses, and inherited traits and characteristics. A division of labor is projected onto the organization of the psyche, the self, the individual as a whole. Each component of the self has a category for its appropriate use and, when the machine works properly, is activated for that use only in the proper context.

As Adorno puts it, "Psychology repeats in the case of properties what was done to property."[27] The ego takes on the role of "business manager," charged with deploying certain traits and characteristics at will to fit different social situations.[28] Is the context a funeral? Then sadness is called for. A popular movie that everyone likes? Cue the laughter and enthusiasm. A fancy meal at an expensive restaurant? Bring on the feelings of satisfaction and enjoyment. Thus, the individual's traits, characteristics, mechanisms, and instincts come to be imagined as malleable external objects: "Character traits, from genuine kindness to the hysterical fits of rage, become capable of manipulation, until they coincide exactly with the demands of a given situation. . . . They are no longer the subject; rather, the subject responds to them as to his internal object."[29] As Adorno says, "Subjectivity itself, knowledge, temperament, and powers of expression" are "reduced to an abstract mechanism, functioning autonomously and divorced both from the personality of their 'owner' and from the material and concrete nature of the subject-matter at hand."[30] Through the process of categorizing mechanisms, the self confronts itself as a conglomeration of objectified parts.

But the management of these parts is left not to the individual, but to the collective authority of society. This is the danger that Adorno associates with psychoanalysis becoming professionalized and organized like a business with "clients." Psychoanalysis, now infiltrated by the authority of mainstream society, became a power working to "calibrate" individuals to work in conventional ways, shaping the appropriate deployment of traits, mechanisms, and impulses.[31] Adorno sees psychoanalysis as instilling in people an "empty, mechanized quality," a "pattern of the reflex-dominated, follow-my-leader behaviour" that is "to be entered to the account not only of their illness but also of their cure."[32] Yet the psychoanalytic "cure" is necessarily violent: "the libidinal achievements demanded of an individual behaving as healthy in body and mind, are such as can be performed only at the cost of the profoundest mutilation, of internalized castration."[33] For Freud, castration anxiety is connected with the fear of a loss of power, whereas psychoanalysis plays the role of helping us recognize and cope with this anxiety. But for Adorno, in another provocative inversion, psychoanalysis itself becomes responsible for the mutilation that deforms and dominates in the name of health.[34]

Ultimately, the "dissection of man into his faculties" and the categorization of mechanisms and complexes that characterized postwar psychoanalysis were tools for control. In a striking hyperbole, Adorno compares psychoanalysis with fascism, saying that the "psycho-analyst's wisdom" became a "technique," a "racket" that bound "suffering and helpless people irrevocably to itself, in order to command and exploit them."[35] But psychoanalysis is a form of domination that operates in subtle and seductive ways: "It is part of the mechanism of domination to forbid recognition of the suffering it produces."[36] The silencing effect of psychoanalysis works in two ways. First, to criticize it is to open oneself to charges of illness, to show oneself to be in need of treatment: "He who calls it by its name will be told gloatingly by psycho-analysts that it is just his Oedipus complex."[37] But, second, even more insidiously, to criticize psychoanalysis is to seem to cling insanely to pain and unhappiness, since such therapy is supposed to be for our own health and enlightenment, to help us enjoy life more. Why would we criticize something that's for our own good, something that promises to make us good, better, and even best?

Adorno was especially sensitive to how American psychoanalysis aimed not just to make the individual "normal," but better than normal. It prescribed exuberant happiness itself, restoring a capacity to take pleasure in mainstream life that was thought to be "impaired by neurotic illness."[38] As he notes, thinking about the problem in these terms is itself problematic. We are conceived as though we have a part whose function is to experience pleasure, but this mechanism can break down and sometimes needs repair. To be "fixed," to be happy, however, the neurotic must compulsively take pleasure in the offerings of mainstream culture:

> Prescribed happiness looks exactly what it is; to have a part in it, the neurotic thus made happy must forfeit the last vestige of reason left to him by repression and regression, and to oblige the analyst, display indiscriminate enthusiasm for the trashy film, the expensive but bad meal in the French restaurant, the serious drink and the love-making taken like medicine as 'sex.' . . . The admonitions to be

happy, voiced in concert by the scientifically epicurean sanatorium-director and the highly-strung propaganda chiefs of the entertainment industry, have about them the fury of the father berating his children for not rushing joyously downstairs when he comes home irritable from his office.[39]

The demand that we be happy, the diagnosis that there must be something wrong with those who cannot take pleasure in conventional modes of living, is itself a form of domination. This demand for conformity with a diseased society effaces the underlying social causes of unhappiness.

Yet the "gospel of happiness" masks itself as a concern for psychological health, as a guide for how one should live life properly: "What a state the dominant consciousness must have reached, when the resolute proclamation of compulsive extravagance and champagne jollity, formerly reserved for attachés in Hungarian operettas, is elevated in deadly earnest to a maxim of right living."[40] The injunction to be happy must be pressed on us with increasing fervor and desperation. The more problematic the social reality, the more society generally and psychology in particular admonish us to be happy and to think we must be in need of treatment if we are not. Instead of fulfilling its early critical promise, psychoanalysis became guilty of promoting a "health unto death," all the while seeming to improve life, normalize it, enhance it, promising enlightenment. Instead of being marked by suffering, those who are most alienated seem determinedly, resolutely happy and healthy. Adorno gives us evocative images of the "sickness of the healthy," saying the traces of their unique illness cover their skin "like a rash printed in regular patterns."[41] For Adorno, the following verses capture the "psychic economy" of postwar America: "Wretchedness remains. When all is said,/It cannot be uprooted, live or dead./So it is made invisible instead."[42]

In postwar America, the negative affective responses that Adorno sees as valuable pathways toward critique are what we immediately try to skip past on the road to happiness. Taken together, the paradigm of biological materialism and the medical model, the conventionalization of psychological illnesses—as well as the American enthusiasm for all things "more," better, longer, and faster—work to drown out the discordant call of the nonidentical qualities of psychic disease. For Adorno, psychoanalysis alienates us from the praxis of thinking, from a potential shared collective endeavor that is a central feature of a life that truly lives. Since the nonidentical qualities that can stimulate critique are contained within the antagonistic features of objects, thinking exists at least as a universal *possibility* for those who can learn to see, listen to, and engage with particularity.[43] Not only is critical thinking, or "open thinking," a praxis that "points beyond itself," but it also is "more closely related to a praxis truly involved in change than in a position of mere obedience for the sake of praxis."[44] There is a "utopian impulse in thinking."[45] Given what is being sacrificed, no wonder Adorno describes the achievements that psychoanalysis associates with health and happiness as "the profoundest mutilation," as "internalized castration," as a testament to the magnitude of the loss.

In addition, the way Adorno defines democracy in terms of critique, as the fulfillment of the human praxis of negation, of thinking and feeling against the conditions we are given as inevitable, further highlights the political dangers of the happiness imperative. The experience of alienation, of damaged life, is a major problem for democracy. When people cannot fully and deeply experience the world around them, they are blocked from the encounters with the nonidentical that prompt them to negate and critique. As we have seen, when people are alienated from themselves, they are also alienated from democracy.

In these ways, Adorno reminds us of what is lost if we listen only to the imperatives to be happy. The conventionalization of psychological illness and the promotion of exuberant vitality lift the burden of critical self-reflection from the individual, shift the focus away from the nonidentical qualities of disease, and redirect energy away from an exploration of the conditions of our personal and social lives. Paradoxically, in the pursuit of happiness, we may participate in a less visible regime of domination. Because of the different ways both eviscerate life and self, Adorno draws unsettling parallels between something as seemingly innocuous as psychoanalysis and something as abhorrent as fascism. Here, too, we see the specter of the happiness imperative: "there is a straight line of development between the gospel of happiness and the construction of camps of extermination so far off in Poland that each of our own countrymen can convince himself that he cannot hear the screams of pain. That is the model of an unhampered capacity for happiness."[46] Adorno did not think he had completely left fascism behind him when he emigrated to the United States. In America he detected strong traces of suppression and domination in a seemingly unlikely place, in the psychoanalytic discourses of health and happiness. Here, instead of enlightening critical self-reflection, was a subtle form of violence, repression, and control. Here alienation took on a new face, but it represented damaged life all the same.

## Attentive Perception, Mindful Attunement, Critical Thinking, and Compassionate Feeling

In this final section, I draw from two novelist-philosophers who both empha-size the larger social and political significance of a certain mode of percep-tion in ways that are sympathetic to Adorno's own views on experience and the promise of democracy. In different ways, Marilynne Robinson and David Foster Wallace help us further appreciate why micro-level practices of atten-tive perception and mindful attunement are politically significant.

For Marilynne Robinson, if democracy means that the people have power and authority, then to fulfill that idea we need to truly respect individual experience, our own and others'. We need to view our own experiences, our own daily lives, as powerful and empowering, and grant this same respect to others' experiences. As she writes, "To identify sacred mystery with every individual experience, every life, giving the word its largest sense, is to arrive at democracy as an ideal, and to accept the difficult obligation to honor oth-ers and oneself with something wholly approaching due reverence."[47] On a practical level, the reverence for individual experience that is a necessary counterpart to the idea that people have power and authority means a relent-less desire to try to see for ourselves, hear for ourselves, and feel for ourselves. We begin by opening our senses more widely. Robinson abides by the imper-ative that "everything always bears looking into, astonishing as that fact is."[48] So, she says, she has spent her life "watching," not "to see beyond the world," but just to see "what is plainly before [her] eyes."[49] She counsels us to "forget definition, forget assumption, watch."[50]

Robinson is concerned with illuminating and experiencing what she calls "complexities," "ambiguities," and "countervailing experience" in ways that are sympathetic with Adorno's understanding of the nonidentical.[51] She wants us to pay attention to all those things that don't fit into the categories we are given. Here we can see how her critique of ostensibly universal and all-encompassing categories and definitions is strikingly similar to Adorno's critique of "identity thinking" and the systematizing logics of modernity in general. Robinson, too, is concerned with how these categories tend to operate violently on those things that they cannot encompass. When we let preformed definitions, categories, assumptions, and norms shape our knowl-edge of, and action in, the world, we let conventional wisdom do the think-ing and feeling for us. But because our daily lives are so much more complex and mysterious than any form of received knowledge allows, these habits of avoiding what our own senses tell us lead to an impoverished and mechanical—but also dangerously certain and arrogant—way of life that falls far short of the ideal of democracy.

Especially in the modern era, she thinks that we are plagued by a "tendency to fit a tight and awkward carapace of definition over humankind, and to try to trim the living creature to fit the dead shell. . . . We inhabit, we are part of, a reality for which explanation is much too poor and small."[52] She thinks that our "attempt to impose definitions on indeterminacy and degree and exception is about the straightest road to mischief that I know of, very deeply worn, very well-traveled to this day."[53] We are mysteries to ourselves and each other, and "if it is agreed that we are in this respect mysterious, then we should certainly abandon easy formulas of judgment."[54] So perceptive attention and mindful attunement to everyday life are important because of the respect they grant to individual experience—our own and others'—but they are also important because of how they chasten politically dangerous fundamentalisms. In a way that is very sympathetic to Adorno's own vision, Robinson thinks that using our senses and paying close attention to the complexity of the world immediately around us stimulate our critical capacities in ways that work against blind certainty and stubborn arrogance. Here, opening wider the senses that we associate with the body primes us for the kind of skepticism, questioning, and critical thinking that we associate with the mind. As is true for Adorno, for Robinson mind and body work together to facilitate the kind of heightened experience that the idea of democracy requires and that is necessary if we are to be fully empowered as individuals.

These concepts come from Robinson's essays, but the figures populating her fiction also exhibit a capacity to recognize the illusory nature of the seemingly firm structures and foundations that surround them—whether those be social norms, conventions, doctrines, houses, or towns. Her unconventional heroes—Sylvie and Ruth in *Housekeeping,* Reverend Ames in *Gilead,* Jack and Glory in *Home*—adopt an attitude of open perception and mindful awareness to the unfathomably mysterious and ultimately unknowable world around them, apart from the disciplining and comforting constraints of assumptions and categories.[55] They work carefully to avoid being judgmental, and their own attitudes of acceptance, flexibility, and forgiveness powerfully highlight the repressive judgments and constraining conventions of others. Through their open perception her heroes find the new, the strange, the unexpected, the disruptive, the unusual in what lies close at hand. They exemplify this democratic ethos by reminding us that what is local and familiar is always also exotic and exciting, that what seems known and comfortable can always also be strange and mysterious, and by emphasizing how the new can spring up within the terrain of the old. Her heroes perform a kind of immanent critique on comfort, familiarity, on the ideological landscape of "home," finding active, vital, and vibrant contradictory value in what might initially seem given, natural, and inert, or even pathological and problematic.

David Foster Wallace also sees certain forms of direct sensory experience as threatened by the forces of modernity but vitally important to our collective lives together. In his now famous commencement speech, "This Is Water," Wallace explores the platitude that a good liberal arts education is valuable for teaching you "how to think," but he takes this in new directions and develops a meditation on how a certain mode of thinking can allow us to experience a unique form of freedom in the midst of the "day-in-day-out" of everyday life.[56] Further, like Adorno's view, like Robinson's view, Wallace's understanding of "thinking" is about perception, experience, and a kind of deep respect for and compassion for other bodies, for other people. Wallace begins with a story about how fish don't know what water is, because it is *all* they know: their senses are immune to the things that surround them in the most immediate and direct way. For us too, "the most obvious, ubiquitous, important realities are often the ones that are hardest to see and talk about."[57] We tend to go through life operating on our "default settings," mechanically, not using our senses, not being alive, conscious, attentive, mindful, or aware. If the liberal arts teach me how to think, this is really supposed to mean teaching me "to be a little less arrogant, to have some 'critical awareness' about myself and my certainties . . . because a huge percentage of the stuff that I tend to be automatically certain of is, it turns out, totally wrong and deluded."[58]

Wallace wants us to use our bodies and our minds to overcome the most primary default setting, the feeling that everything revolves around us. He gives us, we might say, an image of the ideal liberal subject, self-interested, atomistic, independent, and to quote Wallace, "uniquely, completely, imperially alone, day in and day out."[59] "Here," he says, is "one example of the utter wrongness of something I tend to be automatically sure of. Everything in my own immediate experience supports my deep belief that I am the absolute center of the universe, the realest, most vivid and important person in existence."[60] To get outside this default setting, you need to use your senses, to try to "stay alert and attentive instead of getting hypnotized by the constant monologue inside your head."[61] Ultimately, for Wallace, "'learning how to think' really means learning how to exercise some control over *how* and *what* you think. It means being conscious and aware enough to *choose* what you pay attention to and to *choose* how you construct meaning from experience."[62] And this is advice that really matters for how we live our lives and how we live with others. This is advice that can affect the quality of our collective lives together.

Wallace gives an example of how this way of thinking can change how we engage in the drudgery of adulthood, of mindless, repetitive tasks such as fighting rush hour traffic after work to drive to a crowded grocery store, filled with confusing choices, long lines, and rushing, grumpy, distracted people, then fighting traffic to get back home to cook dinner and eat. This is the kind of thing that adult life is filled with, and "the point is that petty, frustrating crap like this is exactly where the work of choosing comes in."[63] Because if I don't make a "conscious decision about how to think and what to pay attention to, I'm gonna be pissed and miserable every time I have to food-shop" because of the natural default setting that tells me I am the center of the universe and focuses only on "my hungriness and my fatigue and my desire to just get home and it's going to seem, for all the world, like everybody else is just *in my way*."[64] But if we can try to get outside our own head, then we can experience our own lives and other people in an entirely different way. Instead of being frustrated with other people, we can be compassionate and imagine the struggles they themselves might be going through. Instead of being bored or angry, we can use our senses and our ability to extend beyond ourselves to find joy in unexpected places—even in supermarkets and rush-hour traffic. Ultimately, if you really learn how to pay attention, "it will actually be within your power to experience a crowded, hot, slow, consumer-hell-type situation as not only meaningful, but sacred, on fire with the same force that lit the stars—compassion, love, the subsurface unity of all things."[65]

And for Wallace, this is a kind of freedom. It's not the freedom of the liberal capitalist individual. It's not the "freedom all to be lords of our tiny skull-sized kingdoms, alone at the center of all creation."[66] But it's a more precious and more important kind of freedom, one that we don't hear much about in the "great outside world of winning and achieving and displaying."[67] But this other kind of freedom, in which we consciously *choose* how to experience the world around us, this "really important kind of freedom involves attention, and awareness, and discipline, and effort, and being able truly to care about other people and to sacrifice for them, over and over, in myriad petty little unsexy ways, every day."[68] This continual striving to stay conscious and alive to our world and to be compassionate to the experience of others, this is "the real value of a real education, which has nothing to do with grades or degrees and everything to do with simple awareness—awareness of what is so real and essential, so hidden in plain sight all around us, that we have to keep reminding ourselves over and over: 'This is water.' 'This is water.'"[69]

Wallace is also advocating a way of life that combines body and mind, that uses the senses and the imagination to heighten our capacity to experience the world beyond our normal, conventional robotic settings. Like Adorno, and like Robinson, Wallace advocates widening our senses to take in our world more deeply—paying attention, staying conscious, being aware—to learn to think differently and to move beyond what seems given, natural, inevitable. Further, Wallace, like Robinson, like Adorno, advocates sensing the world more deeply, directly, and immediately as a pathway to greater skepticism about the reality we are given. And finally, Wallace, like Robinson, helps us better appreciate how, in Adorno's work too, all this sensation, attunement, attention, and perception take place in service of larger ideals such as freedom and democracy. All these thinkers elevate these concepts beyond their conventional definitions and ask more of them, and ask more of us who try to fulfill the potential of these promises.

And for all three, thinking is not valued for its own sake, but for the way it can change our way of being with others in the world. For Robinson, Wallace, and Adorno, thinking (and the heightened mode of experience that prompts us to think) works in service of compassion, in service of attentiveness to the pain and suffering of others, in service of greater respect and reverence for other bodies. The sympathies among these three thinkers also serve the purpose of reframing the conventional wisdom about Adorno's excessive intellectualism. In fact, Adorno draws complex connections between the mind and the body, between somatic experience and cognitive capacities, between our ability to sense the world around us and our ability to think critically about it. The mind works in service of these other, larger goals, then. As Wallace says, this is as it should be: "Think of the old cliché about 'the mind being an excellent servant but a terrible master.'"[70]

The final stars in Adorno's constellation of ideas are education and democratic pedagogy. Ultimately, for Wallace, as for Adorno, education is also in service of these larger goals of truly experiencing our daily lives, thinking for ourselves, practicing compassion, and enjoying an unconventional kind of freedom. The real task of education, for Wallace, is to cultivate this greater capacity for compassion, this ability to get outside the imperial self. For Adorno, education is vitally important for teaching us how to think critically. Thus, education is understood as a broadly civic project that moves beyond the institution of the school and aims to foster people's ability to identify the nonidentical currents and the countertendencies of their own daily lives. Education cultivates this attentiveness to the contradictions, disjunctures, disharmonies, and dissonances of our own bodies and minds and of the world around us. In this way, education is also about encouraging us to experience our lives more deeply and with greater attention. But education, importantly for Adorno, should show us how to be softer, less hard, less cold, less steely in the face of the pain and suffering of other bodies. Learning how to think against conventional society and learning how to feel against it are both part of the educational program that Adorno introduces, as we will see in the next chapters.

# 4

# Democratic Leadership

## Egalitarian Guidance and a Plan for Empowering the People

> Today perhaps more than ever, it is the function of democratic leadership to make the subjects of democracy, the people, *conscious of their own wants and needs as against the ideologies which are hammered into their heads by the innumerable communication of vested interests.* They must come to understand those tenets of democracy which, if violated, logically impede the exercise of their own rights and reduce them from self-determining subjects to objects of opaque political maneuvers.
>
> —Adorno, "Democratic Leadership and Mass Manipulation"

In 1950 Adorno published an essay, written in English, titled "Democratic Leadership and Mass Manipulation" in the volume *Studies in Leadership: Leadership and Democratic Action,* edited by Alvin W. Gouldner. The volume aims to analyze leadership in ways that, as the editor says, "promise some help to people engaged in democratic action."[1] It seeks to analyze leadership as a "social problem," as something that can be fixed. Leadership skills are presented as things that can be acquired, and the book is driven by a sense that widespread alienation and the rise of modern dictators make this an especially pressing social problem. The volume brings together an impressive roster of social scientists whose names have stood the test of time into our own era: Robert Merton, Paul Lazarsfeld, Daniel Bell, Seymour Martin Lipset, and David Riesman, to name a few. The tenor of the volume is left-leaning, with citations to Erich Fromm and Herbert Marcuse in the editor's introduction and essays that, as Gouldner notes, frequently appeal to common sources such as Marx, Freud, Durkheim, and Weber. The book is divided into sections that look at different types of leaders (such as bureaucrats, agitators, and informal leaders), leadership in group settings (such as social classes, unions, grass-roots labor, ethnic and racial minority groups, as well as the nascent feminist movement), authoritarian and democratic leaders (propaganda versus democratic modes of leadership), and the ethics and techniques of leadership (how to deal with apathy, stressful situations, and problems of succession).

In the editor's introduction to *Studies in Leadership*, Gouldner gives an overview of the dominant ways that leadership was conceived of at the time, while differentiating his book's approach. Traditionally, leadership studies were characterized by "great man" theories, a kind of aristocratic social theory arguing that it was "men of a distinctive stamp, predestined by their possession of unusual traits, who led events and molded situations."[2] Under this theory, scholars focused on studying the traits possessed by leaders, their distinctive ways of acting, their personality characteristics. Here the particular attributes of the individual were what permitted him or her to become an effective leader. The next category of leadership studies that Gouldner discusses, the Situationists (distinct from the later Situationist movement of the late 1960s), emerged out of a polemic against the "traits" and "great man" school of thought. The Situationists "developed the antithetical position— that it was the situation that determined the leader's traits," a position shaped by their "adherence to democratic values, the belief that leaders were not born but made."[3]

Gouldner's volume is more sympathetic to this democratic theory of leadership, but he thinks the Situationists were ultimately co-opted by the bureaucracy. Bureaucratic organizations funded many studies that in turn limited the scope of this school of thought. Situationists became too much governed by the research needs of bureaucracies, characterized by highly formalized offices, limited and specific situations, and delimited areas of responsibility and authority.[4] The knowledge gained from these studies focused on articulating what kind of person could be effective in these specific situations, but this "radical emphasis on leadership traits in relation to concrete situations and roles, narrowly conceived, while useful to bureaucratic organization, is not of equal value to democratic organization."[5]

Gouldner's volume is firmly committed to carving out space for democratic forms of leadership over and against the antidemocratic and authoritarian social tendencies of the day. As he says, "In short, it is a frankly partisan book," one that supports democratic values, but this is its only commitment: no other values are insisted on by the editor.[6] This is a book that seeks to examine leadership in a way that is useful to those engaged in democratic action: "The problem confronting democrats is how to use leadership for realizing their goals, rather than how to get along without leadership."[7] Gouldner's volume seeks to analyze leadership with a focus on the wide variety of situations and problems that arise in democratic societies like the United States, with an eye toward specific challenges such as apathy and propaganda. He is interested in exploring the role of leadership in democratic social action, in how to organize effectively in ways that are also democratic.

Adorno's contribution to the volume is sympathetic with these broad concerns. But his essay does not conform with the definition of democratic leadership that Gouldner sets out in his introduction, a definition to which the other essays in the volume generally adhere. Gouldner is not interested in the "attainments" or "traits" possessed by great leaders; he is interested instead in "the varied modes of ascendancy of leaders" in a democratic society, their "techniques and problems."[8] But his volume does subscribe to other mainstream components of the concept of leadership. Leaders are described, in the literature, as those "whose status is recognized as superior to others engaged in the same activity" and as those who "emit stimuli that are 'responded to integratively by other people.'"[9] Regarding the first component, though some scholars want to measure status informally, Gouldner asserts that "an approach to leadership *suitable for use on the action level* must include those characteristics of leaders, such as power, prestige, and authority, which in large degree accrue to and are reinforced by formal statuses."[10] Under a democratic model, formal and informal norms, as well as the skills needed for specific situations, work by popular selection to allow some to rise in status. Regarding the second component of this definition, leaders also generate followers in the group. The book as a whole is guided by this definition of leadership: "A leader will, then, here be considered as any individual whose behavior stimulates patterning of the behavior in some group. By emitting some stimuli, he facilitates group action toward a goal or goals, whether the stimuli are verbal, written, or gestural. Whether they are rational, nonrational, or irrational in content is also irrelevant in this context. Whether these stimuli pertain to goals or to means, cluster about executive or perceptive operations, is a secondary consideration, so long as they result in the structuring of group behavior."[11]

For the purposes of Gouldner's volume, leaders legitimately and rightfully guide group behavior because of their knowledge and expertise, their unusual capabilities, by how their appointment and activities are validated by traditional or legal norms, or because they exemplify "other qualities valued by the group."[12] These are individuals whose leadership is importantly sanctioned and supported by the group. Also, "leadership" is seen not as the trait of any one individual, but as a role different people in the group may take on at different times: "A leader is not a total personality, but a person who in certain situations emits legitimate group-patterning stimuli."[13]

Adorno speaks of leadership in an entirely different vein, in two major ways. First, he focuses on what leaders *do*, in terms of how they accomplish their goals with respect to their target audience. He analyzes their method, not who they are, or what skills they have attained, or how their authority is legitimated, or how they are received by their fellow group members. He explores the actions of the leader, his or her praxis. He does not speak of leaders as having any special status in terms of their position or their educational credentials. Democratic leaders, in Adorno's sense, are simply those who converse with other people, to work with them toward becoming more meaningfully democratic in their own practice, toward attaining that sense of true empowerment and greater autonomy and self-determination that Adorno calls "democratic enlightenment." Anyone who can help other people learn to experience the world around them in a way that fosters encounters with the nonidentical is a democratic leader. Anyone who can stimulate other people's capacity for critical thinking is a democratic leader.

Second, Adorno speaks of democratic leaders entirely outside the context of an action group. There is no group that the leader leads or that patterns itself on his or her behavior or responds to his or her stimuli. Adorno's "democratic leaders" are not leading any particular group or social action organization: there are no followers. He seems to be saying that anyone who reads his essay and understands this process—of stimulating the capacity for critique, of highlighting people's own contradictory countertendencies, and working against various forms of authoritarianism—could be considered a democratic leader. These seem to be people who would try to integrate various kinds of consciousness-raising conversations as part of their everyday lives, engaging the people they come into contact with, working with people wherever they are to try to move them toward greater empowerment and autonomy. Ideally, we would all strive to be democratic leaders. For Adorno, democracy gains its normative, authentic, and robust meaning from the everyday critical practices of individuals. And his democratic leaders are people who try to cultivate this capacity for critique, but not in any official way or on the basis of any official position. This is consistent with Adorno's view that critique is a universal human praxis that is equally available to anyone who can open himself or herself up to the nonidentical. Thinking and feeling against given conditions are possibilities that are available to us all as a part of our humanity, and guiding others toward this practice is a kind of leadership we should engage in as fellow humans.

Third, the project as Adorno outlines it here looks a lot like a form of therapy or psychoanalysis. Twice he notes that the democratic leader cannot engage in psychoanalysis on a large scale, both because it is not feasible and because of his own problems with mainstream forms of psychology. Adorno says that "full fledged analysis" is "out of the question," but still "attempts will have to be made."[14] But despite his own critique of psychoanalysis, there is still something therapeutic about the kind of leadership he envisions. He starts with people where they are, in their own specific concrete conditions, and describes one-on-one discussions and interviews in which "democratic leaders" talk through people's conscious and unconscious fears, desires, and prejudices. The goal is to work with people to find the "levers" that make authoritarianism attractive to them, and to push on these "nerve centers" in ways that redirect this energy toward the cause of democracy, while also drawing out the subterranean countertendencies and contradictions that can further incline people toward a more meaningful practice of democratic citizenship. Ultimately, democratic leaders guide others through their encounters with the nonidentical, help them make sense of these experiences and draw meaning from them, and then use these moments as a stimulus for action.

All this is very similar to the open way that Adorno defines the educator, as we will see more clearly in the next chapter. He defines both the democratic leader and the practitioner of democratic pedagogy in terms of what they *do*, in terms of specific practical moves, and encourages energetic people who have a mind to foster this kind of change to take up the activities of leading and educating outside the conventional spaces and places we would associate them with: outside a specific organized group, outside the school. As this chapter and the following will demonstrate, ultimately Adorno sees democratic leadership as a form of democratic pedagogy. The moves he associates with both practices map onto each other: leadership is about education and education is a form of leadership, and both start with people where they are, in their immediate, concrete, material circumstances, to talk with them about the discordant, contradictory, antagonistic desires, impulses, emotions, or thoughts they might experience but then deny or disavow. The role of the educator or leader, for Adorno, is to focus the individual's attention on these experiences of the nonidentical as a form of interruptive agency, and to work with them to identify the nascent critique of existing conditions that is contained in these forces and feelings. Both the leader and the educator would walk with the individual through this process of critique, to cultivate a different mode of experiencing the world that regularly attends to the nonidentical instead of ignoring or repressing it and to ultimately encourage action that is based on these insights, in the form of a life lived differently as well as more overt forms of resistance and protest.

Specifically, in his essay on democratic leadership, Adorno envisions working with Max Horkheimer to write a manual that outlines the various tactics used by authoritarian agitators and also contains counteracting strategies. Adorno says the manual is "as yet in a preliminary stage" and notes "there still lies ahead the extremely difficult task of translating the objective findings on which it is based into a language that can be easily understood without diluting its substance."[15] This task of "translation" to a broader audience, Adorno notes, "must be accomplished through trial and error, through the testing of the manual's understandability and effectiveness with various groups and by continuous improvements, before the manual can be distributed on a large scale."[16] Part of Adorno's goal here seems to have been accomplished with the publication of *The Psychological Technique of Martin Luther Thomas' Radio Addresses.* But this study of the tactics employed by one particularly popular American radio demagogue does not function so much as a productive and useful manual for democratic leaders as an analysis of the deceptive strategies Thomas employed.

"Democratic Leadership and Mass Manipulation" has the flavor of a proposal for a larger project that the essay itself cannot complete. The essay reads more as a précis than anything else. But a précis of what? Reading "Democratic Leadership and Mass Manipulation" alongside his writings on education, it becomes clear that Adorno's plan for democratic leadership is really a plan for a civic education project that operates through radically democratic forms of pedagogy. If Adorno never fully accomplished this goal or completed his intended project of translating his findings into a manual that would be useful for democratic leaders, the writings I analyze in this book give us a sense of that larger project. In this essay he speaks of the need to communicate his ideas to the *demos* in a more direct and immediate way, to distribute these ideas "on a large scale," working to translate and introduce a theory of democratic leadership that represents a nascent practice of negative dialectics to a broader audience. Essentially, the present volume pieces together the uncompleted project he titles "Operation Boomerang" to get a sense of what Adorno's manual for democratic leadership would have looked like if he had been able to finish translating it, introducing it to the *demos,* and distributing it on a large scale.

By examining this essay alongside his writings on education, composed largely after his return to Germany, we can see Adorno working to lay out an understanding of how democratic leadership can take the form of a specific kind of democratic pedagogy. In this way, Adorno's piece on democratic leadership provides an illuminating lens through which we can better understand the strategies he undertakes in texts such as *Current of Music, The Psychological Technique of Martin Luther Thomas' Radio Addresses,* and even *The Stars Down to Earth.*

## Operation Boomerang

Adorno's essay is placed in the section of the volume on authoritarian and democratic leaders and, at first glance, it seems to focus more on a critique of authoritarian leaders and the manipulation tactics they use to undermine American democracy. Adorno makes connections between Hitler and American demagogues who also take on fascist methods, appealing to people's sense of powerlessness, manipulating them, and also stirring up anti-Semitism. But Adorno's essay actually balances itself between authoritarian modes of leadership and the counteracting form of truly democratic leadership that would be its obverse. He explores what makes American demagogues so popular, and then focuses on how we can use this knowledge to create a robustly democratic form of leadership that will be able to cultivate more truly democratic citizens. He is concerned with how an ostensibly democratic American landscape actually bears strong resemblance to Hitler's Germany, populated with "hollow and inflated leaders" who demonstrate a "phony charisma" and prey on the powerlessness and impotence of citizens to cultivate obedience and irrationality. Adorno's starting point is that the promise of democracy in America is not being fulfilled. In fact, "today, democracy breeds antidemocratic forces and movements."[17]

Adorno begins by noting that democracy in the United States is being undermined by threats to autonomy in official and institutional political and economic realms. He cites, as just two examples, the rise of modern parties and their subservience to the world of finance and other vested interests in society, as well as the fact that democracy is increasingly equated with voting and elections that are controlled by the established leadership.[18] Institutional factors undermine citizens' everyday practices of democracy, with dire consequences. When "the people feel that they are unable actually to determine their own fate" and are "disillusioned about the authenticity and effectiveness of democratic political processes, they are tempted to surrender the substance of democratic self-determination and to cast their lot with those whom they consider at least powerful: their leaders."[19]

Democracy, for Adorno, is not defined in a "merely formalistic way," in terms of institutions, representation, or the will of the majority.[20] Rather, the "*content* of democratic decisions" matters, as well as how people reach those decisions. In addition, meaningful democracy is about what Adorno calls, at one point, "the dialectics of lived experience."[21] By this he means that democracy is a practice, a *doing*, rather than a *being*: it is not something you have, but something you strive to enact. For Adorno, as we have seen, democracy is defined by people's ability to engage in the praxis of thinking in their everyday lives, but also by their ability to attend to the nonidentical elements of the world (including pain, suffering, and psychic unease) that encourage critique if we can hear their call. So democracy, in terms of the dialectics of lived experience, is about thinking and feeling against the world we are given. As we have seen, Adorno's theory issues a kind of ethical imperative for us to attend to suffering, to let our gaze rest on pain, and to resist hardening ourselves and becoming cold. These corporeal, somatic, and affective elements are part of the practice of critique and thus are important elements of fulfilling the promise of democracy.

And if, as we have seen, Adorno identifies many de-democratizing forces in American society as well as a "thought-controlling mass culture," the situation is not entirely bleak. In this short essay on leadership, Adorno emphasizes how "grass-roots democracy, as opposed to official public opinion, shows amazing vitality."[22] He also says, "Those who prate about the immaturity of the masses" overlook "the mass potential of autonomy and spontaneity which is very much alive."[23] But most important, he argues that there are "strong countertendencies" we can see in citizens that "work against the all-pervasive ideological patterns of our cultural climate."[24] Adorno's proposed form of democratic leadership, which he also calls "democratic enlightenment" has to "lean on these countertendencies" and has to draw on all the scientific knowledge available regarding how to appeal to the whole self—the intellectual as well as emotional self—to work with people to help them see how the dominant ideology is actually at odds with some of their own values and beliefs.[25] Adorno understands that what authoritarian leaders do well is to appeal to the cognitive self as well as the passionate self, the conscious as well as the unconscious, but of course they do this in service of antidemocratic causes. Adorno argues that a truly democratic form of leadership can't just "give them the facts" and tell people that what they believe is wrong.[26] It must work with people on a personal, individual level to help them see the contradictions in their own lives and to draw out the lessons of the countertendencies that exist at the level of their beliefs or their practice.

As we have seen, when he speaks of countertendencies, Adorno means the nonidentical energies that course through us as we live in the world. These are the forces that interrupt our tendencies to accept and adapt to given conditions: countertendencies are contradictory, antagonistic currents that make us stop and think. Countertendencies can take the form of affective responses, manifesting as forces, feelings, and intensities that can push us toward change if we can learn to stay with them and draw out their meaning. Instead of ignoring, repressing, or disavowing these interruptions and rushing on to the next thing, Adorno thinks democratic leaders are those people who could help us pause and analyze the significance of these encounters with the nonidentical.

If the democratic leader emerged with the rise of modern democracy as someone who was "supposedly qualified to guide the rank and file through rational argumentation," Adorno thinks that today the "truly democratic functioning of leadership" has vanished, if it ever really existed in the first place.[27] But he does want to hold on to this idea of guiding people through rational argument—through a conversation almost like a therapy session— to help them more clearly appreciate how certain ideologies work against their own stated desires and interests, in ways that go against the grain and create the tensions, contradictions, twinges, and interruptions that he calls countertendencies.

Democratic leaders can help people recognize how their consent is manufactured, so to speak, how their desires and needs are manufactured. But for Adorno, these processes whereby people adapt and conform, however smooth and seamless their internalization of social authority seems to be, don't happen without some part of the self, however small, kicking back. Democratic leaders can help turn these moments of unconscious rebellion into more conscious acts of resistance, through one-on-one conversations, discussions, interviews, and other unspectacular ways of encouraging people to engage in a politics of self-cultivation and transformation.

A truly democratic leader would bring about the "emancipation of consciousness rather than its further enslavement," but Adorno is adamant that there cannot be any "inconsistency between ends and means" because that would "impair the sincerity of the whole approach and destroy its inherent conviction."[28] But Adorno's whole method is based on turning negatives into positives, subverting and inverting authoritarianism for democratic purposes, turning things inside out and upside down, pitting opposing forces against each other to create something productive.

The metaphors Adorno uses to describe his plan for "democratic enlightenment" signal this dialectical method. In "Democratic Leadership and Mass Manipulation" he uses the following terms to describe this plan for democratic leadership. On the most meta-level, the project is called Operation Boomerang because of how he intends "to use the mobility of prejudice for its own conquest," to turn one thing against itself and send it flying in another direction.[29] The other meta-concept Adorno invokes is the idea of the vaccine. He speaks of studying the pathological tendencies of existing democracy in America so as to "derive from them, as it were, vaccines against antidemocratic indoctrination."[30] A vaccine provides protection by working *through* and *with* the disease itself: the cure is created from the pathology. So Adorno's project for democratic leadership and democratic enlightenment will start with people where they are to invoke change and move them to a better place, but it will do so in two related ways: first, by drawing out their internal contradictions and highlighting how their own beliefs and practices contain countertendencies that push against the cause of authoritarianism and toward the cause of democracy; and second, by working with people, in conversation and dialogue, to create vaccines from their own pathologies, to turn their own feelings of impotence, their own longings for genuine relationships—all of which are pathologies stoked by modern mass society—against the fascist agitator, now exposed as a swindling manipulator.

But there is an important secondary level to Adorno's method of democratic leadership. If it operates by immanent critiques, by dialectics, by inversions, reversals, boomerangs, and vaccines, it also works on both a rational and extrarational level. Adorno wants to draw on all the lessons he's learned from studying the authoritarian personality and from analyzing the methods of fascist demagogues. He knows that antidemocratic movements gain traction by appealing to the whole person, playing on a person's fears and passions rather than just appealing to the rational and cognitive self. Consequently, any counteracting effort must also take the whole person into account. In the rest of this chapter, I will further draw out the implications of Adorno's understanding of democratic leadership.

## The "How" of Democratic Leadership

The authoritarian leader keenly connects "stimuli and susceptibility," shrewdly reading the culture and exploiting not just the predominant intellectual beliefs and values of the people, but their fears, desires, and emotions. Antidemocratism "feeds on age-old traditions and strong emotional sources," and the programs of American fascist agitators serve "as an outlet for aggressiveness and pent-up fury."[31] Drawing lessons from the success of antidemocratic movements, Adorno says that democratic leaders must study this "correspondence between stimuli and patterns of reaction."[32] This will enable them to use "the agitator's technique of lies as a guide for the realistic transformation of the truth principle into practice."[33] These susceptibilities represent important "levers" and "nerve centers," which can be redirected toward the cause of democracy and can "induce people to reflect about their own attitudes and opinions, which they usually take for granted."[34] He wants to press these levers and stimulate these susceptibilities, but he intends to turn them around to serve the cause of democratic enlightenment and empower the people toward greater autonomy and self-determination.

In what follows, I look at several specific examples that Adorno cites to get a sense of what this form of democratic leadership would look like in action, to paint a picture of the "how" of democratic leadership. In all these examples, the person who has taken on the role of leader works with other individuals to bring some kind of internal tension or conflict that they harbor to the level of conscious thought and to work with them to think through its larger implications. Leaders enter into the unique worlds of the individuals they are in dialogue with to find their own specific levers, nerve centers, or countertendencies—all of which are ultimately encounters with the nonidentical. The personal nature of these interviews, discussions, or workshops is important. The specific experience of unease or antagonism must be truly meaningful to the individual for him or her to be moved by critically analyzing it.

In the first example, Adorno discusses how certain kinds of individuals might be encouraged to engage in the kind of introspection that he sees as a necessary part of the kind of enlightenment he wants to foster. As he notes, the individual who is susceptible to the authoritarian leader resists serious introspection and is "incapable of finding fault with himself," and instead externalizes all problems onto the outside world.[35] And yet this person is also deeply insecure and internally conflicted: "The unwillingness to search in oneself is first of all an expression of the fear of making unpleasant discoveries."[36] At the same time that he avoids any real or serious introspection, however, the insecure person is likely to consult "quacks of every description, from the astrologer to the human-relations columnist."[37] This, at least, shows a "distorted" desire for some greater level of self-awareness. This is a lever, a nerve center, that can be drawn on productively in service of the truth principle. These individuals would benefit from, and also perhaps be flattered by and feel a narcissistic pleasure in, personal interviews that would help them uncover the motivations that lead to their feelings of prejudice, their desire to submit to an authority, and so on. As Adorno notes, "Such interviews might provide the prejudiced persons with a kind of relief and ignite what some psychologists call an 'aha-experience.'"[38] Here the democratic leader would foster a deeper mode of experience by working with the individual to confront his or her inner conflicts and insecurities and misplaced desire for greater understanding. These forms of psychic uneasiness are valuable countertendencies that could be turned into transformative critical insights.

To give another example of what this project might look like in practice, Adorno discusses how the arbitrary nature of the prejudiced person's object of hatred can be mobilized in the fight against antidemocratic feeling. He notes how studies have shown that even strongly prejudiced people show "a certain mobility in regard to the choice of their object of hatred."[39] For example, someone who demonstrates the kind of character traits that might make him anti-Semitic happens to be married to a Jewish woman, so the target of prejudice is deflected elsewhere, onto Greeks or Armenians, for example. Additionally, "he may not even remain faithful to his chosen foe."[40] These are all levers that can be pressed: the "feebleness, arbitrariness, and accidentality of the object choice *per se* may be turned into a force which would make the subjects doubtful about their own ideology. When they learn how little it matters whom they hate as long as they hate something, their ego might cease to side with hatred and the intensity of aggressiveness might subsequently decrease."[41] By working with individuals in specifically personal terms that pertain to their own lives and their own immediate circumstances, the democratic leader could draw out the internal contradictions at the root of this prejudice. But again, these kinds of conversations don't work in the abstract. The individual's own deeply contradictory feelings must be involved, and the democratic leader must press on the countertendency represented by the man's love for his Jewish wife and his hatred of other "others." Because of the ways that encountering these nonidentical elements and drawing out these countertendencies involve feelings and affective responses, the discussions must focus on people's immediate, concrete, personal conditions, starting where they are in their own lives.

Adorno gives another set of examples that highlight other countertendencies that are more generally rooted in American culture. Here the levers or nerve centers exist as part of a national identity, as part of the feeling of what it means to be American. For example, the "American tradition of common sense, of sales resistance" and of not wanting to be "treated like a sucker" is a valuable countertendency that can be redirected against the fascist agitator. If the authoritarian leader takes advantage of this susceptibility with specific stimuli—by telling Americans that they are being made into suckers by "the Jews, bankers, bureaucrats, and other 'sinister forces'"—the democratic leader can also make use of this susceptibility. Redirecting these countertendencies in the service of enlightenment, the democratic leader can highlight how, in fact, the fascist agitator is himself "nothing but a glorified barker."[42] If people don't like to be taken advantage of, then highlighting how they are being manipulated in specific ways that prompt them to experience authoritarian leaders differently can foster the realization of a productive antagonism.

A second example that highlights valuable countertendencies draws from American culture and concerns the idea of neighborliness. Adorno describes how the fascist agitator poses as a man of the people, someone just like you, "a neighbor, somebody close to the hearts of the simple folks."[43] He exploits people's desire for "warmth and companionship," and this "cold-blooded promoter of the inhuman" exploits and seizes on Americans' "truly human motive," their "longing for spontaneous, genuine relationships, for love."[44] The agitator "shrewdly attempts to enroll their support by posing as their neighbor," by posing as a "great little man."[45] In an era of mass culture, in which people suffer from alienation, they are especially ripe for this kind of exploitation. In a context in which people feel constantly manipulated and tricked, they nostalgically yearn for meaningful relationships, for true companionship, for real neighbors. And yet "the very fact that people suffer from universal manipulation is used for manipulation" by the authoritarian leader.[46] But this desire for relationships is a countertendency that can also swing against the antidemocratic leader: people will turn on the leader when it is revealed that their "sincerest feelings are being perverted and gratified by swindle."[47] All the emotional desires and yearnings that made people fall for the fascist leader can be used to bring him down, once his own hypocrisy is revealed and it becomes clear that he is not one of the people, not one of the simple folk. Then "the energy inherent in their longing may finally turn against its exploitation."[48]

Finally, Adorno notes how "bad conscience" can also be a productive countertendency. He notes that those who voice anti-Semitic ideas "do so with a somewhat bad conscience" and "find themselves to a certain extent in a conflict situation."[49] Adorno wants to help people "transition from a naive to a reflective attitude," which works to weaken the "violence" of their ideas.[50] As we have seen, Adorno thinks that feelings and different affective responses can be valuable critical indicators of larger social problems. Critique is not generated just by intellectual concerns, but also by feelings such as guilt. Here the democratic leader would try to draw out these feelings and talk through their implications with the prejudiced individual, to turn a nascent feeling of discomfort with one's own professed ideas into a more conscious reflection on the tension between what may come out of one's mouth sometimes and what one's gut—or one's heart—tells one is right.

Throughout these examples and in the essay generally, Adorno is redirecting, inverting, turning things around, inside out, and upside down. He invokes the dialectical language of a countertendency, a boomerang, and—in these examples—a vaccine. Adorno's use of the metaphor of vaccines, like his image of the boomerang, is especially appropriate and illuminating. A vaccine is a prophylactic that improves one's immunity to a particular disease. A vaccine is prepared with a weakened form of the disease-causing microbe or toxin itself. The vaccine works because the weakened form of the disease-causing agent is administered to the body, which stimulates the immune response. Then in the future, when confronted with the real toxin, the immune system recognizes and remembers the disease-causing microorganism and destroys it. Similarly, in his writings on American culture, Adorno focuses on pathological qualities, the disease-causing toxins, we might say. But he thinks that by drawing these pathologies into our consciousness, highlighting their existence, and examining how they operate, we can work toward a "cure," so to speak. But this prophylactic vaccine can be developed only through exposure to the pathologies themselves. Adorno discusses various different pathologies from which we might derive vaccines, but one that he emphasizes is the pervasive American sense of passivity and impotence. The dominant culture of liberal capitalism cultivates a dependent citizen, but this is in contradiction with its ostensibly democratic values of independence and autonomy. By highlighting these nonidentical elements and drawing out specific contradictions, by "exposing" Americans to their own pathologies and disease-causing toxins, a vaccine for these problems might be derived. Indeed, as Adorno writes in a piece on education, "Anyone who wishes to bring about change can probably only do so at all, by turning that very impotence, and their own impotence, into an active ingredient in their own thinking and maybe in their own actions too."[51] Thus, Adorno's form of democratic leadership is one that works to develop prophylactic vaccines by injecting us with a consciousness of the pathology itself.

As we have seen, though, Adorno notes that it would be "naively ideal-istic to assume that it could be achieved through intellectual means alone."[52] Instead, he advocates a form of leadership that highlights these contradic-tions, draws out these countertendencies, and works to create these vaccines, calling it "the Truth principle." Antidemocratic leaders employ forms of manipulation and propaganda to play on people's desires and emotions, and this is expressly forbidden to anyone trying to lead in a truly democratic way: "democratic leadership should not aim at better and more comprehensive propaganda but should strive to overcome the spirit of propaganda by strict adherence to the principle of truth."[53] But Adorno does recognize that to gain the support of the masses "one has to take them as they are and not as one wants them to be; in other words, one has to reckon with their psychology."[54] Further, Adorno recognizes that people actually have a libidinal attachment to propaganda itself. Political propaganda and advertising campaigns excite and stimulate emotions and stir affective responses that people then become attached to: elevated blood pressure, excitement, desire, anger. So "the renun-ciation of propaganda would, therefore, require an instinctual renunciation on the part of the masses."[55] Thus, the democratic leader or the educator has to find a nerve center or lever that is also linked to our affect. The inner conflict or tension that is identified and "pressed" so to speak, also has to be some-thing that we care deeply about, that is tied to our most profound feelings about who we are and what we believe. This is why Adorno gives examples of levers or nerve centers that touch on one's love for one's wife, for example, or one's identity as an American. The democratic leader must work at the same level as those who would manipulate individuals in de-democratizing directions, the level of affect, emotion, desires, and feelings.

This is all a lot for the "Truth principle" to break through. Here Adorno refers to truth in the way he writes about it in other more theoretical works such as *Negative Dialectics*. Truth is attained by drawing out the contradic-tory, nonidentical qualities over and against surface appearances and har-monies. The nonidentical, for Adorno, contains utopian qualities that resist "what is" and the status quo, and drawing out these qualities is tied up with his understanding of truth in a non-positivistic way. Thus, the "Truth prin-ciple" would have to break through the walls of inertia, resistance, and condi-tioned mental behavior patterns.[56] As he puts it, the irrational element has to be "fully considered" and "attacked by enlightenment."[57] Democratic leaders should try to "promote insight into the irrational dispositions which make it hard for people to judge rationally and autonomously."[58] Democratic leaders should seek to "emancipate people" from the "grip of all-powerful conditioning," and the truth that they will spread "pertains to facts which are clouded by arbitrary distortions and in many cases by the very spirit of our culture."[59] Adorno wants to convey information that results in the kind of uncomfortable, disruptive, but productive and illuminating kind of unsettlement that accompanies a confrontation with the nonidentical. As he puts it, "The *shock* evinced by the dawning awareness of such a possibility may well help to bring about the aforementioned lever effect."[60] The democratic leader or educator must push a lever that is compelling enough to the individual that he or she cannot comfortably and blithely pick up his or her life in exactly the same way afterward.

All this demonstrates why the process of working with individuals to turn countertendencies into vaccines must be personal and work directly from the individual's own life context. Adorno recognizes the power of affect in shaping our thought and action, and he appreciates how extrarational forces shape the self. So the democratic leader or the educator must start with an individual's immediate, concrete circumstances and engage him or her on a deep and personal level to be able to speak to the nerve centers that will cause this specific individual to react, to push his or her own particular levers. Leaders must also work with people in an egalitarian way, to encourage them to open up by appealing to them as equals, rather than lecturing them or chastising them in ways that would make them close down in defensiveness. Adorno's plan for democratic pedagogy and his program for democratic leadership converge on all key points. His plan for democratic leadership follows the same principles he outlines in his writings on democratic pedagogy, as we will see in the next chapter. Then, in chapter 6, we will be able to see how Adorno himself puts this plan of democratic leadership as democratic pedagogy into action.

# 5

# Democratic Pedagogy

## Resistance and an Alternative Model for Civic Education

The only real concrete form of maturity would consist of those few people who are of a mind to do so working with all their energies towards making education an education for protest and for resistance.

—Theodor Adorno and Hellmut Becker,
"Education for Maturity and Responsibility"

After his return to Germany in the years following World War II, Adorno wrote a number of essays and gave radio addresses and interviews exploring how schools, teaching, and civic education could change to become less prone to fostering authoritarian tendencies and more conducive to robust democracy.[1] Scholars have begun to note how these essays present an image of Adorno that differs from the (flawed) conventional reading of him. Here he writes with an eye toward productively informing practice, participates in the German public sphere, shows himself to be engaged in postwar politics, and is even, at times, quite optimistic about the ways that education can cultivate meaningful democracy.

The existing scholarly treatments of Adorno and education focus on topics ranging from the profession of teaching to his suggestions for reforms to institutional and cultural education.[2] Ultimately, however, there is a missing piece in all these works.[3] Scholarship on the topic to date fails to recognize how Adorno's writings on education are part and parcel of his more theoretical works, introducing and translating his ideas into different languages to make them more accessible to a wider audience.[4] None of the existing essays on this theme situates Adorno's writings on education deeply enough in his larger theory and practice of negative dialectics.[5] None of them mentions or refers to the role of the nonidentical in his thought as the stimulus to critique.[6] None explores the role of experience and Adorno's thoughts on how we apprehend the material objects of the world.[7] And though several pieces recognize how Adorno's writings on education are important *for* democracy, none fully appreciates how his essays on pedagogy encourage a way of thinking and feeling against what we are given that *is* democratic, that exemplifies the essence of his definition of democracy.[8] In short, despite the valuable ways that scholars advance our understanding of Adorno by shining a spotlight on his neglected and largely unappreciated work on education, and despite the ways they work to reframe the flawed conventional image of him, they fail to link his writings on education closely to the constellation of concepts that are all part of his democratic project: experience, critique, negative dialectics, and leadership. This is where *Adorno and Democracy* builds on the existing literature, showing how his work on education connects to each of these constituent parts of his theory and practice of democracy.

Adorno's thoughts on experience and critique build up to a theory of education that this chapter will parse out and examine. To draw out the democratic value of Adorno's writings on education more clearly and fully and to give us a sense of the radical nature of his work, however, I begin this chapter by putting him into conversation with an unexpected interlocutor: Paulo Freire. Freire's *Pedagogy of the Oppressed* is perhaps the classic text on radical democratic pedagogy, very well known inside and outside the academy for how it outlines a revolutionary form of leadership that prefigures the kind of egalitarian, nonhierarchical, critically transformed world it envisions and idealizes. The book was first published in Portuguese in 1968 and was aimed toward citizens of Latin American countries suffering under the legacy of colonization. Shaped by Marxian analysis, *Pedagogy of the Oppressed* went on to become a foundational text of the critical pedagogy movement and a life-changing text for many teachers and students. Though Freire is famous for his writings on a radical form of democratic education, Adorno is conventionally thought to represent the opposite of these things: complacent as opposed to radical, elitist as opposed to democratic, and someone who writes more about high theory than education. But Adorno began to work explicitly on the topic of education after his return to a German state trying to democratize in the aftermath of fascism. Adorno's writings on education are quite extensive, and they share many of the same fundamental commitments that we see in Freire's work. Freire's alternative model of revolutionary leadership based on a radically democratic pedagogy helps illuminate the significance of Adorno's own writings on education and helps us appreciate how concerns with democratic pedagogy shape his thoughts on leadership, as well as his practice of cultural critique in the United States. The parallels between what Freire presented in a fully fleshed-out style in the late 1960s and what Adorno was pushing toward, in a more scattered way, in the 1940s and 1950s, are striking. In short, putting Adorno into conversation with Freire, and seeing the sympathies and alliances between them, valuably furthers this book's project of reframing and reconfiguring our conventional image of Adorno.

Paulo Freire and Theodor Adorno describe similar social problems. Though they focus on different kinds of societies, in different places and times, the worlds they describe are structured to dominate, stultify, and render humans dependent on oppressive structures of authority. Freire and Adorno describe a landscape where norms, conventions, structures, and institutions work to create a passive, docile, unthinking, and obedient citizenry that feels incapacitated and dependent rather than being an active, critical, thinking, and questioning citizenry that feels itself capable of intellectual emancipation and even revolutionary change. Both see great potential in humans, but the tremendous optimism they project onto human *capabilities* lies in stark contrast with the far more pessimistic portrayals of the structures of modern societies that we find in their work.

But perhaps most important, Freire and Adorno combine a deeply textured portrayal of modern conditions of violence, oppression, and domination with a resolute sense of the human potential to change these conditions. For both, humans fundamentally possess a capacity for critical thinking and intellectual emancipation that is then dulled and deadened by the dependency-inducing culture of modernity. The challenge, then, concerns how to unleash those capabilities and potentials in the context of a society that works to contain them. Both thinkers struggle with the question of how to move from the point A of oppression and dependency to the point B of emancipation and revolutionary agency. But even more crucially, they struggle with the question of how to do this in a radically democratic way. For Freire and Adorno, there can be no intellectual vanguard pushing the deluded masses into this new day. There is no faith in this kind of leadership and no sense that a party of the few can force revolutionary cultural change. But neither do they believe that the cultural contradictions of class will automatically stimulate a consciousness-raising experience on the part of the dominated. So there must be a way of making space for the growth, development, and unleashing of these critical capacities that will allow humans to be the subjects of their own history in a way that is democratic as opposed to authoritarian, egalitarian as opposed to hierarchical, dialogic as opposed to monologic, and engaged as opposed to elitist. There must be a form of education that can move people from point A to point B in a way that is itself consistent with the democratic values that are supposed to characterize point B itself; there must be a *process* that is consistent with the possibility that is being projected. Adorno and Freire both articulate a democratic form of pedagogy in which the means reflect the ends in just this way. I will discuss Freire first, then show how Adorno's thoughts on education resonate with this more famous and radical pedagogy of the oppressed.

## Paulo Freire's *Pedagogy of the Oppressed*

Freire's own work dealt with oppressed peoples in Latin America, in countries with a legacy of colonialism and violent oppression. But in *Pedagogy of the Oppressed,* he writes of oppression and alienation in broad terms that allow the tools of his book to transcend their original context. Indeed, his advice contains notable parallels with Adorno's and also valuably speaks to the condition of citizens in so-called advanced industrial capitalist nations, countries with their own forms of oppression and their own legacy of cultivating a culture of alienation, silence, and dependency on the part of citizens.[9]

Freire describes a landscape of dehumanizing oppression where the oppressed have adapted to the structures of domination that surround them and have become resigned to their state of unfreedom, coming even to fear the pursuit of freedom. They have internalized their oppression, becoming both alienated and inauthentic. They try to escape from themselves, refusing even "the appeals of their own conscience," and they prefer "gregariousness to authentic comradeship."[10] They suffer a duality in their innermost being, given that they have always known themselves only in terms of the oppression. This state of unfreedom is written into the fabric of their being:

> They are at one and the same time themselves and the oppressor whose consciousness they have internalized. The conflict lies in the choice between being wholly themselves or being divided; between ejecting the oppressor within or not ejecting them; between human solidarity or alienation; between following prescriptions or having choices; between being spectators or actors; between acting or having the illusion of acting through the action of the oppressors; between speaking out or being silent, castrated in their power to

create and re-create, in their power to transform the world. This is the tragic dilemma of the oppressed which their education must take into account.[11]

These forms of oppression are replicated and reified under the dominant model of what Freire calls the "banking" concept of education. Here students are imagined as "containers" and "receptacles" to be "filled" by the teacher: "The more completely she fills the receptacles, the better a teacher she is."[12] But the teacher does not teach the students by starting where they are or by appealing to their immediate material circumstances and their current knowledge, but, rather, fills the students with information that is alien to their own experience of the world. The stream of words that come from the teacher are "emptied of their concreteness and become a hollow, alienated, and alienating verbosity."[13] In this hierarchical form of pedagogy, the students are treated as objects and the teacher is the only subject with power or agency: the "teacher presents himself to his students as their necessary opposite; by considering their ignorance absolute, he justifies his own existence."[14] The teacher bestows knowledge like a gift on those considered ignorant in a way that works to maintain this hierarchy.

Freire is not concerned with *what* the students learn, but *how* they are being taught, not just the substance of education but the style of it: the relationships it creates, the consciousness it cultivates, and the feelings it generates. Under the traditional model, the students are positioned as passive figures, devoid of agency, capable of adapting to the world only as it is given to them. The banking concept of education works to create obedient subjects who do not question this world; it stifles their creative and critical energies in ways that maintain existing power relations that serve the interests of their oppressors. Like all authoritarian systems, this form of education also works to present the existing reality as the only possible reality, unchangeable, just the way things are, as "motionless, static, compartmentalized, and predictable."[15] Freire notes how the banking model may wear the cloak of humanism, but this only "masks the effort to turn women and men into automatons—the very negation of their ontological vocation to be more fully human."[16]

For Freire, this form of education not only stultifies the student's capabilities, but also acts violently on the qualities of critique and praxis that he sees as fundamental to our humanity. This is why he emphasizes how alienated students are under the banking model. They have lost the critical and creative capacities that define us as humans. The banking model speaks to students in a hierarchical, authoritarian voice instead of entering into dialogue with them. But because Freire sees this kind of dialogue—the words that we use to build our world—as a right of every human being, the banking model of education alienates people from something essential to their being in the world. For Freire, "human beings are not built in silence, but in word, in work, in action-reflection."[17] Like Adorno, Freire sees this capacity for critical thinking, and for the dialogue that helps us analyze and rebuild the world, as the praxis of all humans, not just the province of intellectuals: "But while to say the true word—which is work, which is praxis—is to transform the world, saying that word is not the privilege of some few persons, but the right of everyone."[18] And further, he sees dialogue as an "existential necessity," because "it is in speaking their word that people, by naming the world, transform it."[19] Without this, people experience a form of violence and oppression, an alienating loss of self.

This has overt political implications for Freire. There are many overlaps between the argument he lays out here with respect to education and the argument that the Marxian critical theorist and psychologist Erich Fromm makes in his classic book *Escape from Freedom,* first published in 1941. Fromm was trying to trace the roots of Nazism and fascism and, combining Marx and Freud, trying to diagnose what prompted modern people to submit willingly to authoritarian rule. Adorno is concerned with the same problem, especially as it plays out in the ostensibly democratic landscape of the United States. For Freire, the tendency to submit to authoritarian leaders is rooted in people's own sense of powerlessness and impotence. This alienating loss of self, and the fear of freedom that has been built into people, makes them ripe for manipulation by charismatic leaders of all stripes: "Populist manifestations perhaps best exemplify this type of behavior by the oppressed, who, by identifying with charismatic leaders, come to feel that they themselves are active and effective."[20] Indeed, "Attempting to liberate the oppressed without their reflexive participation in the act of liberation is to treat them as objects which must be saved from a burning building: it is to lead them into the populist pitfall and transform them into the masses which can be manipulated."[21] This is why the *how* of education, or we might say also, the *how* of politics, is so important; people must be educated in ways that themselves prefigure the egalitarian ideal that is ultimately being sought.

To work against these oppressive conditions, Freire proposes an alternative model of education, which he calls the "problem-posing method." This form of education teaches students to appraise the status quo critically and to see the world that they are given as contingent and always in a process of transformation. If "the banking method directly or indirectly reinforces men's fatalistic perception of their situation," then "the problem-posing method presents this very situation to them as a problem."[22] The problem-posing method fosters the students' critical and creative powers and encourages them to intervene in the world around them, to see themselves as subjects of history who also possess agency. But these changes must all take place, in Freire's view, in a radically egalitarian, nonhierarchical, horizontal, and dialogic way that is itself empowering. He wants to foster liberation in a way that is itself consistent with a projected alternative vision of the world that is itself deeply empowering and meaningfully democratic. For Freire, "The central problem is this: How can the oppressed, as divided, unauthentic beings, participate in developing the pedagogy of their liberation?"[23] For this to happen, the radical educator who is truly committed to human liberation must work "*with,* not *for,* the oppressed (whether individuals or peoples) in the incessant struggle to regain their humanity."[24] True solidarity "requires that one enter into the situation of those with whom one is solidary; it is a radical posture."[25] Talking *with,* not *for* or *to,* the people and entering into a dialogue are the central tools for a pedagogy of the oppressed. This alternative kind of educator "does not consider himself or herself the proprietor of history or of all the people, or the liberator of the oppressed; but he or she does commit himself or herself, within history, to fight at their side."[26]

So there is a process whereby the educator fosters the creation of a critical consciousness, but this does not take the form of the sort of emancipation whereby the teacher enlightens the student by bestowing his or her wisdom in a hierarchical fashion. The development of this critical consciousness happens through conversation that starts where the student is and works from his or her existing experience of reality. This pedagogy of the oppressed, then, requires a change not just in the students, but also in the teacher. The teacher must be open and flexible to having his or her own worldview changed. The student and the teacher are co-creators, collaborators: "The students—no longer docile listeners—are now critical co-investigators in dialogue with the teacher. The teacher presents the material to the students for their consideration, and re-considers her earlier considerations as the students express their own."[27] Freire describes a process of "conversion to the people" that "requires a profound rebirth."[28] Educators who "authentically commit themselves to the people must re-examine themselves constantly. This conversion is so radical as not to allow of ambiguous behavior. To affirm this commitment but to consider oneself the proprietor of revolutionary wisdom—which must then be given to (or imposed on) the people—is to retain the old ways. The man or woman who proclaims devotion to the cause of liberation yet is unable to enter into *communion* with the people, whom he or she continues to regard as totally ignorant, is grievously self-deceived."[29]

This model of education calls for the use of words, thinking, and reflection as a praxis to remake the world. Freire says this is not calling for an "armchair revolution," but the kind of "true reflection" that "leads to action," and "authentic praxis."[30] For Freire, as for Adorno, "critical reflection is also action."[31] But this praxis transpires through dialogue that requires the teacher to trust in the students' *capabilities,* to trust in the students' potential for reason, and to have faith in their ability to overcome their legacy of oppression through this alternative form of education: "Whoever lacks this trust will fail to initiate (or will abandon) dialogue, reflection, and communication, and will fall into using slogans, communiqués, monologues, and instructions."[32] Those who engage in true dialogue with the people have a faith in their abilities that prevents their work from falling into a pattern of "paternalistic manipulation."[33]

But it also becomes clear that Freire sees education as the root of all revolutionary change and that true political leaders must also adopt the alternative pedagogy he proposes. He says that he seeks to "defend the eminently pedagogical character of the revolution."[34] He sees the only "effective instrument" for change as a "humanizing pedagogy in which the revolutionary leadership establishes a permanent relationship of dialogue with the oppressed."[35] But in drawing out the consequences of his alternative pedagogy for larger social and political change, Freire also reworks traditional notions of leadership. Freire's definition of leadership seems one and the same with his understanding of the role of the teacher. In this way Freire connects his form of radically democratic pedagogy with an alternative model of revolutionary political leadership, in ways that are surprisingly sympathetic to the project Adorno will both propose and enact. Freire gives us a valuable model with which to appreciate the larger political significance of Adorno's own writings on education.

## Adorno's Democratic Pedagogy

Adorno's writings on education assume a landscape of oppression that is quite similar to the one Freire's teachings work to overcome. For Adorno, too, modernity operates to produce alienated selves who have lost their essential human capacity for critical thought, the defining praxis that Freire also emphasizes. Additionally, Adorno shows how conventional forms of education work in problematically authoritarian ways to reify this kind of obedient and docile subject. Modernity in general and conventional forms of education, for Adorno, encourage us to adapt to the world as it is, fit ourselves into an existing mold. The world is presented as static, fixed, something we cannot change. We are treated as, and feel ourselves to be, dependent objects as opposed to empowered, autonomous subjects. And for Adorno, as for Freire, these are all violent moves that produce real suffering in the ways that they cut us off from parts of ourselves, from each other, and from a dynamic experience of the world around us. Adorno's alternative model for a democratic form of pedagogy works in opposition to these tendencies, to create a resistant and revolutionary subject. And for Adorno, as for Freire, revolutionary leadership is ultimately about education and begins with a radically democratic form of pedagogy.

Adorno sees critique, democracy, and education as interrelated and interdependent: democracy depends on critique, and education cultivates the capacity for critique and thus also contributes to the broader realization of meaningful democracy. But how exactly does this dynamic work? How can education cultivate this resistance and further the cause of true democracy? In several essays and addresses Adorno gives pragmatic advice, in a tone that is also at times quite optimistic about the cumulative effect that this kind of education might have. As he notes, "It is fashionable to complain about civic education, and certainly it could be better, but sociology already has data indicating that civic education, when it is practiced earnestly and not as a burdensome duty, does more good than is generally believed."[36] Here again, Adorno's attitude is not one of hopeless pessimism. Rather, the other Adorno that this book seeks to uncover emerges quite clearly in his writings on education. He insists that education must be about protest and resistance: "Concrete possibilities of resistance . . . must be shown."[37] Despite the scope of the problem, "education and enlightenment can still manage a little something."[38] But what exactly would "a pedagogy that promotes enlightenment" look like?[39] What is Adorno's vision for a democratic mode of pedagogy and how does it anticipate key aspects of Freire's pedagogy of the oppressed?

First, Adorno thinks that democratic pedagogy must cultivate a sense of possibility, a sense that change is possible, that the conditions we are given are not necessary and inevitable but contingent and mutable. The oppressive forces of modernity, like the oppressive forces Freire describes, work to convince people that the world they are given is the only world that is possible. Thus, a revolutionary pedagogy must first unfix and dislocate this sense of hegemony. Toward this end, Adorno says that education should foster the recognition that we are all both subjects and objects, who are neither wholly constructed nor wholly free, but can—at least in small ways—think against and resist the forces that would control and contain us. Education can teach us that "we are neither simply spectators of world history, free to frolic more or less at will within its grand chambers, nor does world history, whose rhythm increasingly approaches that of the catastrophe, appear to allow its subjects the time in which everything would improve on its own. This bears directly on democratic pedagogy."[40] Adorno reminds us that social relations make up the world: "We are not only spectators looking upon this predominance of the institutional and the objective that confronts us; rather it is after all constituted out of us, this societal objectivity is made up of us ourselves."[41] The world makes us, but we also make up the world, and in this "doubleness" lies "the possibility of perhaps changing it."[42]

Second, a democratic form of pedagogy must cultivate people's autonomy, by which Adorno means their ability to trust in themselves, to maturely trust in their own powers. Late modernity in advanced industrial capitalist societies, like the oppressive society Freire describes, tries to construct dependent, obedient subjects, individuals who are fit to be governed by external authorities. So Adorno emphasizes the importance of autonomy and trusting in the self, but as we have already seen in previous chapters, he emphasizes autonomy not as a way of enclosing the self in a solipsistic, atomistic, separate world, but as a way of connecting with, and becoming more receptive to, the material world around us and the other bodies in it. Autonomy, for Adorno, is vital for democracy because of how it pushes individuals to rely on the modes of experience that define our humanity. As we saw in the previous chapter on experience, for Adorno, when we are truly autonomous, we are not closed off to the world around us but radically open to the nonidentical, sensing, perceiving, listening. When we are truly autonomous, we are giving the law to ourselves by relying on our human praxis: being receptive to the dissonant calls of the nonidentical, thinking and feeling against what we are given, being fully conscious, awake, and attuned. And as we have already seen, Adorno thinks we can truly fulfill the promise of democracy only when we are not alienated from this human praxis of thinking, critique, and negation.

In a piece called "Education for Maturity and Responsibility," which takes the form of a back-and-forth question-and-answer session with Hellmut Becker, Adorno emphasizes these connections among autonomy, democracy, and education.[43] Adorno notes, "Democracy is founded on the education of each individual in political, social and moral awareness," and he argues, "The demand for maturity and responsibility seems to be entirely natural in a democracy."[44] The "prerequisite" for democracy, he states, is this kind of awareness, "the capacity and courage of each individual to make full use of his reasoning power."[45] The kind of transformative education that Adorno has in mind, however, requires resisting the many forces in society working to construct individuals who are "heteronomous," which means that "no individual in today's society can, on their own, determine the nature of their own existence."[46] Modern society works to preshape, preform, predigest our experience for us, to "mould people through a vast number of different structures and processes" so that "they swallow and accept everything, without its true nature even being available to their consciousnesses."[47] Adorno is concerned especially with how educational theorists and practitioners of his own day seem to emphasize authority more than autonomy: "In so doing they work, not just implicitly but quite openly, against the basic conditions required for a democracy."[48]

Third, and related to these concerns about autonomy and receptivity, Adorno thinks education also needs to teach us to attend to suffering and overcome modern society's tendency to make us hard and cold, to encourage us to turn away from the pain of others. This is another example of how Adorno's thoughts on critique and education are not just intellectual and cognitive, but also corporeal and sensory. He appeals to the whole range of experience. We can be pushed toward critique not only by thoughts but by feelings. Here Adorno makes it clear that democratic pedagogy aims to cultivate a more sensitive subject. Education has an obligation to teach us not to be barbaric. By barbarism he means "delusional prejudice, oppression, genocide, and torture."[49] When we are barbaric, we are cold and unresponsive to the pain of others. So schools have the task of "de-barbarizing" individuals, to teach them to feel as well as to think. Unfortunately, much of traditional education is still governed by "the ideal of being hard": "This educational ideal of hardness, in which many may believe without reflecting about it, is utterly wrong. The idea that virility consists in the maximum degree of endurance long ago became a screen-image for masochism that, as psychology has demonstrated, aligns itself all too easily with sadism. Being hard, the vaunted quality education should inculcate, means absolute indifference toward pain as such."[50]

Being truly autonomous, for Adorno, means being open and attentive to the suffering of other bodies. The relationship between autonomy and receptivity and, in these writings, between education and democracy that Adorno continually draws may seem strange, until we remember his basic theory that earlier chapters have laid out.

In Adorno's constellation of linked movements, we can be truly autonomous only when we are taking in the world through our own sensations and perceptions, instead of adapting our experience to the conventional vision of the world we are given, seeing what we think we are supposed to see and hearing what we think we are supposed to hear. If we are truly to give the law to ourselves, we must experience for ourselves. And it is only when we are open and receptive to the immediate, material conditions around us that we can listen to the nonidentical elements of the world that push us to think and feel against the given, that push us toward critical thought and action, and—ultimately—that push us to practice democracy in more meaningful ways. So an educational program that works to make us "hard" is dangerous because it encourages us to close ourselves off to the nonidentical elements of the world that may be represented in terms of pain and suffering, encouraging us to become atomistic, imperial selves who cannot feel and thus cannot really think, either.

This brings us to the fourth requirement of education. In the interest of fulfilling the three prerequisites for meaningful democracy—and a fulfillment of our human praxis as autonomous, perceptive, experiencing humans—Adorno thinks that education must teach us to be skeptical of collective movements that often work against these ideals. Not surprisingly, given its focus on autonomy and self-reflection, education also entails cultivating a skepticism of the collective, which Adorno thinks can too easily turn into another form of authority that we blindly obey and which can also harden our sensibilities: "People who blindly slot themselves into the collective already make themselves into something like inert material, extinguish themselves as self-determined beings. With this comes the willingness to treat others as an amorphous mass."[51]

People become alienated from themselves, and when we become alienated from ourselves, as we have seen, we also become alienated from democracy, and humanity turns into barbarism, as Adorno himself witnessed: "My generation experienced the relapse of humanity into barbarism, in the literal, indescribable, and true sense. . . . The pathos of the school today, its moral import, is that in the midst of the status quo it alone has the ability, if it is conscious of it, to work directly toward the debarbarization of humanity. . . . It is up to the school more than anything else to work against barbarism."[52] He continues to develop this theme in "Education after Auschwitz," where he says, "The premier demand upon all education is that Auschwitz not happen again."[53] Auschwitz represents "the barbarism all education strives against."[54]

But the barbarism that was manifested so horrifically in Auschwitz is evident in a less extreme way in the "administered world" generally. The literal killing of the self that took place in the death camps was emblematic, for Adorno, of the devastating potential of the "administered world" of modernity generally. The evisceration of the thinking, feeling, experiencing, perceiving subject is a consequence of the culture industry, the logic of abstract exchange, and the tendency for identity-thinking that characterizes idealism: "One can speak of the claustrophobia of humanity in the administered world, of a feeling of being incarcerated in a thoroughly societalized, closely woven, netlike environment."[55] The weave of this net is dense, making it hard to escape, and "the pressure exerted by the prevailing universal upon everything particular . . . has a tendency to destroy the particular and the individual together with their power of resistance."[56] The metaphor of a claustrophobic net is an apt and vivid way to describe the loss of self that Adorno sees as the dominant threat of modernity. He imagines a net that cloaks and covers us, blocking us off from the experience of the world around us, making it impossible for us to use our senses to apprehend what is around us. We are closed off, rendered insensate, unable to take in the particular things around us. And for Adorno, this destruction of particularity also works to destroy us and our powers of resistance, because we are able to think and feel against given conditions only through our encounters with the nonidentical elements of our world, the little particularities that resist universal systems. So education must work against the deadening net of the administered world by cultivating our capacity for autonomy, which also helps further the ideal of democracy. As Adorno says, "The single genuine power standing against the principle of Auschwitz is autonomy, if I might use the Kantian expression: the power of reflection, of self-determination, of not cooperating."[57]

Fifth, Adorno shows that making these changes in how we understand the role of education also requires rethinking how we teach, both revaluing the work of professional educators as vitally important work for democracy and expanding what *counts* as education to encompass civic education projects outside the classroom. Regarding official instruction in the classroom, in an essay titled "Taboos on the Teaching Vocation" Adorno argues that placing more social value on the profession of teaching is part of the cause of advancing meaningful democracy. Unfortunately, he says, "compared with other academic vocations such as law or medicine, the teacher's profession unmistakably smacks of something society does not take completely seriously."[58] Speaking of the German context in this case, he says that nevertheless "symptoms are evident that permit the hope that, if democracy in

Germany realizes its opportunity and seriously develops further, all this will change."[59]

But education and teaching also need to transcend the classroom. After criticizing others for thinking about education in ways that are too limited, "too much within the framework of the institution, particularly of the school," Adorno makes some suggestions about broader civic education projects.[60] Here, as we will explore more in the next chapter, we begin to see how his ideas of democratic leadership join with his thoughts on democratic pedagogy. Democratic leadership becomes a form of democratic pedagogy in which "those few people who are of a mind to do so [work] with all their energies towards making education an education for protest and for resistance."[61] Two things are especially important about this plan for an alternative form of civic education. First, those who would lead and educate are simply volunteers with a passion for change and some critical insights they want to discuss with others. They have no official status or certification beyond this desire to empower other individuals to experience their world differently. Second, the goal of this form of education is not to fill students with information, but to change their experience of, and response to, the conditions in which they are already immersed.

This education for protest and resistance starts with people where they are, in their existing culture. Adorno describes senior classes of students being taken to see commercially produced films, and "the students could quite simply be shown what a con is being presented, how hypocritical it all is."[62] Or this same thing could happen with radio broadcasts or magazines. For example, "a magazine could be read with them, and they could be shown how, by having their own inner needs and desires exploited, they are being taken for a ride."[63] The important point is that "in order to change this state of consciousness, the normal primary school system . . . cannot suffice." Adorno says he could "envision a series of possibilities": "One would be—I am improvising here—that television programs be planned with consideration of the nerve centers of this particular state of consciousness. Then I could imagine that something like mobile educational groups and convoys of volunteers could be formed, who would drive out into the countryside and in discussions, courses, and supplementary instruction attempt to fill the most menacing gaps."[64] As we will see in the next chapter, the radio programs that Adorno produced were centrally tied to his project of democratic cultivation.

So one becomes a true educator, in Adorno's view, not through being officially certified, but simply, as he said above, by being "of a mind" to work with others to help cultivate our common human capacities for critique. In the broadest terms, these civic projects of democratic pedagogy would work to cultivate people's capacity for critical self-reflection: "What we can do is give people contents, give them categories, give them forms of consciousness, by means of which they can approach self-reflection."[65] Here Adorno reminds us that the educator's task is to work with people where they are, starting from their own immediate, material conditions, and work with them to develop new ways of critically analyzing their own impulses, desires, thoughts, feelings, and ways of perceiving their situations.

Ultimately, Adorno's thoughts on education as a whole refer to Kant's essay "What Is Enlightenment?" in which he describes enlightenment as having the courage to use our own understanding and emerge from the tutelage of other authorities. But, for Adorno, we are made into dependent students by a vast array of modern forces—the new "tutors"—that shape our understanding of the world for us. As Adorno says, "To begin with, all we try to do is simply open people's minds to the fact that they are constantly being deceived, because the mechanism of tutelage has been raised to the status of a universal *mundus vult decepti:* the world wants to be deceived. Making everyone aware of these connections could perhaps be achieved in the spirit of an immanent critique, because there can be no normal democracy which could afford to be explicitly against an enlightenment of this kind."[66]

This idea that education is fundamentally about helping us use our own minds and bodies to apprehend the world is helpful in reminding us that education, for Adorno as for Freire, is about working with people in a horizontal and egalitarian way, to develop their *own* critical consciousness. Freire emphasizes the importance of talking *with*, not *to* or *for*, people and entering into relationships of solidarity with them to work to develop a more critical posture toward their own life conditions.

Using different language to a similar end, Adorno reaches toward a radically democratic model of pedagogy where the educator is not installed just as the new tutor, the new authority figure. He seeks a kind of pedagogy whereby the means are consistent with the ends of producing autonomous, empowered, critical subjects. This process should unfold, as Adorno says above, by immanent critique, by which he means that those who want to foster change (the "educators," who could be anyone) should enter into the "student's" world and draw out the nascent critique that may already be prefigured by certain impulses, desires, and conflicts. The goal is to enter into relationships with people to talk through, think through, their own internal contradictions, tensions, conflicts, antagonisms, and to work to change their reactions to these nonidentical elements, to encourage them to respond and attend to these interruptions instead of closing them out. Ultimately, Adorno's understanding of this mode of immanent critique is similar to Freire's problem-posing method. Both work on the students' own terms, starting from their own experience of the world, to cultivate a more critical, empowered perspective.

But Adorno is not Freire. My goal here has been to highlight the striking resonances between these two thinkers regarding democratic pedagogy. I hope these sympathies with Freire have served to further uproot the flawed conventional image of Adorno as an apolitical, withdrawn elitist. But I don't want to go too far in the other direction, either. It is safe to say that Adorno never reached the full measure of solidarity with the people that Freire's image of education demands. As we saw, Freire says that entering into solidarity with the people is a process of "conversion" that "requires a profound rebirth."[67] I'm not sure that Adorno underwent a complete conversion and rebirth, though I do think that his move to the United States pushed this concern with the problems and possibilities of democracy to the forefront of his thinking. As this book shows, Adorno's time in the United States brought the language of democracy into his writings in a way that shaped the rest of his thought after his return to Germany. So if he "converted" to take up the cause of democracy in a fundamental way in his theory and practice, as we have seen and will continue to see in this book, this is not quite the same as having been "born again" as part of the people.

Adorno's theoretical aims are consistent with Freire's, but there are also moments of inconsistency and contradiction in his writings on education when he seems to fall back into the kind of hierarchical mode of speech he sets out to avoid. For example, in Adorno's improvised discussion of the forms that this plan for civic education might take—discussed above—he speaks of the "menacing gaps" in the countryside in a way that seems to speak from a privileged position of superiority that actually works against the much more dialogic mode of "working with" people to gain mutual understanding that his invocations of "democratic pedagogy" actually strive toward. To give another example of these sporadic lapses, in "Education for Maturity and Responsibility" Adorno admits that we can't predict the success of his educational methods, but "it is possible to knock something into young people's eyes. . . . I would advocate most strongly this kind of education for 'knocking things down.'"[68] In other ways Adorno's language itself, even emphasizing "maturity" and "responsibility," seems to set up a kind of hierarchy that his own theory protests against. At times his language makes us think that he wants to give people who are deceived a good shake by the shoulders to wake them up.

Ultimately, in some of these writings Adorno seems to be learning what it means to practice a democratic mode of pedagogy himself, and we hear him, at times, *struggling* to speak in a more egalitarian and engaged voice—to speak *with* the people as opposed to speaking *to* them. (It is notable that Adorno never attempts to speak *for* the people.) But despite his obvious commitments at the level of theory to a radically democratic form of pedagogy, Adorno's own language sometimes misfires, and there are moments when his voice fails his own prescriptions. The ideas that he communicates at the level of theory do not always translate to his own tenor and tone. But he tries. If Adorno is never fully "converted" to the people, his time in America does convert him to the cause of democracy and changes his thinking and action thereafter, as well as his register of communication, despite these occasional tonal misfires. Not only does Adorno work on American democracy, but American democracy also works on him.

Further, Adorno's own occasional struggles bear witness to a valuable dialectical tension that might be said to exist at the heart of these ideas about democratic leadership and pedagogy themselves. The institutions and norms of liberal capitalism work to cultivate a dependent, unthinking, passive citizenry, but how to foster a more critical and robustly democratic practice of citizenship without simply offering new forms of authority to obey? Adorno's project of democratic pedagogy grapples with the tension between speaking to the people and speaking with the people, between speaking as an authority and speaking as a participant, between teaching the people and being taught by the people. To illuminate Adorno's negotiations here is—at least—to work to enrich our understanding of Adorno in America, and—at best—to inform our own attempts to practice a better approximation of democracy in America.

# 6

# Seeing Small-Scale Resistance

Turning Countertendencies into Vaccines
to Strengthen Democratic Practice

> Counterpropaganda should point out as concretely as possible in every
> case the distortions of democratic ideas which take place in the name of
> democracy. The proof of such distortions would be one of the most efficient
> weapons for defending democracy.
>
> —Adorno, *The Psychological Technique of*
> *Martin Luther Thomas' Radio Addresses*

In chapter 3, which focuses on Adorno's practice of critique, I discussed one
category of scholars exploring the political significance of his thoughts on
justice, ethics, aesthetics, resistance, and thinking as a praxis. But there is
a second category of thinkers who seek to *use* Adorno's thoughts to inform
politics today in an even more direct, immediate, and explicit way than the
first group of thinkers discussed earlier. Since this chapter explores Adorno's
more practical political applications, I want to begin by briefly discussing
some of the relevant literature to give a sense of how current scholarship is
working to dislodge the traditional image of Adorno as an apolitical, elitist,
withdrawn aesthete.

One recent volume, titled *Negativity and Revolution: Adorno and Political Activism,* is written by anticapitalist activists who are looking to Adorno's
*Negative Dialectics* and his thoughts on the nonidentical to inform working-class struggle and anticapitalist activism and to deepen their critique of
capitalism.[1] John Holloway's essay in that volume argues that working-class
struggle *is* the nonidentical. Here the nonidentical is the "hero," the "misfit,"

the "rebel who will not submit to party discipline," the "moving force of the world," and as such is "revolutionary," "explosive," and "volcanic."[2]

But the best example of how Adorno's work might productively inform current politics is Paul Apostolidis's book *Stations of the Cross: Adorno and Christian Right Radio.*[3] This book is both an exception in the existing scholarship and a valuable model for the approach of my own project in that Apostolidis draws from Adorno's theory to inform our analysis and consideration of the modern American context. In addition, Apostolidis's book is the only other major scholarly investigation of one of the same English-language texts that I analyze in this project, *The Psychological Technique of Martin Luther Thomas' Radio Addresses.* Apostolidis's cultural critique is informed by the method of negative dialectics generally, but he draws particularly from Adorno's book on this 1930s radio evangelist to mobilize the nonidentical elements of an unlikely cultural object, James Dobson's *Focus on the Family* radio program. Following Adorno's own method of immanent critique, Apostolidis analyzes Christian right radio in a microscopic way, drawing out the internal contradictions of the Christian right to show how evangelicalism gives evidence of utopian moments on the basis of deep criticisms of our post-Fordist social order as well as a desire for greater autonomy.

In sum, though his focus is on evangelicalism, Apostolidis's approach is a good model for my own because of the way he *uses* Adorno's theory to undertake an immanent critique of one key aspect of American culture. He approaches Adorno, from the outset, as a thinker whose work can valuably inform democratic politics today. My project begins with a similar set of assumptions to explore the contours and contributions of a broader set of Adorno's writings on democracy in America, with an eye toward drawing out a different kind of democratic project that surfaces in Adorno's English-language compositions, when read alongside his essays on education and against the backdrop of his theory of negative dialectics.

This chapter shows how Adorno puts into practice the project of democratic leadership as democratic pedagogy that previous chapters have outlined, bringing together the arguments that have been built up so far about this "other Adorno." Here we see him illuminating the small-scale forms of resistance that Americans are already enacting, from within but against, the large-scale pathologies of pseudo-democracy. If they are nurtured and developed, these countertendencies represent the possibility and the hope for a stronger practice of democracy in everyday life. But according to the plan Adorno details in his writings on leadership and education, these more overtly positive and productive moments of his critique arise from and are originally embedded in the problematic aspects of American culture that were outlined in the first chapter of this book. Vaccines are formulated from toxins. What is hopeful and promising, what is utopian, emerges from wrong life, damaged life, sick life.

As I outline in this chapter, for the radio generation, reparative possibilities can arise from what is broken: "There is reason to assume that the loss of some abilities is accompanied by the freeing of certain others, and these are precisely what destines them to carry out changes that would never have been possible for the 'old' individuals."[4] Like a boomerang, the pernicious aspects of the radio generation can be turned toward productive purposes:

> The same people who will no longer allow themselves to think (or do similar things such as read books, discuss theoretical questions, etc.) have become "canny" and can no longer be fooled. . . . It is a matter of pushing this "canniness" so far that it breaks through its bond to the immediate world of action and transforms itself into real thinking. If that succeeds, it is precisely those "crippled" human beings who will be most able to put an end to that crippling. Their coldness can become a readiness to make sacrifices for truth, their improvisation can turn into a cunning in the fight against the giant organization, and their speechlessness can become a willingness— without words or arguments—to do what needs to be done.[5]

These are the transformative reversals that characterize Operation Boomerang. In what follows, I analyze *Current of Music, The Psychological Technique of Martin Luther Thomas' Radio Addresses,* and *The Stars Down to Earth* to show how, in each of these texts, Adorno enacts the project of democratic leadership as democratic pedagogy outlined earlier, by showing how to produce vaccines from these countertendencies.

## *Current of Music:* **Radio and Countertendencies**

### *Twirling the Dial and Searching for "Good Reception"*

Standardization and homogenization are basic features of the radio phenomenon, for Adorno, where the identical material is offered to anyone who listens: "This standardization, in a way, is the essence of radio itself. The abstract fact that an identical content appears at innumerable places at the same time practically coincides with the concrete fact of standardization—

namely, that the same material is impressed upon a great number of people."[6] This, Adorno notes, is self-evident and would not be important were it not also the motivation for several different rebellious responses from the listener; standardization is the "background" against which all the "countertendencies" of radio can be "properly understood."[7]

Channel surfing is one countertendency through which the listener expresses frustration with the homogeneous content of radio. Against standardization, the listener channel-surfs and "twirls the dial," as an expression of a frustrated desire for difference and a frustrated assertion of autonomy, a resistance against "getting the same stuff everywhere."[8] For Adorno, "the man who plays on his radio as if it were an instrument, obtaining ready-made, accordion-like chords dragged into each other in a dilettantish way, is a sort of model for all behavior where individual initiative attempts to alter ubiquity-standardization."[9]

Adjusting the dial to get "good reception" is another countertendency: "behind this desire lies a hidden resistance to ubiquity-standardization."[10] The listener substitutes his desire to influence the phenomena with a fetish for finding good reception:

> Doing the best job for receiving a radio broadcast no longer opposes the ubiquity-standardization but obeys its laws so completely that the listener gets the illusionary self-satisfaction that the workings of the mechanism are his own. Still there is good reason to believe that behind this transformation lies only his original desire to preserve his individuality and "his phenomenon" as his property. When conditions prevent people from fulfilling this desire against a central power, they make the case of the power their own case. The pattern is this: private person resists ubiquity-standardization of his radio set; knows this resistance is futile; finally transforms this wish for individual activity into preparedness to obey the laws of his apparatus; but just in this way loses his relation to the object and the content which he originally sought or pretended to seek.[11]

The individual is frustrated by radio but also confronts it as a powerful object. So rather than reject radio, the listener tries to inhabit and master it. The desire to be "the real master of machinery is a relic" of a frustrated but "genuine spontaneity."[12] The listener develops a case of Stockholm syndrome in relationship to radio; feelings of irritation combine with a sense of impotence culminating in a tendency to identify with the oppressor, to want to connect with the oppressor. As Adorno notes, "One of the only psychological refuges is identification with those very powers, just as a prisoner may grow to love the barred windows of his cell."[13] Engaging with radio, working the dial, in a futile search for "good reception," then, represents this unfulfilled countertendency. Adorno seeks to cultivate the nascent critique that the frustration represents, while removing the sense of impotence and powerlessness that stops the countertendency from developing into conscious resistance.

## *Fan Mail*

Fan mail represents another unlikely countertendency. Adorno speaks of analyzing fan letters, which can display a kind of exuberance that he describes as "standardized enthusiasm." The uniformity of the letters and the tendency to use "rubber stamp phrases" occur not because the writers have had "profound musical experiences" in listening to the radio. This would make them more likely to "stammer and use awkward expressions," struggling to find authentic words to capture their reactions, rather than cloaking their letters in cliché and giving such similar responses.[14] Instead, Adorno argues, there is another explanation: "The listeners were strongly under the spell of the announcer as the personified voice of radio as a social institution, and they responded to his call to prove one's cultural level and education by appreciating this good music. . . . They took refuge in repeating, often literally, the announcer's speeches on behalf of culture."[15] This is essentially a form of manufacturing consent. Adorno notes that the fan-mail writers "identified those songs which they regarded as most popular with those they happened to like themselves" because the announcer plugged certain songs and then people imagined those were their own favorites too.[16] So the fan-mail writer parrots what the announcer has already told him to think, using the same language he has heard on the radio but claiming it as his own. This is just another example of how capitalism and the culture industry cultivate dependent, passive subjects:

> The standardization of production in this field, as in most others, goes so far that the listener has virtually no choice. Products are forced upon him. His freedom has ceased to exist. This process, however, if it were to work openly and undisguised, would promote a resistance which could easily endanger the whole system. The less the listener has to choose, the more is he made to believe that he has a choice: and the more the whole machine functions only for the

sake of profit, the more must he be convinced that it is functioning for him and his sake only or, as it is put, as a public service.[17]

Again, though, there is a countertendency at work here. Even from inside this homogenized and oppressive structure, there is still a small part of the self that resists being told what to like and what to think. This assertion of self, even within a system of standardization, this "pseudo-individualism," takes the unlikely form of fan mail. As Adorno says, "The consumer is unwilling to recognize that he is totally dependent and he likes to preserve the illusion of private initiative and free choice."[18] The very urge to write a letter, no matter the content, Adorno says, is a small attempt by the listener "to impress his will upon broadcasters" and to engage, to participate, to have one's say.[19] These letter writers "feel somewhat lost and neglected in the face of ubiquity-standardization," but "even while they are criticizing the phenomenon, they compensate for this lost feeling by attempting to re-establish personal participation in the phenomenon and by trying to attract the attention of the institution from which it originated."[20] The very fact of reaching out and writing the letter signals a refusal to remain fully within the passive, impotent, dependent position dictated by the culture industry. Writing fan mail is a form of action through which the individual "maintains the original motive of 'individual resistance'" and "does not flatly accept what is offered to him."[21] When we listen closely to the dissonant object of radio, Adorno notes, "facts apparently so far apart as dial-twirling and fan-mail-writing begin to 'speak'" and these important countertendencies become apparent.[22]

### Switching Off

Turning the radio off is the "last chance left for the listener to escape ubiquity-standardization." This countertendency represents the most extreme feelings of frustration and impotence on the part of the listener: "Since it is absolutely impossible for the individual actually to impress his own will, he seeks refuge in one last loophole. He completely destroys the phenomenon."[23] In fact, Adorno argues, the act of switching off, this drive to destroy the radio, is actually a way that individuals signal their cognizance of how the forces of modernity work to condemn them to destruction. But their sense of impotence and dependence also drives a feeling of futility in the face of the liquidation of the individual. Rather than work for change, rather than rebel, the individual feels that no real alternatives exist and thus passively waits for the apocalypse, so to speak. People engage in a "fruitless" gesture of oppression that creates the "illusion of might and power." Adorno says that he has observed that "people switch off their radios with a sort of wild joy, just as if they were shouting 'I shut his mouth for him!'"[24] But this really only means that the erstwhile rebel is "withdrawing from contact with the very public events he believes he is altering."[25] As Adorno notes, the "drive for destruction" represented by switching off "can be described more accurately as a desire of those who are condemned to impoverishment or demolishment; who reflect their own annihilation by annihilating the whole; who console themselves by hoping for what they fear and who even prefer a world catastrophe to a change of conditions."[26]

## Spite and Resentment

Another countertendency is represented in the feelings of spite and resentment people direct toward particular songs, saying how much they hate this song when it comes on the radio, with a disproportionate amount of energy and animus. As we have already seen, listeners feel impotent against the power of radio and the power of the culture industry. Even if they feel nascent frustration against the standardizing, homogenizing, and oppressive aspects of radio, they are also "disillusioned about any possibility of realizing their own dreams in the world in which they live, and consequently adapt themselves to this world."[27] So they can only take a busman's holiday and "escape" *from* the modern world that frustrates them by escaping *to* that same world: "the escape provided by popular music actually subjects the individuals to the very same social powers from which they want to escape" and "makes itself felt in the very attitude of those masses."[28] And so there is no outlet for the frustration people feel except to direct their rage at a certain kind of popular music or a particular song. They can't hate the entirety of the culture industry or the entirety of the radio because they see no alternatives to it and feel that any attempt at real change is futile. And they can't admit their own shameful impotence because "the shame aroused by adjustment to injustice forbids confession by the ashamed."[29] So they channel all this negative energy into hating a particular song. "To dislike the song is no longer an expression of subjective taste but rather a rebellion against the wisdom of a public utility and a disagreement with the millions of people who are assumed to support what the agencies are giving them. Resistance is regarded as the mark of bad citizenship, as inability to have fun, as highbrow insincerity, for what normal person can set himself against such normal music?"[30]

Spite here "becomes drastically active" and is "the most conspicuous feature of the [listeners'] ambivalence toward popular music." Rather than confess their dependence on the culture industry itself—"nothing is more unpleasant than the confession of dependence"—they "turn their hatred rather on those who point to their dependence than on those who tie the bonds."[31]

Here, as in other places, Adorno shines light on the energy people must put into convincing themselves that they actually like the conditions that are forced on them. This is the only way they can maintain the illusion of autonomy. In the modern era, "spontaneity is consumed by the tremendous effort which each individual has to make in order to accept what is forced upon him."[32] Adorno thinks that if people put the same amount of energy into working against those powers that make them dependent as they do into lying to themselves about it, there might be actual change instead of just countertendencies that point toward alternatives.

## Atomistic Listening and the Preponderance of the Parts

Two additional potentially productive countertendencies reside in the qualities of the radio itself as a physical object. Here Adorno focuses not on how people respond or react to the form or content of the radio, but rather on how the physical and material qualities of the radio force us to listen in certain ways that can be potentially valuable. Adorno begins to unpack the first countertendency by explaining how when music is fulfilling its highest potential, it is so intense and transcendent that it overcomes time and moves into space. But the radio causes the symphony to fall "back into time."[33] Symphonies are distorted as the listener breaks them up into parts and loses a sense of the whole: "the symphonic work, in a way, will be atomized when presented by radio. That is, it will appear not as a totality in which each part derives its proper meaning only in relation to the other parts, but rather becomes a rapid succession of 'atom-like' sections, each apperceived more or less in isolation."[34] The radio encourages what Adorno calls "atomistic listening": because of its physical constraints, radio cannot articulate the totality, so it focuses listeners' attention on the parts.

But there is also a potentially valuable countertendency that can be drawn out here. When "the parts become preponderant over the whole," the listener's attentiveness to particularity is sharpened and, whereas elsewhere Adorno speaks of the value of a "microscopic gaze" that allows us to "see" the nonidentical, here he speaks of a kind of microscopic mode of hearing: "One may listen to individual musical sections in radio as if through a microscope."[35] We can learn to hear in a more careful, more attentive, more discerning, more particular way, and these are all qualities that help us become better attuned to the nonidentical elements of the world and help us access that deeper mode of experience that Adorno sees as so valuable for democracy. Radio can, in fact, help us hear in a more particular way. Granting this kind of preponderance to the object has positive "prospective chances": "It might well be that this study of details, free of the 'spell,' will finally lead to a new apperception of the whole which, although totally different from the traditional, may ultimately make good its losses."[36]

And furthermore, this mode of atomistic listening can offer a valuable aesthetic shock of its own. The "nourishment" offered by listening to music in this way doesn't just add "a new substance which helps you feel better and go on," but rather may be "simply a sort of shock" which makes you "doubtful" about your entire "psychical household."[37] For Adorno, there is supposed to be an "antagonism between the work of art and the psyche" that motivates change, that makes you think that, borrowing a line from Rilke, "You ought to change your life."[38] This kind of revolutionary sensibility can even come from listening to radio, which can actually teach us to pay attention to particular things, to cultivate the kind of careful perception that helps us experience the nonidentical.

### Playing the Hear-Stripe

In this example, Adorno focuses on radio's inauthentic reproductive qualities. Here another kind of mechanical limitation of the radio becomes a potentially productive countertendency, and another kind of negative constraint can turn into a positive possibility. Adorno analyzes radio in terms of Benjamin's work of art in the age of mechanical reproduction. Up until the era of mechanical reproduction, "one of the essential elements of the work of art was its 'hic et nunc'—its here and now—its existence unique to the locus at which it can be found," unique to the original. For Benjamin, as Adorno notes, "only the original sustains its authority and the 'aura' of the work of art is only the way this authenticity is expressed in the phenomenon of the artwork."[39] Live music, Adorno notes, has such an aura, but it is vanishing as music is played on a phonograph or over the radio: "The phonograph record destroys the 'now' of the live performance and, in a way, its 'here' as well," and "*in radio the authentic original has ceased to exist.*"[40] Radio symphonies played again and again lose their aura because of their immediacy, "because they can no longer keep their distance from the listeners. They show, instead, a tendency to mingle in his everyday life because they can appear at practically every moment, and because he can accompany brushing his teeth with the Allegretto of the Seventh."[41]

The countertendency that could be drawn out here, amid this large-scale pathology, would entail the radio's ceasing to be an imitation of something else and, instead, playing on itself. For Adorno, this would mean using the sounds that are original to radio to produce radically modernist, atonal compositions that employ distortion and what he calls the "hear-stripe" of radio. The hear-stripe is the background music of the radio, the warping hiss that one could especially hear in the moment when the radio was switched on, before other sounds filled the air. Adorno saw distortion and the hear-stripe as sounds that are authentic to the instrument of radio, which could then be played using these sounds, like any other instrument. Playing on the radio would be kind of like playing the theremin, Adorno notes. This instrument was patented in 1928 by its inventor, Léon Theremin. The device consists of two antennae that transmit electronic signals that are then manipulated by the operator's hands, which control frequency and volume by waving and moving in space like an orchestra conductor's. Something similar could be done to play the hear-stripe of radio. As Adorno puts it, "The idea is that we should no longer broadcast over the radio but play on the radio in the same sense that one plays on a violin."[42] As Robert Hullot-Kentor says in his introduction to *Current of Music*, "Radio would become a musical instrument. Its technique would engage the full productive range of the instrument's electrical phenomena. Distortion would not vie with the normality of sound and the hear-stripe itself would become a compositional source."[43]

This is another way that Adorno gives us evidence of his desire to transform passive radio listeners into active radio composers, to shift our relationship to radio from one where we are positioned as subservient objects to one where we become subjects with creative agency. Playing the hear-stripe could become a way of resubjectifying the radio generation into artists of a distinctly modern style. Distortion itself can become reparative. Radio's function as an inauthentic—and imperfect—reproducer of naturalistic sounds, as evidenced by distortion and the hear-stripe, can become a source of creativity. Thus, here, as in other examples, Adorno tries to turn an aspect of radio that is representative of damaged life into the means of working against that pathology.

## The Psychological Technique of Martin Luther Thomas' Radio Addresses

In the first chapter of this book, we saw the pathological elements that Adorno identified in the addresses of this right-wing radio demagogue. But once again, this is only part of the story. Adorno also sees some small-scale avenues toward resistance, subversion, and change in the dynamics between this authoritarian figure and his American audience. Here, too, he moves beyond a diagnosis of the problem to also discuss tactics for "counterpropaganda" to work against this manipulation in the name of more meaningful democracy.

The most important countertendency he discusses concerns democracy, specifically how, in the United States, even an authoritarian demagogue such as Thomas has to appear to work through the medium of democracy. Thomas must assume a hollow democratic style to appeal to his audience, steeped as Americans are in the rhetoric of democracy. The fascist agitator can be successful only by deforming democratic ideas to his own purposes, but in doing so he still has to appeal to and negotiate them as "living forces," given the prevailing culture. But this strategy can also backfire for Thomas, in productive ways: by "perverting" democratic ideas, he is "always bound to hurt the very feelings which he wants to utilize."[44] If democracy actually is important to Americans, pointing out the manipulations that take place in its name could be an effective pathway toward democratic enlightenment. As Adorno says, "Thomas' persistent references to democracy, to democratic personalities, such as Jackson or Lincoln, and to the American Constitution [are] exceedingly significant from the point of view of counterpropaganda."[45] Adorno advocates drawing out this countertendency by helping the demagogue's audience think through the contradictions, antagonisms, and tensions between Thomas's style and meaningful democracy: "counterpropaganda should point out as concretely as possible in every case the distortions of democratic ideas which take place in the name of democracy. The proof of such distortions would be one of the most efficient weapons for defending democracy."[46]

Adorno ultimately wants to use the desire for democracy as a stimulus for the critical analysis of Thomas's manipulations. This is one of the ways that his understanding of countertendencies and of the nonidentical take into account the whole person. The American desire for democracy is not inherently a rational, intellectual, analytical experience. Rather, the idea that democracy is an unquestioned good is a knee-jerk reaction for most Americans, something that has been bred into them by the larger culture. It is, at first, an irrational desire that involves complex feelings and emotions tied to nation and tradition. As Adorno notes, the American culture is "intrinsically bound up with democratic ideas and institutions" in a way that "has tended to give to some elements of democracy a quasi-magical halo, an irrational weight of their own."[47] But Adorno thinks that this irrational faith can become part of a critical practice whereby Americans come to appreciate the gap between Thomas's authoritarianism and the real meaning of democracy.

As we have already seen, Adorno believes that the capacity for thinking and feeling against the given is a part of our birthright as humans. In this instance, the emotional attachment to democracy can push Americans to think about what this concept would really mean in practice and to realize how far Thomas falls short of that ideal. Adorno ultimately has a different set of assumptions about the audience. He thinks Thomas misjudges his audience. Thomas "reckons with an audience who cannot think, that is to say, who is too weak to maintain a continuous process of making deductions," and instead assumes that its members "live intellectually from moment to moment" and "react to isolated, logically unconnected statements, rather than to any consistent structure of thought."[48] But Adorno reckons with audience members whose nonidentical desires and feelings can become the basis for critique and who can, through conversation and discussion, come to realize that they are being sold a wolf in sheep's clothing. And because of their deep emotional attachment to and faith in democracy—which can foster a more critical and analytical commitment to democracy—this realization can turn their admiration for Thomas into resentment. The same sense of discontent that drew people to Thomas could turn them against him and his kind: people's "objective situation might possibly convert them into radical revolutionaries."[49]

### The Stars Down to Earth

Adorno approaches astrology in much the same way that Marx approached religion, with sympathy for how one might turn to it out of frustration with an alienating existing reality, out of a sense of helplessness and impotence, and out of a desire for something better. Marx is often misunderstood on this point. He actually sees religion as a valuable critical indicator, a symptom of suffering and alienation in the actually existing world. The desire for heaven works as a disavowal of existing reality, a protest against "what is" that points toward a wish for something better. For Marx, "*religious* suffering is at the same time an *expression* of real suffering and a *protest* against real suffering. Religion is the sigh of the oppressed creature, the sentiment of a heartless world, and the soul of soulless conditions. It is the *opium* of the people."[50] Marx is critical of religion because it is a fantasy that humans spin for themselves owing to the impoverished state of their earthly conditions and because it problematically redirects human energies away from creating a heaven on earth. Religion is "only the illusory sun around which man revolves so long as he does not revolve around himself," and thus the call for the "abolition of religion as the *illusory* happiness of men, is a demand for their *real* happiness."[51] Religion is a symptom of human alienation. Turning away from heaven, Marx wants humans to focus their attention on law, economics, and politics. Instead of seeking refuge in religion or solace in visions of an afterlife, Marx calls for people to address the causes of suffering in this world and wants us to work toward universalizing emancipation in the here and now for all humans. There is a kind of religiosity to Marx's writings, and he sees the "religious spirit" as opening up a valuable pathway for change, but he wants the emancipation that might be associated with religion to be the experience of all humans, every day on earth.[52]

Adorno's attitude toward astrology is quite similar. Astrology is a representation of an authoritarian social order, but it also encompasses contradictory elements that might be drawn out to work against the latent threats it poses.[53] But Adorno is concerned not just with highlighting the roots of fascism deep in the heart of what is supposed to be an exemplary democratic nation, but also with drawing out the countertendencies that would allow us to work against it. He says, "We want to utilize our studies of astrology as a kind of key to more widespread social and psychological potentialities."[54] The feelings that motivate people to turn to astrology columns can be more productively turned in other directions, and this seems to be what drives Adorno's investigation. In this way, astrology columns are both part of the problem and potentially part of the solution.

The astrology column mirrors the pathologies of damaged life and reflects the so-called "real world" of late modernity because both appear to be irrational, fetishistic, and inscrutable systems that position individuals as passive, subservient, and powerless. Adorno notes that the "system" of the "real world" also positions individuals as dependent objects in an "all-comprising net of organization with no loopholes."[55] People face the existing world of late modernity as a complicated mechanism that offers "no way out," and they suspect that "this closed and systematic organization of society does not really serve their wants and needs."[56] Given how the "real world" also has a "fetishistic, self-perpetuating 'irrational' quality, strangely alienated from the life that is thus being structured," people find it easy to accept the false world of astrology.[57] Ultimately, even people with a "supposedly 'normal' mind are prepared to accept systems of delusions for the simple reason that it is too difficult to distinguish such systems from the equally inexorable and equally opaque one under which they actually have to live out their lives."[58] And, at least the confusing system of astrology—another kind of "administered world" that positions people as subservient, dependent, and passive objects—seems to come with a manual in the form of the column and promises to offer affirmative guidance.

But there are also nonidentical elements inherent to the writing and reading of astrology columns that can be drawn out to work against its otherwise authoritarian and fascistic elements. If modern life presents itself as a system on which we are dependent, the astrology column also names that dependence and recognizes the frustration that individuals feel. The astrologer's advice exacerbates the irrationality and impotence of individuals, but it also reflects the dismal and retrograde conditions of modernity back to the reader and stimulates a hope for change. If the column makes individuals feel threatened, it also affirms that the threat is real and widespread, that others feel it, too. The astrologer's advice reifies adjustment and accommodation rather than structural change, but it also addresses some real contradictions of modern life. The columns also testify to a desire for change, a desire to act and exert agency, and a hope that things might be otherwise. Despite the ways it conditions them, people "want at the same time desperately to get away from the existent."[59] If astrology is ultimately an "ideology for dependence," a way of coping with dependence instead of changing it, it is also a record of frustration with social conditions under modern liberal capitalism. Adorno wants to put pressure on all the countertendencies contained here, to capture the critical energies that are misdirected into astrology, lost in this irrationality, and use them to generate more substantive structural changes. He wants to take the nonidentical moments seen even in astrology and use them to strengthen meaningful and substantive democracy in America.

The first potential pressure point Adorno describes concerns the knowledge of "wrong life" that the astrologer must have: "The column calculates, probably correctly, that whoever is subject to cold, dehumanized, rigid and alienated social relationships feels insufficiently understood," feels lost, and has a desire to turn to external authorities such as an astrology column.[60] The astrologist has wide and deep knowledge of "the most frequently recurring problems prescribed by the set-up of modern life" and "figures out a number of typical situations in which a large percentage of his followers might at any time find themselves."[61] He is familiar with the "insoluble situations" and "impasses" of modern life, with the threatening conditions that "stimulate each individual's hope for some effective interference from above."[62] In short, to appeal to readers, the astrologer must be intimately acquainted with people's frustrations, their fears, their everyday concerns. Adorno notes, "In order to fulfill such exacting tasks, the columnist really has to be what is called in American slang, a homespun philosopher."[63] The very way that the astrology column is framed provides a kind of witness to damaged life, wrong life, and the pathologies of modern America.

The structure and content of the column also testify to the contradictions that people experience in their lives. The astrology column assumes that people "are incessantly beset by irreconcilable and contradictory requirements of their own psychological economy as well as of social reality. The column constructs its addressee as being 'frustrated.'"[64] People turn to the column because they don't feel free and empowered, despite the promises of liberalism, but feel like dependent objects. Or they turn to the column out of a sense of bewilderment, given the contradictions between American values of independence and the social pressure to conform. For Adorno, the column is witness to the fact that Americans do indeed, on some level, recognize that "classical liberal ideas of unlimited individual activity, freedom and ruggedness are incompatible with the present developmental phase in which the individual is more and more required to obey strict organizational demands made by society," that "the same person can hardly be expected to be thoroughly adjusted and strongly individualistic at the same time."[65] These contradictions are potentially productive countertendencies of the column that could be captured and turned into more conscious and change-oriented critical insights.

Of course, rather than draw out the implications of these negative energies of discontent, the astrologer takes an interest in "hammering over and over again into people's heads ideas to which they are already conditioned but in which they can never fully believe."[66] But even this represents a potential countertendency. The fact that the astrology column has to repeat the ideological imperatives that people are supposed to have internalized indicates that the transmission failed in some ways. Their allegiance to these ideas is imperfect and incomplete and needs continual reaffirmation. These fault lines can become the basis for the kind of resubjectification that is central to Adorno's project for democratic leadership as democratic pedagogy, enacted here in his writings on the *Los Angeles Times*'s astrology column.

Again, as we have seen before, another potentially productive counter-tendency exists in the energy that individuals expend in accepting their own dependence. Adorno emphasizes that it takes a great deal of effort and energy to give up one's individuality, whether to the authority of mainstream society or to the authority of the astrology column: "giving up one's individuality requires the same effort and investment of libido formerly needed in order to develop individuality—in a way, the same 'ruggedness.'"[67] This is another moment when efforts could be redirected toward making structural changes that work to strengthen individuals' autonomy instead of reify their dependency. People do not want to think of themselves as dependent, and something in them resists it, even as they recognize their own powerlessness: "For, while people recognize their dependence and often enough venture the opinion that they are mere pawns, it is extremely difficult for them to face this dependence unmitigated."[68] What the astrology column does, then, is help people make sense of their own feelings of dependency, explain to them why they feel powerless, give them categories to understand their feelings of impotence. The astrology column is not just an "expression of dependence," but is actually an "ideology for dependence," a kind of handbook that instructs readers how to navigate their own painful condition. But if astrology is something that people turn to, on a daily basis, to make sense of their feelings of dependence, they might also be given other categories, other theories, other explanations, other ways to invest their discontented energies. In *The Stars Down to Earth* Adorno enacts the practice of democratic leadership as democratic pedagogy toward turning these nonidentical moments into conscious critique, toward working against the ideology of dependence and toward greater autonomy.

## Adorno's WNYC Radio Addresses

In the final section of this chapter I would like to examine an instance in which Adorno's critique is followed up by an active attempt on his part to correct the problem he identifies and educate people directly in an alternative way. Here Adorno is not just outlining his overall plan for democratic leadership as democratic pedagogy, or enacting it through writings on American culture, but he is working to cultivate people's capacity to think and feel against the given in a more immediate way. Adorno undertook a study of NBC's *Music Appreciation Hour* as a companion piece to his essay "'What a Music Appreciation Hour Should Be.'" Together, these two pieces provide a written exposé of the problems he identifies in NBC's program. But

"'What a Music Appreciation Hour Should Be'" also provides the text for a series of radio programs that Adorno himself put together, wrote, and aired on WNYC that attempted to expose listeners to music in a different way. In *Current of Music*, there is a list of twelve lectures that begin the course.[69] He also aired a number of radio programs based on this model on WNYC. The inaugural program aired on 22 February 1940, and the remainder were broadcast in spring of that year.

In the analytical study of NBC, Adorno highlights a number of short-comings that his own radio show then aims to remedy.

> The purpose of the present study is to point out that radio, at its "benevolent" best, in a nation-wide, sustaining program of purely educational character, fails to achieve its aim—namely to bring peo-ple into actual living relation with music. . . . It will be shown that not only is the purely musical part of this program insufficient musi-cally and pedagogically, but that it also leads to a fictitious musical world ruled by personalities, stylistic labels, and pre-digested val-ues which cannot possibly be experienced by the audience of the *Music Appreciation Hour,* since the program presents the material in a way designed, wittingly or unwittingly, to foster conventional, stereotyped attitudes, instead of leading to concrete understanding of musical sense.[70]

At root, the problem lies with the conflict between the appreciation of music and the place of radio in general and NBC in particular as a part of corporate culture, embedded in a capitalist mode of production. The idea of promot-ing music appreciation in this way is especially problematic given how the system "uses its own putative unselfishness and altruism as an advertising medium for selfish purposes and vested interests."[71] In ways large and small, NBC's *Music Appreciation Hour* is tied up with this larger system, whether in terms of sponsorship, of promotions, or of the way it seems to present knowl-edge of music—ability to identify and recognize classical music—as a kind of cultural capital that might elevate the "masses."

Musical education primarily takes the form of drilling students so they can recognize themes and identify composers, rather like a spelling bee. It inculcates a kind of "musical Babbittry" and ultimately promotes a kind of "pseudo-culture."[72] The listener, the pupil, is "bored by the formalistic scheme and, at the same time, fed empty phrases about intellectual effort and skill, which must either repel him or spur him on to erudite babbling."[73]

The program emphasizes that its job is to make music "fun," but "fun" is conceived as recognizing a composer, for example, as if one is trying to win a contest: "These principles, borrowed from the sphere of commercialized entertainment and shallow in themselves, lead, even if excusable as pedagogically expedient in inducing people to listen, to distortions of musical sense and cultural absurdities."[74] During the *Music Appreciation Hour,* there is a "shifting of the 'fun' from a living-relationship with music to a fetishism of ownership of musical knowledge by rote."[75] As a result, music "is actually transformed into property," made "our own" in the act of identification "instead of being lived by the listener."[76] As Adorno notes, "The *Music Appreciation Hour* destroys respect for the work, its meaning, and its achievement, by transposing it into the effect it has upon the listener and inculcating in him composer-fetishes which become virtually identical with the 'fun' he derives from viewing a World Series baseball game."[77] Adorno is also concerned with the way the show cultivates an attitude of hero worship toward the composers and also toward the program host, framed as the listener's "spiritual leader."[78] It tends to deify the composer and produce a "false halo" around his head. Ultimately, "the authoritarian structure of this type of musical education, promotes a cult of persons instead of an understanding of facts."[79] Adorno is also critical of the deep sentimentalism of the program: "Musical Babbittry celebrates it greatest triumph when it enters the emotional sphere: no one is more sentimental than the tired businessman and there's no one more willing to endorse such statements as 'all of us are happy at some times and sad at other times.'"[80]

Adorno follows up this critical analysis with his own attempt at a better alternative outlined in the section of *Current of Music* titled "'What a Music Appreciation Hour Should Be': Exposé, Radio Programmes on WNYC and Draft." He sets out the goals of his own program for "correct listening," which means grasping a given piece through the act of direct, spontaneous perception, "as a semantic unity in which every aspect has its function within the whole."[81] Adorno wants to present music in a way that appeals intuitively to individuals, "to destroy the taboos that seal it off," and, instead, convey a "living understanding of music" that doesn't preach to the individual but follows "from the living musical experience that one can assume among the audience: from the musical language they speak themselves."[82] Here, too, we can see that, as in his other writings, he emphasizes the importance of starting with his audience where they are and appealing to their own particular context, their own concrete experiences. He assumes his audience already has a way of listening to music, a way of talking about music, and he will build from these concrete experiences. Adorno says, "We are expecting listeners of high school and college age, and will appeal to their experience without pandering to it."[83] Just as he sees the capacity for critique, and for thinking and feeling against the given, as a human praxis that we all possess that can be activated as long as we can open ourselves up to a deeper mode of experience, he also assumes that music is a human force that will move people, so long as they can open themselves up to the experience of truly hearing. Serious music contains a nonidentical element that helps stimulate our critical capacities, that shocks us out of our comfortable numbness. And just as Adorno's other writings show us how to open our senses to this mode of experience—this democratically valuable mode of experience—his course on music appreciation hones participants' capacity for spontaneous listening.

Adorno's course is also consistent with the program for democratic leadership as democratic pedagogy that we have outlined in previous chapters. He enacts a democratic, horizontal, egalitarian style of leadership in his course. He proposes guiding participants through the experience of listening in a way that is intended to empower them and increase their own feelings of agency, to help them realize themselves as empowered subjects rather than dependent objects. Adorno's audience will be treated as mature, autonomous individuals: "Avuncular undertones, personality cult, and authoritarian elements should be avoided to the same extent as any superficial test or contest tastes. On the contrary: these should in fact be eroded through the course, also in a broader pedagogical sense extending beyond the music itself as far as possible."[84] His course aims to unseat authorities, including himself. He does not aim to tear down the hosts of other music appreciation programs to put himself in their place. Rather, Adorno wants to cultivate participants' sense of their own authority. In his program, the listener will not be constructed as a dependent sitting at the feet of the great men: "No final value judgments will be communicated. One should abstain in particular from attempting to convince listeners and advertising music, or praising masterpieces and great composers. . . . One should guide listeners towards true discernment and serious, critical independence."[85] Indeed, he imagines something that is dialogic: "Listeners should be encouraged to respond. Questions or objections voiced in letters should be addressed for a few minutes in each session. Possibly one could also arrange discussions with listeners."[86] Ideally, this would be a dialogic, conversational, discussion-based model of education, reflecting the contours of Adorno's program for democratic leadership as democratic pedagogy.

Finally, his music appreciation program also entails a critique of capitalism and the culture industry. He notes how, in his course, the "human force" of music will be emphasized, its aesthetic power, instead of selling it as a "fun" commodity: "It will also be shown that the notion of 'having fun with music' is not suited to genuine musical experience. The notion of having fun is modelled on *commercial entertainment,* and is thus transferred from that realm and applied to aesthetic objects to which it is not suited."[87] Adorno thinks that serious music can prompt a critique of the alienating, conforming, identifying forces of modernity. Serious music prompts the kind of encounter with the nonidentical that pushes one to think and feel against the given world of the culture industry. A living experience of music is not "fun" but, rather, stimulates the human praxis of thinking. For Adorno, "it is actually impossible with serious music to have the kind of fun that is derived from commodities."[88] Ultimately, then, even the experience of listening to music is connected with Adorno's overall democratic project, because music stimulates the capacity for critique, on which democracy depends. It now becomes clear why democracy is a theme that threads through *Current of Music:* what we listen to and how we listen are politically important. Depending on the nature of this listening, music can either advance or retard our practice of meaningful democracy, our ability to sense and experience the nonidentical elements that push us to think and feel against what we are given and act to change our world.

## Conclusion

This chapter has brought together all that we have learned about Adorno's democratic project, showing what his plan for democratic leadership that works through a democratic form of pedagogy looks like in action. Here we see him putting into practice a nascent form of negative dialectics as well as the lessons laid out in his writings on leadership and education. Here, too, Adorno works through, step by step, the democratic theory that this book has drawn out from all the various texts that have been analyzed. *Adorno and Democracy* began by tracing the relationship between the constellation of concepts around which this book revolves: the material objects of the world; the nonidentical elements that surround us; thinking, feeling, and the capacity for critique; the universal praxis of humans; alienation; negative dialectics; leadership; education and pedagogy; and democracy. This chapter illustrates the dynamic relationship among all these concepts, applied to specific cultural objects.

Adorno's starting point concerns the pathological elements of pseudo-democracy. In this chapter we see him analyzing cultural objects that work primarily to uphold the dominant political and economic culture of liberal capitalism in the United States, which works against its ostensible values, making citizens passive, obedient, and cultivating a sense of infantile helplessness. But as a materialist, Adorno thinks that even these largely retrograde objects contain dissonant nonidentical qualities that prompt and push us to think and feel against the given conditions. This is why cultivating a new mode of perception and experience is so vital for Adorno. By opening ourselves up to the countertendencies that run through these objects, we confront the contradictions that ask us to engage in the practice of thinking and turn what is initially a raw, reactive form of resistance into something more conscious. Thinking and critique, then, begin with this attentiveness to the world around us, this coming to consciousness of the kind of countertendencies this chapter has analyzed. And since, for Adorno, critique is the essence of democracy, the processes laid out in this chapter are all part and parcel of his efforts to cultivate a more robust political practice at the level of everyday life among American citizens. Furthermore, in introducing and translating these ideas in more accessible language as well as over the airwaves, Adorno himself undertakes the program for democratic leadership in the form of democratic pedagogy that he advocates in the texts analyzed in earlier chapters of this book.

His plan for democratic leadership as democratic pedagogy works through an analysis of the small-scale, unspectacular, everyday twinges, pauses, interruptions, and anxieties that we all experience when we are open to the world around us. Turning our nascent experience of countertendencies into more conscious forms of resistance is the goal of Adorno's overall democratic project. The image of a phoenix arising from the flames is far too dramatic an image of rebirth to really capture what Adorno imagines. And yet there is, in his writings on democracy in America, a sense of recreation and renewal, a redemption of latent democratic forms in American culture that he wants to foster and facilitate, a world-building enterprise that he undertakes as a political theorist and a democratic theorist.

# Conclusion

# Adorno and *A Postcapitalist Politics*

In this book we have seen Adorno lay out the theoretical underpinnings for a democratic politics, outline a plan to put it into action, and begin to enact that project in his own writings and radio addresses. My goal has been to connect the dots between Adorno's writings in a way that seems true to his intentions, in hopes of convincingly and persuasively demonstrating how his work as a whole has a surprisingly compelling and productive democratic project at the core. As a way of continuing that work of articulation and development, here I want to put Adorno into conversation with another text that has received a great deal of attention in recent years among students of leftist politics, J. K. Gibson-Graham's *A Postcapitalist Politics*.[1] J. K. Gibson-Graham is the pen name of Julie Graham and Katherine Gibson, who coauthored the book. (Because they see themselves as creating a new joint entity or persona when they write together, I refer to Gibson-Graham as a single author for verb number [i.e., "Gibson-Graham focuses . . ."] while also referring to the authors as "they.")

*A Postcapitalist Politics* has become popular with theorists on the left for the way it cuts through the melancholy pessimism about the totality of neoliberal hegemony to show how, in fact, there are all kinds of hidden ways that ordinary people engage in counter-hegemonic acts that participate in a diverse community economy to dislocate and resist capitalism. Ultimately, Gibson-Graham has become a kind of go-to text for thinkers on the left who want reassurance that resistance is not, in fact, futile, and that there are micropolitical ways of unsettling the neoliberal capitalist system that can seem so totalizing. If we work with the traditional view of Adorno as a gloomy, apolitical elitist, then there would seem to be a chasm of difference between his writings and this text. If Adorno has tenaciously but erroneously been held up as the poster child for gloomy pessimism and despair, Gibson-Graham is a representative for productive optimism and hopefulness. But at the close of this book, we have the complete architecture of a remodeled Adorno in front of us—another Adorno—and are positioned to recognize the overlaps and points of agreement between these seemingly divergent thinkers.

Gibson-Graham focuses on capitalism, whereas this book has explored Adorno's writings with a particular emphasis on democracy. But the distinction matters less in practice, given how Gibson-Graham values postcapitalist politics that are radically democratic in nature, and given how Adorno's critique of existing democracy is also always tied to a critique of capitalism. Both Gibson-Graham's critiques of capitalist hegemony and the alternative politics they illuminate have many points of sympathy with the project I have outlined here. Indeed, though Adorno does not figure into their book at all, the micro-political community-action research projects that Gibson-Graham describes sympathize with the plans Adorno outlines and tried to put into action. Because of how closely their work follows his own ideas, we can in fact see Gibson-Graham's research projects as examples of what a more fully fleshed-out version of Adorno's plans might have looked like if carried out on a wider scale. Thus, as a final way of pulling the pieces of Adorno's project together and emphasizing the productive nature of his novel theory and practice of democracy, I make parallels between Adorno's project and the community-action research projects that Gibson-Graham undertakes and explicates.

Gibson-Graham's projects work on thought, action, affect, and emotion to remap the political landscape and make way for an emergent imaginary that discloses economic practices that unfix and interrupt the dominance of capitalism. They want to show how, despite our habit of thinking of "the economy" only in terms of capitalism, and despite our tendency to view it as an all-inclusive and totalizing system, in everyday practice people participate in a "diverse economy" that reveals alternatives to capitalism. For example, Gibson-Graham illuminates a wide variety of practices people engage in that are not part of the capitalist norm of receiving wages in return for production in a profit-oriented firm. The diverse economies that people are already participating in consist of unpaid household work and family caretaking; cooperative labor; work for welfare; participating in ethical and fair-trade markets; bartering; serving as a neighborhood volunteer; gift giving; hunting, fishing, gathering, and gleaning; cooperative exchanges; or self-provisioning labor.[2] Further, Gibson-Graham also shows how ordinary people act in ways that contain nascent critiques of capitalism and how their practices and thoughts contain energies that can be drawn out to realize alternatives to capitalism.

Toward amplifying these tendencies, their overall project has three primary aims. First, a postcapitalist politics involves a "politics of language," creating new discursive spaces that widen "the field of intelligibility to enlarge the scope of possibility."[3] Second, Gibson-Graham's work undertakes a politics of the subject. They engage in practices of "revolutionary self-cultivation" and "resubjectification" to address the parts of the self that accommodate capitalism as well as oppositional parts of the self. They recognize that individuals are both "powerfully constituted and constrained by dominant discourses, yet also available to other possibilities of becoming."[4] Understanding the subject as a "zone of possibility," they work to cultivate modes of thinking and feeling, dispositions and attitudes, emotions and desires that can foster the wider realization of the emergent alternatives to capitalism. Third, their project moves beyond the subject to engage in a politics of collective action, a "micropolitics" that "involves conscious and combined efforts to build a new kind of economic reality."[5]

Gibson-Graham works to realize these goals, in part, through a number of community-action research projects. The two projects they focus on the most in their book were located in the Latrobe Valley in Australia and the Pioneer Valley in Massachusetts. In the Latrobe Valley project, they worked with people who were marginalized and displaced by mainstream visions of "developing" the region: people who were unemployed, people whose jobs had been retrenched, and single parents.[6] In the Pioneer Valley, economic and social "development" was also a goal of planners and business leaders who wanted to attract business to the region. The Pioneer Valley is composed of diverse regions, some economically depressed and deindustrialized, some thriving. In both research projects, much of the work was undertaken by community researchers who were themselves local. The researchers responded to advertisements and were hired part-time to work in the community with other local participants on specific community-based projects and enterprises that worked outside the logics of capitalism. The research projects were explicitly based on Paulo Freire's idea that participation in research could try to, as Gibson-Graham puts it, "break down the power differential between the researched and the socially powerful by enabling the oppressed to become researchers of their own circumstances."[7] For example, in the Pioneer Valley Rethinking Economy project, seventeen local community researchers were

trained to conduct interviews with other locals who were active in noncapitalist sectors of the diverse economy, over several months. In other instances,
one-on-one interviews and discussion sessions were held between researchers and participants that allowed for in-depth exploration of their views and
opinions. Focus-group sessions were also conducted with business and community leaders.

It is important to note that the participants in these projects were by
no means all like-minded critics of capitalism. They were just local people
who had been affected in different ways by economic changes to the regions.
And the research projects were not simply aimed at indoctrinating the participants against capitalism. The goal, instead, was to empower people to
broaden the category of "economy" to recognize, appreciate, amplify, and
extend the informal community economies—the diverse economies—that
their community already participated in and to value and "develop" these
economies as well. Their community-action research projects explicitly took
in the whole subject in their efforts to prompt individuals to engage in a
process of resignification, reframing, and renarrativizing themselves. The
projects aimed to empower the participants as subjects in ways that would
encourage them to take control of their own community economy, instead
of positioning themselves as dependent objects waiting for conventional economic development to save them: "The people engaged in our research conversations had a chance to encounter themselves differently—not as waiting
for capitalism to give them their places in the economy, but as actively con-
structing their economic lives, on a daily basis, in a range of noncapitalist
practices and institutions."[8]

Ultimately, Gibson-Graham's community-action research projects give
us an example of what an expanded version of Adorno's Operation Boomerang might look like. His thoughts on experience and encountering the
nonidentical, his project for democratic leadership and pedagogy, and his
analysis of countertendencies and vaccines all find resonance with Gibson-
Graham's projects. First, if Adorno describes a specific form of democratic
leadership as democratic pedagogy to draw out the lessons of the countertendencies and contradictions he finds, Gibson-Graham undertakes
community-action research projects with a similar goal and intent. Like
Adorno, Gibson-Graham works to illuminate possibilities, but additional
forms of leadership and education are also necessary to fully realize the possibilities they identify, to widen these openings. But for our purposes, what
is most important is how the community-action research projects coordi-
nated with local people to draw out their own nascent critiques and empower

them to think, feel, and act with a new sense of their own possibilities. These research projects worked with people in their immediate conditions to awaken different noncapitalist economic possibilities, in a way that revolved outward from the participants' own thoughts and actions. The projects collaborated with the participants in a nonhierarchical, egalitarian, and democratic way, starting where they were to walk together to a new point along their path. These community-action research projects and community-partnership projects worked to "listen to [people's] experiences of subjection and to identify the energies and intensities that might be harnessed by a politics of becoming."[9]

In his writings on leadership and education, Adorno also describes how his own proposed form of democratic pedagogy needs to take place outside the classroom, how it needs to be deinstitutionalized from schools and cultivated throughout society in a kind of broad civic-education program. The type of community-action research projects that Gibson-Graham undertakes provide an excellent model that gives us a better sense of how Adorno's goals could be met and how the form of democratic leadership that he envisions could be carried out. The process Gibson-Graham describes is one that is deeply situated in the community, and all the work that the projects undertake is both in and for the local people, drawing from the nearby population and taking place in a particular place with a history and present conditions with which the researchers are familiar.

Indeed, Paulo Freire's work on the pedagogy of the oppressed is a node connecting Adorno with Gibson-Graham. We have seen how Adorno's writings sympathize with Freire's emphasis on working *with* the people and starting from their own experiences of the world and their immediate conditions; Freire's work is also a touchstone for Gibson-Graham. What Adorno wants to do, and what Gibson-Graham also does, is to turn ordinary people into leaders, to make into a leader anyone who can help others cultivate critical insights about their own internal contradictions and countertendencies. Leaders, for Adorno, are not people who possess special status or credentials, as we have seen. "Democratic leaders" are, rather, people who can experience the nonidentical elements of the world around them in ways that prompt them to recognize the contingency of given conditions and engage in critical negation and then work with others in an egalitarian way to help them reach similar insights.

A second point of sympathy between Gibson-Graham and Adorno concerns the kinds of reactions, responses, and behaviors that they seek out to cultivate as pathways to change. For Adorno, the nonidentical elements of the world that can prompt a more meaningful practice of democracy can take various forms, manifesting themselves as feelings of uneasiness, contradictory desires, and negative affective responses. He looks to develop and cultivate the nascent forms of resistance represented in these countertendencies, but political change begins with these humble, modest, small-scale changes in how we experience the world around us, how we process our thought, how we learn to think against what we are given and ultimately feel empowered to act as subjects to engage in wider world-building activities. Gibson-Graham's community researchers look for similar moments in their discussions and start small. The language that they use maps onto Adorno's understanding of the nonidentical.

In their conversations, community researchers searched out "momentary eruptions that break familiar patterns of feeling and behavior [and] offer glimmers of possibility," and their projects worked to "cultivate these glimmers," according to Gibson-Graham.[10] Two kinds of "openings" proved most productive in Gibson-Graham's efforts to encourage these processes of empowerment and resignification. They looked for "the discursive 'nonclosures' signaled by contradictory ways of thinking and speaking, and the ethical opening of persons to one another that conversation provokes and enables."[11] Borrowing a term from William Connolly, they searched for and guided the "fugitive currents of energy" that were released by the conversation and "the process of collective reflection."[12] Gibson-Graham sees these micro-political energies as the starting point for more macro-political movements and the basis for a politics of becoming; they quote Connolly, who states that macro-political proposals will not get far until "micropolitical receptivity to [them] has been nurtured across several registers and constituencies."[13] For Connolly, fugitive energies "release subjects from 'preset judgements that sanctify the universality or naturalness of what [they] already are,' thus allowing them to participate in new and surprising movements."[14]

The kinds of reactions that Gibson-Graham looks for as openings are also often affective, embodied, and emotional responses. We saw earlier how Adorno's understanding of the nonidentical encompasses both thinking and feeling against the given and how his understandings of the pathways toward change involve both the mind and the body. Similarly, Gibson-Graham recognizes that "the process of becoming a different economic subject . . . is not so much about seeing and knowing as it is about feeling and doing."[15] Changing the world is about changing the self and "the project of history making is never a distant one but always right here, on the borders of our sensing, thinking, feeling, moving bodies."[16] They are looking to prompt changes in habits, dispositions, and the ways of being "prior to reflection" that "we almost never think about."[17]

But what is most helpful about Gibson-Graham's work is how they show what all these moves and moments look like in action, through the discussions that take place in their community-action projects. Gibson-Graham's work shows how effective Adorno's vision of democratic leadership as democratic pedagogy might be, how practical it is, and how it could be replicated in these kinds of community-action research projects across the country. For example, at a focus group composed of business and community leaders, Gibson-Graham descrivbes a discussion of proposals to bring new forms of traditional economic development to the Latrobe Valley, "attracting 'good' jobs by recruiting major capitalist employers, via subsidies and other inducements, to locate in the region," trying to attract new businesses to the area to revitalize a deindustrialized and depressed economy.[18] But beneath the surface enthusiasm for these traditional ideas about economic redevelopment, it became clear that there were also a lot of reservations and a fear that traditional economic development also brought with it costs and possibilities of social failure. For example, people spoke about their concerns that there would be no one left at home to raise children and that the younger generation would suffer:

> These fears and vulnerabilities erupted through the smooth surface of rational interchange and destabilized the explicit closures and certainties of development. We encountered an unspoken, embodied acknowledgment that capitalist economic development might be a dependent rather than a self-sufficient process, and that social well-being has multiple wellsprings and determinants. As the sufficiency of capitalist development to regional well-being unraveled before our eyes, a dislocation took place. We recognized a discursive nonclosure, a breakdown of sorts, an unsettling of the subjects of a capitalist economy. Over the course of the project, we would return to this moment as an emotional opening for a counterdiscourse of the "household-based neighborhood economy" and its contributions to social well-being and economic development.[19]

Later, through a question-and-answer session, the participants began to chart the previously invisible diverse economy that characterized the community and the strengths, capacities, and assets of the community. This kind of conversation was typical of their work. In discussions with community researchers, participants worked to expand each other's ways of thinking about the

economy and to map out a sense of how the community was already participating in many activities that worked outside the capitalist hegemony.

The discursive reframing and renarrativizing made people aware of how
they were subjects of a diverse economy with agency of their own, not just
objects of a capitalist economy outside their power and control. They engaged
in "asset-based community development," wherein participants listed their
personal assets and capabilities to develop a sense of themselves as skillful
and competent, as opposed to being victims.[20] The goal here was to redirect
the habitual pessimistic attitude of people in the valley, to give people a sense
of their own capabilities rather than making them feel that the only hope for
their community came from attracting businesses from outside. And it seems
to have worked: "At the end of the session, one participant noted the shift that
had occurred in his own understanding and sense of possibility—a shift that
had resulted from being placed in a different relation to the formal economic
'identity' and familiar downbeat narrative of the valley."[21] Gibson-Graham
is also struck by the change in affect that accompanied this process of resignification: "Over the course of the two-hour conversation, the participants
had moved from an emotionally draining narrative of regional destruction
at the hands of the SEC, to outbreaks of raw emotion occasioned by retelling
this painful story in the sympathetic presence of witnesses/listeners, to open,
even exuberant responses to our questions about counterstories and alternative activities."[22]

In working with men in their forties or fifties who had been "retrenched"
or whose jobs had been made redundant, the community researchers found
it especially necessary to move beyond working with language and discourse
and to address these men's emotional lives and habitual affective responses of
hopelessness and frustration. For example, through a question-and-answer
session with a community researcher, one man's views changed: "Where the
man had felt pain and anger associated with past experiences of Economy,
under Yvonne's patient cultivation he moves toward pleasure and happiness
associated with a different way of being. Her questioning shifts his attention
away from a narrative of impotence and victimization and into a hopeful sce-
nario that positions him as skillful and giving, endowed with an identity in a
community economy."[23]

As we can see from these examples, the work of the community researchers and the participants in these projects generally was part education, part
therapy, part support group. The kind of world-building activities directed
toward realizing a postcapitalist politics that Gibson-Graham envisions
require this type of closely and carefully engaged discussion. This, in general,

captures the flavor of Adorno's vision of Operation Boomerang. But the projects Gibson-Graham describes were also discussions among equals in ways
that exemplify Adorno's vision of democratic leadership. What we see here is
a process in which people are first unmoored from their assumptions. People confront countertendencies or fugitive energies that unsettle them from
their seemingly firm foundations and habits. They are then caught between
two worlds: they are leaving one subject position behind, but they need support and encouragement in building a new one. This is what the discussion
groups provide, helping individuals navigate from the "dissatisfactions and
disappointments" of what they used to know, toward developing the "satis-
factions and surprises of what is new, but hard to fully recognize."[24] The discussions of the community-action research projects provide the individual
with "nourishment and encouragement from without to sustain acts of self-
cultivation, to see changing selves as contributing to changing worlds."[25] The
groups provide necessary support for the acts of resubjectification that participants undergo as they discuss, learn, and change.

Ultimately, Gibson-Graham helps us appreciate how Adorno, who might
usually be seen as an exemplar of what Eve Sedgwick would call the "paranoid" style of theorizing, takes on a "reparative" style of reading the surrounding culture in the writings that are the focus of this book.[26] For Sedgwick, the
"paranoid" style of theorizing wants to know the whole world in advance.
It produces "strong" theories that describe the world in monolithic terms,
as an all-encompassing ordered system that is predictable and stable. Paranoid styles characterize those on the left who bemoan regimes and systems
of oppressions and repression that seem to offer no escape. The exemplar of
paranoid strong theories, for Gibson-Graham, is the narrative of neoliberal
global capitalism as a hegemonic regime. This is a theory that maps out the
whole world with certainty, but if it "definitively establishes what *is*," it also
"pays no heed to what it *does*."[27] Neoliberal global capitalism is described as
a phenomenon that has "colonized" the economic landscape, as well as our
imaginations. This totalizing theory of our contemporary world "affords the
pleasures of recognition, of capture, of intellectually subduing that one last
thing," but it is also hopeless in its certainty and "offers no relief or exit to a
place beyond."[28]

This kind of strong theorizing leaves no possibility for interruptions, exits,
alternatives, or redirections, in ways that also satisfy a desire for a kind of paranoid control that submits the world to rational order. Those on the left can be
guilty of a paranoid attachment to *knowing* the world in a systemic and predictable way, even if this means being attached to a disposition of melancholy

and hopelessness. Walter Benjamin recognized the possibility of this form of "left melancholia," where an attachment to one particular analysis of the world or one specific identity becomes a force preventing the birth of a better alternative, an emergent possibility. So if paranoid readings of the world produce strong theories, they may also be characterized by a desire to cling to the known past, even if this prevents the realization of the better future. In contrast, for Sedgwick, "reparative" readings work against systematizing strong theories to *open up* possibilities, to interrupt, to highlight exits. Reparative modes of theorizing are characterized by an affective disposition of hopefulness, creativity, and opportunity as opposed to melancholy loss. Reparative readings are weak modes of theorizing that are not all-encompassing, all-knowing, or totalizing, but leave space for something unexpected to happen, something new to emerge. In this vein, Gibson-Graham works to practice weak theory, adopt reparative motives, and cultivate positive affects. As they write, "What if we believed, as Sedgwick suggests, that the goal of theory were not only to extend and deepen knowledge by confirming what we already know—that the world is full of cruelty, misery, and loss, a place of domination and systemic oppression? What if we asked theory to do something else—to help us see openings, to help us to find happiness, to provide a space of freedom and possibility?"[29] Their goal is to try to get outside our colonized imaginations and to disarm and dislocate the "naturalized hegemony" to make space for new becomings, "ones that we will need to work at to produce."[30]

Traditional ways of interpreting Adorno cast him as an exemplary paranoid reader of the world. This view of Adorno engages in strong theory and takes a kind of melancholy pleasure in finding his own dismal and gloomy characterization of modernity confirmed, looking down on the devastation, so to speak, from the comforts of the Grand Hotel Abyss. As we have seen, however, such a characterization of Adorno was never accurate in the first place. His mode of critique and the practice of negative dialectics are oriented toward highlighting the rebellious nonidentical elements of the world that interrupt totalizing systems and open up the contradictory fractures that exist even in things like the culture industry. Adorno's affective disposition, of course, does usually tend toward a stance of lament and loss—his "reflections" are, after all, on "damaged life"—and his dialectics is indeed a "negative" one, not just because it thinks against given conditions, not just because it critiques "wrong life," but also because of the alienated sense of loss that characterizes much of his work. Further, his stylistic practice of exaggeration and provocation can make him seem like an exemplar of strong theorizing, until we remember that cracks, fractures, and alternative possibilities also pervade what seem to be known systems.

But the writings that this book analyzes make it clear that another Adorno is actually engaged in a reparative mode of reading the world that tries to open up and extend alternative possibilities. Furthermore, his affective stance in these writings is much more hopeful, creative, and positive. This other Adorno is more obviously committed to realizing the emergent imaginary of a more meaningful democratic politics and more explicitly focused on drawing out the countertendencies that interrupt and can productively recalibrate the existing pseudo-democracy. More experimental, more speculative, and less attached to certainty, the Adorno this book illuminates is doing reparative work on democracy, trying to fix its problems and cultivate its greater possibilities.

We see Adorno undertaking the kind of critical analysis that defines the subfield of political theory, moving between the real and the ideal, the empirical and the normative, and engaging in the art of thinking that brings creative vision, political imagination, and inspired world building to bear on the present. Traditionally, Adorno has certainly been seen as a critical theorist and a social theorist. And though he has been read, analyzed, and written about by political theorists, he himself is not usually designated as a "political theorist" or associated closely with these particular words because of the complicated relationship he has been seen as having with the political. But this book revises this conventional wisdom to the point that we can now appreciate this critical theorist fully as a political theorist, indeed a democratic theorist. Critique is an important part of political theory, and Adorno's credentials here are impeccable. But the subfield also involves other normative, productive, creative, and imaginative work that has not traditionally been associated with him.

Political theory moves back and forth between "what is" and "what ought to be" or "what might be" and brings philosophical wisdom to bear on current problems. As Hannah Arendt explains, "The dichotomy between seeing the truth in solitude and remoteness and being caught in the relationships and relativities of human affairs became authoritative for the tradition of political thought."[31] Despite their personal antipathy to each other, this is a point on which both Adorno and Arendt agree. Adorno also explores the truth and the utopian possibilities that are contained in the "now" and complexly represented in the nonidentical, but which point toward the future. Second, political theory is described as having an "irreducibly normative component," whatever focus and method it takes up and whatever its stripe.[32]

In the same way, we see Adorno illuminating and trying to draw out and realize the utopian possibilities represented in the nonidentical elements of the world around us. He also shares political theory's "concern with the demands of justice and how to fulfill them" as well as "the presuppositions and promise of democracy."[33] Third, political theory is productive and practical, a way of thinking that also works on us and the collectivities of which we are part, a civic activity. Political theory is not just something you read: it is something you do. Political theory gives us frameworks for thinking about politics, but it is not just academic. It also productively works on us, shaping us into different kind of subjects, fostering the cultivation of new subjectivities, new ethical positions, new ways of being in the world. Indeed, as Sheldon Wolin puts it, political theory "is primarily a civic and secondarily an academic activity. In my understanding this means that political theory is a critical engagement with collective existence and with the political experiences of power to which it gives rise." As he says, "Political theory might be defined in general terms as a tradition of discourse concerned about the present being and well-being of collectivities."[34] This is the aspect of political theory that has, perhaps more than any other, worked to exclude Adorno from the subfield. But as this book shows, Adorno was in fact deeply invested in the problems and possibilities of American democracy during the World War II era and developed pedagogy to critically engage and inform the collective lives of U.S. citizens. In this book we see Adorno engaging in explicitly civic and not just academic enterprises, trying to lead and educate in specifically democratic ways.

Ultimately, then, political theory is a world-building activity. It combines all the elements noted above to critique our existing world in ways that also try to foster, prompt, and cultivate the creation of new worlds. Theory does not engage in descriptions of the world as it is, but as Jane Bennett puts it, it "aspires to help us live better—to identify, invent, and pursue paths through which a more vital, less violent, more sustainable collective life might unfold." As she emphasizes, "The hope here is that careful theoretical reflection upon the concepts, ideals, narratives, perceptions, arguments, comportments, spatial arrangements, and mood of public life can, however indirectly and tentatively, help *build a better world.*"[35] Or, as Wendy Brown puts it, theory is not a descriptive enterprise but a "meaning-making enterprise" that "depicts a world that does not quite exist, that is not quite the world we inhabit." Theory does not "simply decipher the meanings of the world but recodes and rearranges meanings to reveal something about the meanings and incoherencies that we live with," and it works to illuminate, provoke, and incite "thought, imagination, desire, possibilities for renewal."[36] Theory "fabricates the world" as it "interprets the world," and, thus, "theory's most important political offering is this opening of a breathing space between the world of common meanings and the world of alternative ones, a space of renewal for thought, desire, and action."[37] Adorno undertakes just this sort of a world-building enterprise in his work generally, even if this has not always been recognized.

The very practice of negative dialectics is a form of critique that is also a world-building project, given the ways it draws alternative future possibilities out of the nonidentical qualities of the present. But this book shows how Adorno's efforts to introduce and translate his nascent theory of negative dialectics to an American audience, writing in English and in a more accessible register, really highlights the democratic, civic, and pedagogic aspects of his work as a whole in the most explicit way. If Adorno's work is always actually political theory—though perhaps unrecognized as such—then his work on, in, and for America makes it impossible to deny how his work is part of the productive, political, and imaginative world-building enterprise that defines the subfield. Here Adorno is directly aiming at educating people to see the world around them in a different way, to perceive, experience, and sense in ways that court the disruptive, unsettling, and interruptive encounters with the nonidentical elements of the material and ideological components of everyday life in ways that dislocate and denaturalize what seems real, solid, and inevitable. After adopting a mode of vision that recognizes this contingency and working to experience the world more deeply than the blinding, numbing, incapacitating forces of modernity usually allow, the next step is to draw out the rebellious lessons of the nonidentical and act against the assumptions, norms, structures, and institutions of the status quo. In transmitting these lessons, Adorno aims to model a form of leadership that is itself democratic.

He tries to anticipate and put into practice the kind of egalitarianism and autonomy that are part of his ultimate vision. In other words, he tries to create a more democratic collective using democratic modes of communication and education. His means of world building prefigure his end. But there is also a micro-politics of world building at work here. His lessons work through the individual, and he implies that we change the world by changing ourselves. Throughout the writings I have analyzed, Adorno outlines, models, and encourages a certain kind of transformative work on the self that changes how we experience, that pushes us to inhabit new ethical positions and new subjectivities that are not just more critical but also more attuned to feeling, that are more sensitive, more compassionate, less hard, less cold, less numb, less alienated, less barbaric.

Still, the Adorno who has been presented here doesn't tell us everything we would want to know or need to know to address all the problems of our modern neoliberal capitalist landscape. What I lay out is all that's there, and it's far more than we had from Adorno in terms of a political theory. Ultimately, however, the portrait of democratic leadership in the form of democratic pedagogy that this book paints is not everything, and it's still not enough. But it's also not nothing. Adorno's democratic theory deepens and develops our understanding of him. It gives us a new sense of how a commitment to democracy fits into his theory of negative dialectics and his materialism, while also showing how his American writings promote and put into practice a plan for strengthening democracy through a form of pedagogic leadership. But in keeping with Adorno's vision of autonomy and his faith in the critical capacities that can be stimulated by our engagement with the nonidentical and our attentive experience, the rest of the story is up to us. The alternative he envisions would derive its basic contours from his Marxist principles, of course, but the substance of that collective world-building enterprise is not prefigured; it is left up to the *demos*. In Adorno we now have another valuable resource with which to inform leftist politics that work against neoliberal capitalism. Now that he has checked out of the Grand Hotel Abyss once and for all, we can deepen our efforts to read him as a political theorist, as a democratic theorist, whose thoughts on the America of the past can inform the problems of the present and even help usher in the alternatives of the future.

# Acknowledgments

It's a pleasure to have the opportunity to acknowledge the people who have invested their time and energy in reading and responding to this project. In chronological order, I would like to thank Paul Apostolidis for the valuable feedback he gave me as chair of a panel I co-organized at the April 2011 Western Political Science Association conference, titled "Adorno and Democracy: Complexity and Contradiction, Possibilities and Potential." Thank you also to the other panelists, Michael Bray and Andrew Douglas, for their insights on Adorno generally and my paper specifically. I would like to thank the participants of the American Democracy Forum conference at the University of Wisconsin at Madison, in May 2011, for inviting me to present a paper drawing from this book and for providing a stimulating space for discussion: thanks especially to John Zumbrunnen, Elizabeth Beaumont, Jack Turner, and Jimmy Casas Klausen. I would also like to thank the organizers of a graduate student conference at the University of Chicago, titled "Exile on Main Street: Fascism, Emigration, and the European Imagination in America," for inviting me to present a paper on this project. Thanks especially to Hadji Bakara for inviting me to one of the most fun and interesting conferences I've ever attended and for his attention to my work. Thanks also to the University of Chicago's Social Theory Workshop, especially to David Gutherz and Patchen Markell, for an enjoyable and productive conversation about this project. Both these events took place in November 2011. Thanks to the other panelists of the "Cultivating Democratic Citizens: Pedagogy, Policing, and Practice" panel at the March 2012 meeting of the Western Political Science Association conference. Megan Thomas and Matthew Voorhees provided especially useful feedback. I would also like to thank the Political Science Department at Johns Hopkins University for inviting me to present at their Fall Seminar in October 2012 and for engaging in such a vibrant and helpful discussion about my work. I'm especially grateful to Jane Bennett for her support of this project, for her suggestions for revision, and for questions that helped me clarify key aspects of my argument. It's a unique pleasure to also thank my former student Katie Glanz, now a political theory doctoral student at Johns Hopkins, for productive questions and a very useful conversation about autonomy at the seminar.

Southwestern University supported this project at the very beginning by awarding me a Brown Junior Faculty sabbatical and another sabbatical midway through the project. I've also received several grants from Southwestern to fund this research. Particular thanks also go to Eric Selbin and Michael Bray at Southwestern for reading the manuscript in part or whole and for interesting conversations about Adorno and critical theory.

Thank you also to Steve Wrinn and Allison Webster at the University Press of Kentucky. At every step along the way, I have been reminded that I made an excellent choice in deciding to send my manuscript to them. All authors should get to work with such humane, enthusiastic, supportive, and professional editors.

I would like to thank the members of my weekly writing group, also dear friends, for providing a fun, friendly, and collegial way to keep myself accountable to goals and deadlines. These weekly lunches with Corinne Pache, Tim O'Sullivan, David Rando, Tom Jenkins, and Nicolle Hirschfeld are nourishing to body, mind, and soul, thanks in large part also to the truly wonderful people who welcome us every Friday at Saigon Express.

There are also many people beyond academia who have contributed to this project by supporting and sustaining me in the most important ways. My deepest thanks go to my family, especially my parents, Robert and Jeanne Mariotti, for being my biggest fans, for always believing I could do anything I set my mind to, and for taking the time to ask about Adorno even when we could just be talking about Walter; love and thanks also to Barbara Rando, to Jason Rando, and especially to Marianne Rando, for all her generosity, support, and good advice on our shared journey through motherhood. Some friends are like family: thank you to Sam Frederick and Maryam Murday Frederick, and Bill and Barbara Sullivan, for all that we have shared. Thank you to David Liss and Claudia Stokes, for your friendship and support, and all you have given to Walter. And thank you to our beloved Karen Trujillo, for always being there for our family and all your love, care, and attentiveness to Walter.

Words fail when it comes to acknowledging the two most important people in my life, the sources of my joy and happiness: my husband, David Paul Rando, and our son, Walter Robert Rando. They mean everything to me and this book is dedicated to them.

# Notes

## Preface

The epigraphs are from Georg Lukács, *The Theory of the Novel* (Cambridge: MIT Press, 1994), 22, and Theodor Adorno and Max Horkheimer, *Towards a New Manifesto* (New York: Verso, 2011), 61 (this dialogue was recorded in spring of 1956).

1. Tocqueville's experience of nineteenth-century democracy in America, recorded in *Democracy in America and Two Essays on America,* trans. Gerald E. Bevan (New York: Penguin, 2003), prompted him to say, "I know of no country where there is generally less independence of thought and real freedom of debate than in America" (297). In American democracy, "the majority has staked out a formidable fence around thought" (298). The tyrannical tendency that Tocqueville describes acts violently, but not on the body. As he says, formerly "princes had, so to speak, turned violence into a physical thing but our democratic republics have made it into something as intellectual as the human will it intends to restrict. . . . But in democratic republics, tyranny does not behave in that manner; it leaves the body alone and goes straight to the spirit" (298).

2. Theodor Adorno and Max Horkheimer, "The Culture Industry: Enlightenment as Mass Deception," in Adorno and Horkheimer, *Dialectic of Enlightenment* (1972; repr., Stanford: Stanford University Press, 2002), 105.

## Introduction

The epigraph is from Adorno, *Current of Music: Elements of a Radio Theory,* ed. Robert Hullot-Kentor (Malden, Mass.: Polity, 2009) 62.

1. As Detlev Claussen writes, "The émigré community living in the shadow of Hollywood experienced its deepest gloom in the years 1940–1943, after which optimism returned among those identified with the workers' movement. This was the precise moment in which Horkheimer and Adorno discussed the idea of critical theory as a message in a bottle. Horkheimer had used the term in a letter from New York in 1940 to Salka Veirtel, Eduard Steuermann's sister: "In view of everything that is engulfing Europe and perhaps the whole world, our present work is of course essentially destined to be passed on through the night that is approaching: a kind of 'message in a bottle.' The idea of the message in a bottle belongs to the pre-

history of *Dialectic of Enlightenment.* It reflects the loss of the traditional addressees of the critical theory of society." Claussen then relates the story of the beach party; Detlev Claussen, *Theodor W. Adorno: One Last Genius* (Cambridge: Belknap Press of Harvard University Press, 2008), 161. There is a similar version of the same anecdote cited in Adorno, *Essays on Music,* ed. Richard Leppert, trans. Susan H. Gillespie (Berkeley: University of California Press, 2002), 70n 224: "At the beginning of the war some of the émigré Institute members were on the beach in Southern California when suddenly Adorno, overcome with melancholy, said: 'We should throw out a message in a bottle.' To which Eisler responded—with sardonic humor—that the message should read: 'I feel so lousy.'" The original source of this anecdote is given in the note as Leo Lowenthal, "The Utopian Motif in Suspension: A Conversation with Leo Lowenthal," interview by W. Martin Lüdke, trans. Ted R. Weeks, in *An Unmastered Past: The Autobiographical Reflections of Leo Lowenthal,* ed. Martin Jay (Berkeley: University of California Press, 1987), 237.

2. Adorno, *Minima Moralia: Reflections from Damaged Life,* trans. E. F. N. Jephcott (London: Verso, 1974), 209. The original German reads: "Schon damals war die Hoffnung, in der Flut der hereinbrechenden Barbarei Flaschenposten zu hinterlassen, eine freundliche Vision"; Adorno, *Minima Moralia: Reflexionen aus dem beschädigten Leben,* in *Gesammelte Schriften,* vol. 4, ed. Rolf Tiedemann et al. (Frankfurt am Main: Suhrkamp, 1951), 239.

3. Adorno, "Radio Physiognomics," in Adorno, *Current of Music,* 62.

4. Ibid.

5. Ibid.

6. In a chapter titled "Approaches to Adorno: A Tentative Typology," Peter Uwe Hohendahl maps out different interpretations of Adorno in ways that highlight the tenacity of the image of him as withdrawn, distanced, a defender of high culture, an unhappy exile in America, and politically problematic. Hohendahl's typology helps us see the contours of the conventional framing of Adorno, though this is not his own view of Adorno. Hohendahl emphasizes the political value of Adorno's aesthetics and the social and political character of works of art. Peter Uwe Hohendahl, *Prismatic Thought: Theodor W. Adorno* (Lincoln: University of Nebraska Press, 1995), 3–20.

7. The list of publications that Adorno originally composed in English is quite extensive: *Current of Music; The Psychological Technique of Martin Luther Thomas' Radio Addresses* (Stanford: Stanford University Press, 2000) (also in his *Gesammelte Schriften,* vol. 9); *The Authoritarian Personality* (with Else Frenkel-Brunswik, Daniel Levinson, and Nevitt Sanford) (1950; repr., New York: W. W. Norton, 1993); *The Stars Down to Earth and Other Essays on the Irrational in Culture,* ed. Stephen Crook (1994; repr., New York: Routledge, 2001); "Anti-Semitism and Fascist Propaganda," in *The Stars Down to Earth* (also in his *Gesammelte Schriften,* vol. 8, bk. 2); "Freudian Theory and the Pattern of Fascist Propaganda" (in his *Gesammelte Schriften,* vol. 8, bk. 2); "Democratic Leadership and Mass Manipulation," in *Studies in Leadership: Leadership and Democratic Action,* ed. Alvin Gouldner (1950; repr., New York: Rus-

sell and Russell, 1965) (also in *Gesammelte Schriften,* vol. 20); *Composing for the Films* (with Hanns Eisler) (1947; repr., New York: Continuum, 2007).

8. For a sense of the importance of radio in the United States during the WWII era, see Michele Hilmes, *Radio Voices: American Broadcasting, 1922–1952* (Minneapolis: University of Minnesota Press, 1997); Susan J. Douglas, *Listening In: Radio and the American Imagination* (Minneapolis: University of Minnesota Press, 2004); Alfred Balk, *The Rise of Radio: From Marconi through the Golden Age* (Jefferson, N.C.: McFarland, 2006).

9. For example, most of the essays compiled in Adorno's *Critical Models: Interventions and Catchwords* (first English ed. 1998) were initially German radio addresses broadcast in the 1950s and 1960s, then later published as essays. Here is the original broadcast information for these lectures: "Why Still Philosophy?" ("Wozu Philosophie heute?"), Hessischer Rundfunk, 2 Jan. 1962; "Philosophy and Teachers" ("Lehrer und Philosophie: Ansprache an Studenten"), originally a lecture in the Studenthaus, Frankfurt, broadcast by Hessischer Rundfunk, 7 Dec. 1961; "The Meaning of Working through the Past" ("Was bedeutet: 'Aufarbeitung der Vegangenheit'?"), Hessischer Rundfunk, 7 Feb. 1960; "Opinion Delusion Society," lecture held in Bad Wildungen during the University-Weeks for Continuing Education in Political Science, conference sponsored by the Hessen State government, Oct. 1960; "Notes to Philosophical Thinking" ("Meditationen über das Denken," Deutschlandfunk, 9 Oct. 1964; "Reason and Revelation," theses for a discussion with Eugen Kogon in Münster, broadcast by Hessischer Rundfunk, 20 Nov. 1957; "Progress," lecture at Münster Philosophers' Congress, 22 Oct. 1962; "Gloss on Personality" ("Persönlichkeit: Höchstes Glück der Erdenkinder?"), Westdeutscher Rundfunk, 2 Jan. 1966; "Free Time" ("Freizeit: Zeit der Freiheit? Leben als Konterbande"), Deutschlandfunk, 25 May 1969; "Taboos on the Teaching Vocation" ("Der Lehrerbreuf und seine Tabis"), Hessischer Rundfunk, 9 Sept. 1965; "Education after Auschwitz" ("Pädagogik nach Auschwitz"), Hessischer Rundfunk, 19 Apr. 1966; "On the Question: 'What Is German?'" ("'Was ist Deutsch?' Versuch einer Definition"), a contribution to the series of the same title, Deutschlandfunk, 9 May 1965; "Scientific Experiences of a European Scholar in America" ("Wissenschaftliche Erfahrungen in den U.S.A."), Hessischer Rundfunk, 31 Jan. 1968; "Critique"("Kritik"), broadcast in the series *Politik für Nichtpolitiker* by Sudeutscher Rundfunk, 26 May 1969; "Resignation" ("Aus gegebenum Anlab"), Sender Freies Berlin, 9 Feb. 1969. These addresses are directed toward the German *demos,* but there are similar instances in which he speaks to the American *demos,* in English.

10. Paul Apostolidis, *Stations of the Cross: Adorno and Christian Right Radio* (Durham: Duke University Press, 2000), is both an exception to the existing scholarship and a valuable model for this project in that Apostolidis seeks to *use* Adorno's theory to inform our analysis and consideration of the contemporary American context. In addition, Apostolidis's book is one of the few existing scholarly investigations of *The Psychological Technique of Martin Luther Thomas' Radio Addresses.* Apostolidis draws from Adorno's work to mobilize the nonidentical elements of an unlikely cul-

tural object, James Dobson's *Focus on the Family* radio program. Following Adorno's own method of immanent critique, Apostolidis analyzes Christian right radio in a microscopic way, drawing out its internal contradictions to show how this form of evangelicalism gives evidence of utopian moments based on deep criticisms of our post-Fordist social order as well as a desire for greater autonomy. For Apostolidis (following Marx and Adorno), "a radical approach to religion does not merely dismiss it as a pack of capitalist lies, but tries to convert its protestative strength into different modes of historically concrete expression" (7). Apostolidis undertakes an immanent critique of *Focus on the Family* to show how left democratic politics might more effectively engage evangelicalism, rather than dismissing Christian right discourse entirely.

   11. Two valuable recent books on Adorno in America—David Jenemann's *Adorno in America* (Minneapolis: University of Minnesota Press, 2007) and Thomas Wheatland's *The Frankfurt School in Exile* (Minneapolis: University of Minnesota Press, 2009)—discuss some of the writings I explore here. But whereas my project aims to bring Adorno's theory and practice of negative dialectics fully to bear on his writings on democracy in America, these other scholarly treatments are explicitly disconnected from the theoretical dimensions of his work. Jenemann's *Adorno in America* provides a social history of the America that Adorno was immersed in, highlighting his extensive and penetrating encounters with mass culture. Jenemann give us a sense of Adorno's experience in America and his intellectual concerns during this exile, drawing on various archival materials: memos, letters, unpublished documents relating to the culture industry, internal documents of entertainment and advertising firms that Adorno had access to through the Princeton Radio Project, NBC and CBS promotional materials and educational manuals, publicity and advertising materials that give insight into consumer culture at the time, and even Adorno's own FBI files. But Jenemann is clear that his book is a social history of the America of Adorno's exile rather than a theoretical analysis of Adorno's writings in and on America. Similarly, Wheatland approaches Adorno and the Frankfurt School not as a theorist, but as an historian: "I am a historian of Critical Theory, not a Critical Theorist. My goal has been to build on the work of Jay and Wiggershaus in an effort to clarify our understanding of the Frankfurt School by situating it in a significant and largely unexplored sociohistorical context that shaped its development and reception—the United States" (4).

   12. I note this difference because of the interesting discussion of the American reception of Adorno in David Jenemann's *Adorno in America*. Jenemann addresses issues of reception in ways that highlight the challenges facing the American reader who is not a native German speaker but who wants to study Adorno, especially Adorno's writing *on* America itself. As Jenemann says, "Anyone who studies Adorno will have faced the near-mandatory caveat that the English translations of Adorno are imperfect at best, mutilating at worst. Since I first began reading Adorno as a student, I have always felt that these warnings were both daunting and discouraging,

as though I was being told that unless I could read Adorno in German, my understanding would always be second-rate. These dire warnings smacked of their own type of elitism, in part because they seemed to deny that an American reader could possibly find something powerful and resonant in Adorno's writings, even though so many of them were written in this country and, at some fundamental level, about the American experience" (xxx). Jenemann is frustrated with the idea that native English speakers can never fully grasp Adorno's German writings, even when he is writing about the American context. As Jenemann says, "I reject that idea. What's more, I believe that the insistence on what an English speaker *cannot* understand threatens to undermine what an American reader *can* take from Adorno as a critic and as a vital intellectual force. It is true: Perhaps more than any other writer, Adorno can probably only be fully understood in German; the very structure of his sentences, and the way the German syntax aids in those sentences' ability to negate their own meanings, help convey those meanings. But the Adorno I'm interested in is the American Adorno: not just the Adorno who wrote some of his most important critiques of the mass media in English, but the Adorno whom Americans get to know through his translated works. The choice not to make too much of translation difficulties reflects my commitment not to derail or demean the reader, but it also represents a tacit acknowledgment that this book is about Adorno in America, the Adorno we're stuck with, both the long-neglected day-to-day existence of the actual, historical figure and also his texts, the ones that we in this country get to read" (xxx–xxxi). In light of these problems of translations, Jenemann sticks to Adorno as he has been translated to Americans who are native English speakers: "And so, with a few exceptions, where I have had to make brief translations of letters or archival documents, I have decided to use preexisting translations rather than to try to bring the English closer to its German home. They might be flawed and messy, but they are also powerful, and funny, and sad, and destabilizing, and like Adorno, even in their 'damaged' American form, they are still very much alive" (xxxi). Jenemann raises some interesting issues here, and he perhaps highlights a (unnecessary? exaggerated?) tension between Adorno's German and American readers. I don't think we have to, or should, try to "claim" proprietary ownership of Adorno for primarily German readers or English readers: the unusual circumstances of his life gave him a foot in both places, in both cultures, and legitimately open his corpus up to both kinds of readers. And, indeed, Jenemann is right to note that Adorno's American audience might have some unique insights into his writings, just as his German audience has other unique insights. At any rate, however, Jenemann's concerns are not my concerns, given that my primary texts are indeed written in English and aimed at an English-speaking American audience. These relatively unexplored texts are an important resource for thinking through the questions of democracy in America that prompt my project.

13. Herbert Marcuse, *One-Dimensional Man: Studies in the Ideology of Advanced Industrial Society,* 2nd ed. (Boston: Beacon Press, 1991), 3.

14. See these recent analyses of Adorno's politics: Apostolidis, *The Stations of*

*the Cross;* Rolf Wiggershaus, *The Frankfurt School: Its History, Theories, and Political Significance,* trans. Michael Robertson (1993; repr., Cambridge: MIT Press, 1995); J. M. Bernstein, *Adorno: Disenchantment and Ethics* (New York: Cambridge University Press, 2001); Martin Morris, "Recovering the Ethical and Political Force of Adorno's Aesthetic-Critical Theory," in Morris, *Rethinking the Communicative Turn: Adorno, Habermas, and the Problem of Communicative Freedom* (Albany: State University of New York Press, 2001); Russell Berman, "Adorno's Politics," in *Adorno: A Critical Reader,* ed. Nigel Gibson and Andrew Rubin (Malden, Mass.: Blackwell, 2002), 110–131; J. M. Bernstein, "Negative Dialectics as Fate," in *Cambridge Companion to Adorno,* ed. Tom Huhn (New York: Cambridge University Press, 2004); Brian O'Connor, *Adorno's Negative Dialectic: Philosophy and the Possibility of Critical Rationality* (Cambridge: MIT Press, 2004); Lorenz Jäger, *Adorno: A Political Biography,* trans. Stewart Spencer (New Haven: Yale University Press, 2004); Stefan Müller-Doohm, *Adorno: A Biography,* trans. Rodney Livingstone (Malden, Mass.: Polity Press, 2005); J. M. Bernstein, "Intact and Fragmented Bodies: Versions of Ethics 'after Auschwitz,'" *New German Critique* 97 (Winter 2006): 31–52 (see also this special issue of *New German Critique,* on the topic of "Adorno and Ethics," 97 [Winter 2006]); Paul Apostolidis, "Negative Dialectics and Inclusive Communication," in *Feminist Interpretations of Theodor Adorno,* ed. Renée Heberle (University Park: Pennsylvania State University Press, 2006), 233–256; Espen Hammer, *Adorno & the Political* (New York: Routledge, 2006); Richard Wolin, *The Frankfurt School Revisited, and Other Essays on Politics and Society* (New York: Routledge, 2006); Roger Foster, *Adorno: The Recovery of Experience* (Albany: State University of New York Press, 2007); Marianne Tettlebaum, "Political Philosophy," in *Adorno: Key Concepts,* ed. Deborah Cook (Stocksfield, U.K.: Acumen, 2008); John Holloway, Fernando Matamoros, and Sergio Tischler, eds., *Negativity and Revolution: Adorno and Political Activism* (London: Pluto Press, 2009); Gerhard Schweppenhäuser, *Theodor W. Adorno: An Introduction* (Durham: Duke University Press, 2009); Andrew Douglas, "Democratic Darkness and Adorno's Redemptive Criticism," *Philosophy and Social Criticism* 36, no. 7 (2010): 819–836. See also Shannon Mariotti, "Critique from the Margins: Adorno and the Politics of Withdrawal," *Political Theory* 36, no. 3 (2008): 456–465.

15. See especially Apostolidis, *Stations of the Cross;* Apostolidis, "Negative Dialectics and Inclusive Communication."

16. See, for example, Hohendahl, *Prismatic Thought;* Peter Uwe Hohendahl, *The Fleeting Promise of Art: Adorno's Aesthetic Theory Revisited* (Ithaca: Cornell University Press, 2013).

17. Dana Villa notes this conversation, which took place in Berlin in 2006, in his essay "From the Critique of Identity to Plurality in Politics: Reconsidering Adorno and Arendt," in *Arendt and Adorno: Political and Philosophical Investigations,* ed. Lars Rensmann and Samir Gandesha (Stanford: Stanford University Press, 2012), 90.

18. See, for example, Martin Jay, "Adorno in America," in *Permanent Exile: Essays on the Intellectual Migration from Germany to America* (New York: Columbia Uni-

versity Press, 1986), 124; Claus Offe, "Theodor W. Adorno: 'Culture Industry' and Other Views of the 'American Century,'" in Offe, *Reflections on America: Tocqueville, Weber, and Adorno in the United States* (Malden, Mass.: Polity, 2005), 69–92; Detlev Claussen, "Intellectual Transfer: Theodor W. Adorno's American Experience," *New German Critique* 97 (Winter 2006): 5–14; Jenemann, *Adorno in America;* Russell Berman, Ulrich Plass, and Joshua Rayman, eds., special issue, "Adorno and America," *Telos* 149 (Winter 2009). See also Joshua Rayman, "Adorno's American Reception," *Telos* 149 (Winter 2009): 6–29; Shannon Mariotti, "Damaged Life as Exuberant Vitality in America: Adorno, Alienation, and the Psychic Economy," *Telos* 149 (Winter 2009): 169–190; and Wheatland, *The Frankfurt School in Exile.*

19. In this way, my interpretation is more like Detlev Claussen's. In contrast to both Jay and Offe, who emphasize an unresolved disjuncture between the American Adorno and the German Adorno, Claussen sees Adorno as engaged in a more complex dialectical negotiation between his American experiences and German influences and implies that the perceived anti-American slant of *Minima Moralia* has been overemphasized. As Claussen notes, "Horkheimer and Adorno returned from America not as disappointed revolutionary critics but as dialecticians of enlightenment. The essence of the American experience—of what was new to the enlightened Europeans—consisted of what Adorno called the 'experience of substantive democratic forms.' Those Germans who read *Minima Moralia* when it appeared in 1951 could hardly understand this, for democracy was for most of them still largely an imported good brought by the occupying power. The anti-American slant inherent to many of the German interpretations of *Minima Moralia* over the years should be viewed in terms of this socio-historical context"; Claussen, *Theodor W. Adorno: One Last Genius,* 9. Claussen also emphasizes the value Adorno places on the substantive forms of democracy, based on his experiences in America, after his return to Germany.

20. Offe, "Theodor W. Adorno," 92; emphasis in original.

21. Wheatland, *The Frankfurt School in Exile,* 4.

22. Jenemann, *Adorno in America,* xxxiv.

23. On the theme of experience, see O'Connor, *Adorno's Negative Dialectic;* Foster, *Adorno: The Recovery of Experience.* See also, importantly, J. M. Bernstein's work on the critical and ethical importance of Adorno's thoughts on the nonidentical and the significance of letting our gaze linger on suffering; Bernstein, *Adorno: Disenchantment and Ethics.*

24. On the theme of education, see Jaimey Fisher, "Adorno's Lesson Plans? The Ethics of (Re)Education in 'The Meaning of "Working through the Past,"'" in *Language without Soil: Adorno and Late Philosophical Modernity,* ed. Gerhard Richter (New York: Fordham University Press, 2010), 76–98; Henry Giroux, "What Might Education Mean after Abu Ghraib: Revisiting Adorno's Politics of Education," *Comparative Studies of South Asia, Africa and the Middle East* 24, no. 1 (2004): 3–22; K. Daniel Cho, "Adorno on Education; or, Can Critical Self-Reflection Prevent the Next

Auschwitz?" *Historical Materialism* 17, no. 1 (2009): 74–97; Volker Heins, "Saying Things That Hurt: Adorno as Educator," *Thesis Eleven* 110, no. 1 (2012): 69–82.

25. Brown argues that the concept of democracy "has historically unparalleled global popularity today yet has never been more conceptually footloose or substantively hollow"; Wendy Brown, "We Are All Democrats Now . . . ," in Giorgio Agamben et al., *Democracy in What State?* trans. William McCuaig (New York: Columbia University Press, 2011), 44–57. See also Wendy Brown, "Neoliberalism and the End of Liberal Democracy," in Brown, *Edgework: Critical Essays on Knowledge and Politics* (Princeton: Princeton University Press, 2005), 37–59; Wendy Brown, "American Nightmare: Neoliberalism, Neoconservatism, and De-Democratization," *Political Theory* 34, no. 6 (2006): 690–714.

26. Berman, "Adorno's Politics," 111.

27. The number of modern theorists taking up these questions is too numerous to list, but for a sense of the relevant debates, see the essays by Giorgio Agamben, Alain Badiou, Daniel Bensaïd, Wendy Brown, Jean-Luc Nancy, Jacques Rancière, Kristin Ross, and Slavoj Žižek in Agamben et al., *Democracy in What State?*

28. Robyn Marasco, *The Highway of Despair: Critical Theory after Hegel* (New York: Columbia University Press, 2015), 5; emphasis in original. Marasco defines despair "not as pathology or paralysis, but in connection with the passions of critique and the energies of everyday life" (3). Despair is "the negative imprint of hope" (17). Despair is not retreat or resignation but the "restlessness of the negative, or the energetic force with which consciousness keeps moving" (31). She says that "critique . . . *is* the work of despair" and turns despair into something productive, moving, energetic (31). Ultimately, "Despair is the refutation of the end of history: It is that dynamic and restless passion that keeps things moving as earthly projects and purposes fall into disrepair" (14). In a passage that captures the key questions of the book, Marasco asks: "What if there are no rational grounds for hope? Does this mean there is no hope? Or does it mean instead that the proof of hope lies in the persistence of despair, that to speak of despair is also to bespeak of hope" (87).

29. Shannon Mariotti, *Thoreau's Democratic Withdrawal: Alienation, Participation, and Modernity* (Madison: University of Wisconsin Press, 2010).

30. Marasco, *The Highway of Despair,* 81; emphasis in original.

31. Ibid.

## 1. Seeing the Large-Scale System

The epigraph is from Adorno, *The Psychological Technique of Martin Luther Thomas' Radio Addresses,* 50.

1. As one marker of the interest in exploring the constitutive and dialectical relationship between Adorno and America, the journal *Telos* published a special issue dedicated to analyzing these themes in an interdisciplinary way, focusing on his views toward (and reception by) social scientists in the United States, his work on music, film, and aesthetics, as well as his thoughts on psychoanalysis and his experience of

exile. Berman, Plass, and Rayman, eds., special issue, "Adorno and America," *Telos* 149 (Winter 2009). Historians and social biographers have also emphasized how life in the United States shaped Adorno's thought in a constitutive way. In *The Frankfurt School in Exile*, Thomas Wheatland studies archival evidence and oral histories and explores the writings of New York intellectuals to trace a transatlantic social history of ideas that analyzes the two-way influence and decades-long "intellectual migration" between what Wheatland calls the Horkheimer Circle and New York intellectuals. His study begins with the Frankfurt School's move to Columbia University in the early years of their American exile but continues into the 1970s (when their ideas were taken up again by the New Left student groups). As we already saw, Wheatland approaches Adorno and the Frankfurt School not as a theorist, but as a historian. In *Adorno in America*, David Jenemann also draws from a wide range of U.S. archival materials. Like Wheatland's book, Jenemann's analysis also tends to set aside the theoretical aspects of Adorno's work. He is clear that his is a "hybrid book": his study "seeks to provide a sense of the texture of Adorno's American experience without hewing to any one particular methodology" (xxxiv). Jenemann thinks that writing about Adorno in America while at the same time engaging his theory will unnecessarily muddy the waters: "To those readers of Adorno looking for an intricate reworking of the collected mass of Adorno scholarship or for erudite twists and turns as I go trundling down every theoretical rabbit hole, I am afraid I must say that this is not that book. The reasons I made this choice have to do with my desire to make the book clear and coherent, coupled with my firm belief that what has precluded many Americans from truly appreciating the power and importance of Adorno's thought has been the tendency among some Adorno scholars to portray him as obtuse, convoluted, and aloof from the America he criticized, even while they are defending him against charges of being obtuse, convoluted, and aloof" (xxxiv). But as Jenemann says, "I am also aware that my decision not to survey the full corpus of Adorno literature may lead to a number of omissions and violate some of the accepted protocols of academic writings. My only defenses for this tactic are that I tend to prefer legibility to pyrotechnic displays of erudition, and that giving every writer who has expressed an opinion on Adorno his or her due would mean a much longer, more cumbersome book" (xxxv). His book is a social history in which Adorno is the main character, though not the only character, and to give a full sense of the texture of Adorno's temporary and paradoxical home in America, Jenemann argues that he could not fully explore all the dimensions of, and scholarly interpretations of, his theory.

2. Martin Jay's "Adorno in America," published in 1984, was the first essay to try to show how, contrary to the prevailing wisdom at the time, Adorno actually did learn valuable lessons about democratic life in the United States that he later tried to import back into Germany. Jay's was the inaugural essay on this theme, which worked to dispel the predominant stereotype of Adorno as an elite mandarin who did not engage with American culture but isolated himself in "German California" and bemoaned his exile in the cultural wasteland of the United States. Without deny-

ing Adorno's uneasy relationship with America, Jay complicates this one-dimensional picture considerably by showing how deeply Adorno's years in America affected his thought and by emphasizing the valuable lessons he learned about the "substance of democratic forms" that penetrated "the whole of life" in America (124). In Jay's view, Adorno sought to import some valuable political lessons from his time in America to Germany after the war, to help bring democracy out of the formal institutional sphere and into the sphere of everyday life.

3. The chapter titled "The Philosopher in Exile" in Hohendahl, *Prismatic Thought,* emphasizes Adorno's "traumatic" experience of alienation in the United States and his "distance" from the political context, but it also valuably reminds us: "Adorno's intellectual position in the United States during the 1940s was less isolated than some scholars have assumed. In several respects his own development (within the Frankfurt School) and that of intellectuals of the American left show similarities—despite the fact that Adorno probably knew little about the United States when he arrived" (29). Again, though, as *Adorno and Democracy* highlights, the picture we get of Adorno depends on which texts are included in the analysis. Hohendahl notes that "the democratic nature of the political system" in America "did not play a major role in his evaluation of the country" (41). Hohendahl argues, "It was only after his return to Germany in 1949 that the matter of the political system became more central to Adorno's view of America. His involvement with the project of German reeducation as a professor of philosophy at the University of Frankfurt significantly changed his evaluation of American democracy" (41). My book shows how democracy is a much more fundamental concern of Adorno's overall theory and practice.

4. In 2003, during Germany's centenary celebrations of Adorno's birth, Detlev Claussen lamented that Jay's earlier warnings to avoid clichés and distorting anecdotes about Adorno in America had tended to go unheeded. Instead, the "old legends" of the "intellectual elites of Weimar" who languished in the cultural wasteland of "German California" were repeated until they hardened into stereotypes. Instead of this false legend, Claussen, in "Intellectual Transfer," argues for an understanding of the dialectical, transatlantic transfer of Adorno's experience: in the United States Adorno drew on his German experiences, while in Germany he later drew on his American experiences. As Claussen notes, "The ostensible literature of remembrance thus tells us yet again how the intellectual elites of Weimar escaped the Nazis by fleeing into the cultural wasteland called America, and how, after finding a place for themselves in the paradise of California during its golden age, they seemed to want nothing more than to return to their native Germany, the land of *Dichter und Denker.* Alas, no documentary evidence, and certainly nothing from Adorno's pen, has retired these hoary narratives" (6). Claussen's essay argues against seeing America and Germany as self-contained entities: Adorno came to understand himself through his experience of exile. Claussen believes that "without America, Adorno would never have become the person we now recognize by that name" (6). Claussen also emphasizes the value of what Adorno called his "experience of substantive democratic forms" in America (9).

5. Offe, *Reflections on America,* 88–89. Offe is only the most emphatic voice expressing a general trend in the existing scholarship: the sense that there is a stark difference between Adorno's early and late writings on life in the United States. Offe argues that "during the exile in California, America was experienced and theorized as the harbinger (or a mere variant) of totalitarian reification," as an exemplary observation post from which to study the trends toward monopoly capitalism, conformism, and the totalitarian drive to eradicate difference, in short, to analyze "the structures and tendencies of Western modernity as a whole" (88, 80). But in later years, mostly after the return to Germany, Offe says that Adorno does an about-face and "suddenly makes a series of markedly positive statements concerning America at the micro-level of direct interaction at work and in everyday life" (85). Adorno praises the open-mindedness of Americans, their democratic spirit of cooperation, and their positive attitude: "looking back from Frankfurt at his American experiences, Adorno developed a diametrically opposite picture of the United States as a beacon of civil freedom that Europe, and especially defeated Germany in its state of moral catastrophe, had to take and study as its model" (88).

6. Adorno, "Radio Physiognomics," 94.

7. Adorno, "A Social Critique of Radio Music," in *Current of Music,* 136.

8. Ibid., 137.

9. Adorno, "The Problem of a New Type of Human Being," in *Current of Music,* 464.

10. Ibid., 463.

11. Adorno, "On Popular Music," in *Current of Music,* 309.

12. Ibid.

13. Ibid., 316.

14. Adorno, "The Problem of a New Type of Human Being," 466.

15. Ibid., 465.

16. Ibid., 464.

17. Ibid., 462.

18. Adorno, "Radio Physiognomics," 69.

19. Ibid., 44.

20. Ibid., 71.

21. Ibid., 47.

22. Ibid., 70.

23. Ibid.

24. Ibid., 47.

25. Ibid.

26. Ibid., 69.

27. Ibid., 70.

28. Ibid.

29. Ibid.

30. Ibid., 70–71.

31. Adorno, *The Psychological Technique of Martin Luther Thomas' Radio Addresses*, 74.

32. These tactics can be found ibid. on the following pages: the "lone wolf" tactic (4), the "emotional release" device (6), the "persecuted innocence" technique (10), the "indefatigability" device (13), the "messenger" tactic (15), the "great little man" strategy (18), the "human interest" device (24), the "listen to your leader" device (37), the "fait accompli" technique (42), the "democratic cloak" technique (50), the "if you only knew" tactic (53), the "dirty linen" device (58), the "tingling backbone" device (61), the "last hour" tactic (64), the "black hand" device (68), the "speaking with tongues" trick (78), the "personal experience" strategy (87), the "anti-institutions" trick (91), and the "faith of our fathers" technique (100).

33. Ibid., 52.

34. Ibid., 51.

35. Ibid., 52.

36. Ibid., 3.

37. Ibid., 50.

38. Ibid., 51.

39. Ibid., 9.

40. Ibid., 20.

41. Ibid., 42.

42. Ibid., 52.

43. Ibid., 1.

44. Ibid.

45. Ibid., 27.

46. Ibid., 44.

47. Ibid., 45.

48. Ibid.

49. Ibid., 66.

50. Ibid., 70.

51. Ibid., 131.

52. Ibid., 2.

53. Ibid., 37.

54. Ibid., 33.

55. Ibid., 104–105.

56. Adorno, *The Stars Down to Earth*, 55.

57. Ibid., 48.

58. Ibid., 57.

59. Ibid., 74.

60. Ibid., 153.

61. Ibid., 142.

62. Ibid., 80.

63. Ibid., 74.

64. Ibid., 164.
65. Ibid.
66. Ibid., 92.
67. Ibid., 61.
68. Ibid.
69. Ibid.
70. Adorno, "The Problem of a New Type of Human Being," 462.
71. Ibid., 466.
72. Adorno says that people may indeed be sick, but "they are at least no sicker than the society in which they live" ("The Problem of a New Type of Human Being," 466).

## 2. Experience as a Precondition for Meaningful Democracy

The epigraph is from Adorno, "Critique," in *Critical Models: Interventions and Catchwords*, trans. Henry Pickford (1998; repr., New York: Columbia University Press, 2005), 284.

1. Michael Hardt, "Foreword: What Affects Are Good For," in *The Affective Turn: Theorizing the Social*, ed. Patricia Ticineto Clough with Jean O'Malley Halley (Durham: Duke University Press, 2007), ix–xiii.

2. Ibid., x.

3. Ibid.

4. Ibid.

5. In recent years the topic of experience has been a rich terrain for philosophical treatments of Adorno's work, such as O'Connor, *Adorno's Negative Dialectic*, and Foster, *Adorno: The Recovery of Experience*. Both Foster and O'Connor argue against reading Adorno's work as aporetic, pessimistic, or futile, and both seek to recapture positive and productive elements of his critical theory through a focus on the recovery of a certain kind of experience. O'Connor and Foster both emphasize that there is indeed a coherent critical project at the heart of Adorno's philosophy of negative dialectics, exploring the different ways that his philosophy seeks to rescue a type of experience that penetrates beyond surface appearances and to stimulate valuable forms of critical thought. But neither makes a political argument about Adorno's thoughts on experience. More specifically, neither appreciates the close links between Adorno's concept of experience and his thoughts on democracy.

6. In *Adorno's Negative Dialectic* Brian O'Connor explores negative dialectics itself as the theoretical foundation of the critical mind-set required by critical theory, but he studies this way of thinking on its own terms, in isolation from Adorno's work on cultural theory and sociology. O'Connor identifies an "epistemological normativity" in Adorno's thought, a sense of "how we ought to think," but he also posits that the exercise of the critical rationality that Adorno enacts and prescribes actively "contributes to *the way things ought to be*" (1; emphasis in original). O'Connor argues that the negative dialectic offers us ways to "recognize the distortions of experience"

and question the view of reality we are given. Adorno shows that there are "radical alternatives" to the given reality and claims that "reality is available to us in ways which go beyond appearances" and, in this way, helps "rescue" a certain kind of experience based on "reciprocity" and "transformation" (x). O'Connor argues that existing scholarship has neglected a full exploration of Adorno's idea of negative dialectics on its own terms. Accordingly, he seeks to "consider Adorno's negative dialectic in isolation from the sociological specifics of his critical theory" and to "explore the structure of Adorno's dialectic, its key concepts, and its historical influences" (xi). O'Connor argues, "Contrary to a conventional line of thought on Adorno, that his position has no positive contribution to make as it is purely negative and critical," for Adorno, "experience is the process in which ideally, that is, in its fullest possibility one (a subject) is affected and somehow changed by confrontation with some aspects of objective reality (an object). Experience has, in a sense, a structure of reciprocity and transformation" (2–3).

7. Roger Foster's *Adorno: The Recovery of Experience* also focuses on this theme, but for him the role of negative dialectics is to disclose loss and suffering by highlighting the impoverishment of language in revealing what he calls "spiritual experience," an "outbreak attempt" that tries to "arrange words around a concept, so that the experiential substance of that concept becomes visible" in a way that also works to rupture repressive subjectivity, instrumental rationality, and modern disenchantment generally (4). Foster understands "spiritual experience" as "a type of interpretation that saturates the object with meanings derived from how it appears as significant or meaningful for a subject"—whether it be a piece of music, a concept, or a social artifact—that works to understand this object in the entirety of its context, that helps the object "speak" about the world it is a part of, as a response to the disenchantment of the world (1). Foster focuses especially on Adorno's philosophy of language and epistemology and places him in dialogue with Bergson, Wittgenstein, and Husserl, as well as Marcel Proust. For Foster, the "project of a recovery of spiritual experience, and the construction of a type of philosophical experience that would be able to put this into practice, is the unifying core to Adorno's strikingly multidisciplinary oeuvre" (1). Adorno seeks to recuperate "spiritual experience" and develops it as a response to the disenchantment of the modern world, "in the context of a radical critique of the model of philosophical cognition as classification under concepts" (3). Foster observes, "What negative dialectics makes us aware of is something that our use of language as a tool for communication, or a medium for transferring contents, makes us forget. It is the potential of language to disclose experience through its expressive moments. I have suggested throughout that Adorno conceives this view of the cognitive potential of language in terms of its making possible what he calls spiritual experience. . . . To 'spiritualize' something on Adorno's account simply means to interpret that item . . . as a surface on which experiential meaning has been expressed. As spiritual, these items 'speak' about the world of which they are a part, because the world is ultimately revealed in the full disclosure of their experiential significance. Thus all phenomena, as monads, are windows onto the world" (199).

8. As Espen Hammer, *Adorno & the Political,* notes, "Adorno's Marxism is at best highly selective, leaving much of the apparatus of Marx's analysis of capitalism's injustices in the background while emphasizing the more Weberian elements of Lukacs' account in which late capitalism represents the victory of the forces of rationalization with the effect of freezing social relations and ultimately replacing them with the subject-transcendent mechanisms of systematically enforced exchange (the bureaucracies, the market and so on)" (35).

9. "The mode of production in which the product takes the form of a commodity or is produced directly for exchange, is the most general and most embryonic form of bourgeois production." Karl Marx, *Capital,* vol. 1, *A Critique of Political Economy* (New York: Penguin, 1992), 328.

10. As Marx writes, "On the one hand all labour is, speaking physiologically, an expenditure of human labor-power, and in its character of identical abstract human labour, it creates and forms the value of commodities. On the other hand, all labour is the expenditure of human labour-power in a special form and with a definite aim, and in this, its character of concrete useful labour, it produces use-values" (ibid., 312).

11. Ibid., 309.

12. Ibid., 307.

13. Ibid., 305.

14. Ibid., 319.

15. Ibid., 328.

16. Ibid., 321.

17. Ibid.

18. Ibid., 322.

19. Ibid.

20. Despite how deeply he is influenced by their thought—especially by Kant's own critiques—Adorno rejects the ways that the idealisms of Kant and Hegel strive for holistic systems, for reconciliation, for closure. As Hammer notes in his discussion of Adorno's critique of Hegel in *Adorno & the Political:* "Pure identity, stated in Hegelian terms, is tantamount to the successful identification of identity and non-identity. . . . On Adorno's reading, this is violent because the movement of negation is such that it always conceives particularity, difference, and nonidentity as being abstract or immaterial, and real only insofar as it is mediated by the integrating universal" (100). Given this drive to construct a positive system of thought, "unfolding the truth content of Hegel's philosophy required 'reading him against the grain,' i.e., confronting its claims and contradictions with its own aspirations and criteria, as well as with the limits and necessities imposed on it by the social context within which it was conceived" (99–100). Adorno's thought is defined by a negative form of critique, a negative disruptive, deconstructing dialectics, that then forms the basis for his alternative practices of resistance.

21. Adorno, *Kant's "Critique of Pure Reason (1959),"* trans. Rodney Livingstone (Stanford: Stanford University Press, 2001), 110.

22. Ibid., 111.

23. Ibid., 25.

24. Ibid., 114.

25. Ibid., 18.

26. Ibid., 66–67.

27. "More generally, the logic of commodification itself allows a thing to appear only insofar as its use-value—which for Adorno becomes a cipher for everything that can possibly contain a utopian promise: difference and heterogeneity, otherness, the qualitative, the radically new, the corporeal, in short what he calls 'the non-identical'— becomes subordinate to its exchange-value"; Hammer, *Adorno & the Political*, 31.

28. Adorno, *Negative Dialectics*, trans. E. B. Ashton (New York: Continuum, 1973), 8.

29. As Susan Buck-Morss notes, "logical breaks," "ambiguities and contradictions, were the philosophical details upon which Adorno focused his interpretive efforts"; Susan Buck-Morss, *The Origin of Negative Dialectics* (New York: Free Press, 1977), 80.

30. Adorno, "Resignation," in *Critical Models*, 202.

31. Buck-Morss, *Origin of Negative Dialectics*, 80.

32. Hammer, *Adorno & the Political*, 36.

33. Adorno, *Negative Dialectics*, 27.

34. Ibid., 19.

35. Ibid., 185.

36. Ibid., 19.

37. Ibid., 85.

38. Ibid.

39. Ibid., 203.

40. Ibid., 85.

41. Ibid.

42. Adorno, "Critique," 285.

43. Ibid.

44. Ibid.

45. Bernstein, *Adorno: Disenchantment and Ethics*, 4, 451.

46. As Bernstein notes, "it would be nothing but full, unreduced experience in the medium of conceptual reflection"; ibid., 35.

47. Here I am in agreement with Ann Cvetkovich, who writes, "I have to confess that I am somewhat reluctant to use the term *affective turn* because it implies that there is something new about the study of affect when, in fact, . . . this work has been going on for some time"; Ann Cvetkovich, *Depression: A Public Feeling* (Durham: Duke University Press, 2012), 4.

48. Melissa Gregg and Gregory J. Seigworth, "Introduction: An Inventory of Shimmers," in *The Affect Theory Reader*, ed. Gregg and Seigworth (Durham: Duke University Press, 2010), 7.

49. See, for example, Lauren Berlant's response to the colleague who says he "hates her archive" and her explanation of the necessity for her own "frame break-

ing" methodology of undertaking a "counterpolitics of the silly object" and specific kinds of "experimental or unusual storytelling" and "textual performance." She defends her archive of low culture and ephemeral objects, from *The Simpsons* to "'The Contract with America." But her interesting and valuable method of cultural studies bears a good deal of resemblance to the kind of analysis of various cultural objects that Adorno undertakes (as we will see in this book), from analyzing the *Los Angeles Times*'s astrology column to studying the radio demagogue Martin Luther Thomas. Additionally, Adorno invokes the necessity of using experimental styles of writing to analyze unusual cultural objects, such as the fragmentary, aphoristic style we see in *Minima Moralia*. Ultimately, here as in other instances, the seeming novelty of certain aspects of affect theory comes, in part, through a kind of forgetting of what has come before to pave the way for this kind of scholarship. See the section on methodology in Lauren Berlant, *The Queen of America Goes to Washington City: Essays on Sex and Citizenship* (Durham: Duke University Press, 1997), 10–15. See also Sara Ahmed, *The Promise of Happiness* (Durham: Duke University Press, 2010), where she describes the methods she must employ to "follow" the concept of happiness and "to attend to how happiness is spoken, lived, practiced" (15). She calls for a method that employs "critical and creative writing" as well as "thick descriptions of the kinds of worlds that might take shape when happiness does not provide a horizon for experience" (14). In *Depression: A Public Feeling*, Ann Cvetkovich tracks specific "keywords," to develop "new conceptual categories and new modes of description" that are necessary "to capture these feelings" (13). Cvetkovich also finds it necessary to write a personal "critical memoir" as a kind of "performative writing" that helps her create the "thick description" of the feeling of depression (15).

50. Cvetkovich, *Depression,* 4.

51. Quoted in Gregg and Seigworth, "Introduction: An Inventory of Shimmers," 11.

52. Ibid., 2–3.

53. Ibid., 1; emphasis in original.

54. See Teresa Brennan, *The Transmission of Affect* (Ithaca: Cornell University Press, 2004), 1, where the first line asks, "Is there anyone who has not, at least once, walked into a room and 'felt the atmosphere'?"

55. Cvetkovich, *Depression,* 158.

56. Quoted in Gregg and Seigworth, "Introduction: An Inventory of Shimmers," 20.

57. Cvetkovich, *Depression,* 10.

58. There is a notable sympathy between Adorno's work on the "happiness imperative" in *Minima Moralia* and Sara Ahmed's *The Promise of Happiness.* Ahmed explores happiness from the standpoint of "feminist cultural studies of emotion and affect" and analyzes the consequences of the cultural imperative, the duty, to be happy, especially in terms of its normative power to fit people into a conventional model of the good life (13). She explores figures who reject and challenge the attachments to particular objects or social ideals that are supposed to make us happy, while also analyzing the effects of making our own happiness contingent on other people's

happiness, as embodied in the statement "I'm happy if you're happy." In a similar way, in *Minima Moralia* Adorno analyzes the duty to be happy that shapes American life in the postwar era, describing a unique form of alienation that masks itself as "exuberant vitality." Given these sympathies, Adorno's work would seem to be an important influence on Ahmed's work, but he appears in her book only in one footnote. She observes that "Theodor Adorno exposes how 'admonitions to be happy can be a form of dominance in *Minima Moralia*. . . . He describes how 'it is part of the mechanism of domination to forbid recognition of the suffering it reproduces.' . . . Or we might say that forms of suffering and sadness are permitted as long as they not involve recognition of domination" (278n8).

59. Cvetkovich, *Depression,* 5.

60. Ibid., 5–6.

61. As Cvetkovich notes ibid., 6, queer theory "rethinks distinctions between positive and negative feelings so as not to presume that they are separate from one another or that happiness or pleasure constitutes the absence or elimination of negative feeling."

62. Ibid., 110.

63. Gregg and Seigworth, "Introduction: An Inventory of Shimmers," 9–10.

64. Cvetkovich, *Depression,* 3.

65. Ibid., 12.

66. Gregg and Seigworth, "Introduction: An Inventory of Shimmers," 10.

67. Lauren Berlant, *Cruel Optimism* (Durham: Duke University Press, 2011), 14.

68. Ibid., 13.

69. Ibid., 48. Ultimately, for Berlant, the utopian hope and possibility captured in these optimistic attachments turn out to be "cruel" because many of the objects we desire to fulfill our vision of the good life turn out to be life threatening. She notes, "A relation of cruel optimism exists when something you desire is actually an obstacle to your flourishing," when "the object that draws your attachment actively impedes the aim that brought you to it initially" (1). Berlant explores, for example, how our relationships to homes and food in the contemporary neoliberal American landscape have become toxic. She writes, "This book is about what happens to fantasies of the good life when the ordinary becomes a landfill for overwhelming and impending crises of life-building and expectation whose sheer volume so threatens what it has meant to 'have a life' that adjustment seems like an accomplishment" (3).

## 3. Critique and the Practice of Democracy

The epigraph is from Adorno, "Critique," 281.

1. Wiggershaus, *The Frankfurt School: Its History, Theories, and Political Significance,* as the title suggests, foregrounds an exploration of the politics of the institute as a whole and of Adorno's politics in particular. Muller-Doohm, *Adorno: A Biography,* highlights the political dimensions of Adorno's practice of critique and describes the complex ways in which Adorno was deeply committed to democracy and served as

an important voice in public affairs in Germany, without losing sight of the complex and often paradoxical ways that he also distanced himself from conventional politics. In addition, Claussen's biography, *Theodor W. Adorno: One Last Genius*, weaves a sympathetic understanding of the ethical and political significance of Adorno's work into this portrayal of his personal life. In contrast to these works, Jäger, *Adorno: A Political Biography*, devotes a great deal of energy to characterizing Adorno's political views and attitudes toward political action, especially the student movements of the 1960s. Jäger, however, tends to reify the image of Adorno as a resident of the Grand Hotel Abyss, arguing that Adorno saw democracy and positive political action as impossible and presenting his theory as aporetic, ultimately as a failure. See also my essay-length review of these works, Mariotti, "Critique from the Margins."

2. Schweppenhäuser, *Adorno: An Introduction*, strikingly foregrounds an image of Adorno that emphasizes the political commitments of his theory. For Schweppenhäuser, Adorno's project aims to recuperate the possibility of a more autonomous individual and has a deeply utopian impulse. Adorno saw the "just life" as necessarily tied to a "just politics" that is in turn indissolubly linked to the "structure of society," and his critical theory was relentlessly motivated by the "drive to bring a humane social order into being" (71, 144). See also my review of this volume, Shannon Mariotti, "Communicating to the Demos," *Review of Politics* 72 (Summer 2010): 561–563. In addition, Deborah Cook's edited volume titled *Adorno: Key Concepts* also emphasizes the political dimensions of his work; Marianne Tettlebaum's entry in this work, "Political Philosophy," in particular explores themes such as freedom, the individual and the state, class, democracy, and education, as well as theory and praxis, offering a good overview of the political dimensions of Adorno's thought and emphasizing the way that a concern with democracy unifies various aspects of his thought. As Tettlebaum says, "The political dimension of Adorno's work, I suggest, lies in the spaces between the possibilities, the spaces, that is, between what was, what is, and what ought to be. His political thought aims at analyzing and understanding the 'societal play of forces,' to use his term, that comprise this space, determining both the occupants' expectations and the actual outcome. This 'play of forces' involves everything from a society's history and economic structure to the concrete experiences of the individuals who comprise it. Only a thorough understanding and critique of all these aspects, rather than some kind of immediate action, can achieve anything resembling the second possibility of freedom while excluding anything resembling the first" (132). She also notes the threat that capitalism and conformity posed to the true functioning of democracy: "Breaking this spell of indifference is, for Adorno, especially crucial to the functioning of democracy. Although he believed in the potential of a democratic form of government, he also held that democracies, like any other form of state organization, are easily co-opted, leading to the unfreedom rather than the freedom of individuals" (138).

3. In "Adorno's Politics," Russell Berman shows how political concerns run throughout his writings, sometimes in an abstract philosophical register, sometimes

veiled in the language of critical theory, but at other times "he grapples with political questions in a relatively direct fashion" (114). This "expressly political stratum"
of Adorno's work concerns Nazism, "the character of the state in twentieth-century
capitalism," Roosevelt and the New Deal, the critique of orthodox Marxism, German conservatism, the potential for democracy after 1945, and "his sympathy for
student radicalism" (127). Berman also argues that aesthetics was a central tool of
resistance for Adorno, but if "political resistance had migrated into the work of art,
art was not its only location. Adorno directed his attention to the quite explicitly
political question of the viability of German democracy" (124). Ultimately, for Berman, "reviewing Adorno's engagement with these issues, one discovered a thinker
deeply concerned with the political structure of domination and the urgency of resistance to it, although unwilling to transform theory into a mere alibi for an activist
praxis with no prospect for success" (114).

4. See Morris, *Rethinking the Communicative Turn*. With a somewhat similar
focus on moments that are highly charged with ethical and political importance,
Morris's book, especially his chapter "Recovering the Ethical and Political Force of
Adorno's Aesthetic-Critical Theory," makes a case for the democratic value of the
"mimetic shudder" that awakens us to the nonidentical and can usher in a new mode
of political being.

5. With similar ambitions to correct the flaws in the traditional image of
Adorno, J. M. Bernstein's *Adorno: Disenchantment and Ethics* highlights the "ethics of
nonidentity" that is at the heart of his critical theory as a way of responding to critics
who complain about the lack of practical, political, or ethical dimensions in Adorno's
work. Bernstein explores how Adorno's unique ethics derive from the particularity
of the object, characterizing these moments as "fugitive ethical experiences" that are
fleeting and momentary, but that also have a utopian promise in the way they resist
"wrong life," even offering a sense of transcendence in their promise of an alternative, and valuably motivating critical, ethical, and political impulses. Bernstein notes,
"No reading of the works of T. W. Adorno can fail to be struck by the ethical intensity of his writing, sentence by sentence, word by word" (1). Everything he wrote
was a vehicle "for his sombre ethical vision of a world grown inhuman in which the
primary task of the intellectual had become critical vigilance: an accommodation
was exacerbation of the worst" (2). These ethical moments are stimulated by letting
the gaze linger on suffering: "Fugitive ethical experience is forged in resistance, it is
determined by the sight of the disenchanted body as suffering that disenchantment"
(451). But after experiencing these ethical "stirrings," we also draw out the implications of the nonidentical toward a broader critique of modern society. Our ethical
and critical impulses are stimulated by these encounters with disruptive particularity.
Though he was a critic of modernity, Adorno was not, as Bernstein notes, a critic of
Enlightenment itself or of an "expanded conception of reason": Adorno "unswerv-
ingly affirmed the values of Enlightenment, and believed that modernity suffered
from a deficit rather than a surplus of reason and rationality" (4). Adorno thus seeks

to "expand reason" and "expand the scope and character of cognitive life, of knowing" to more capaciously be able to take in these "fugitive ethical experiences" that derive from sensuous particularity (4). Combining sensual experience with the cognitive process of thinking means that philosophy must give itself over to experiencing "the diversity of objects that impinge upon it"; "it would be nothing but full, unreduced experience in the medium of conceptual reflection" (35). Just as Bernstein amplifies the political significance of Adorno's work by putting his thought into dialogue with ethics, he also highlights how a deep commitment to justice figures into Adorno's thought. In an essay titled "Suffering Injustice: Misrecognition as Moral Injury in Critical Theory," in Richter, *Language without Soil,* Bernstein explores Adorno's commitment to an "emphatic" notion of justice that seeks to eliminate injustice in the form of suffering. Bernstein remarks, "In abjuring the language of injustice, Adorno made his thought appear more politically impotent than in fact it is; that his philosophy is not politically or ethically idle no longer needs demonstrating. However, making perspicuous what it means for social thought to sustain the idea that injustice is the medium of justice does still require elaboration" (32). For Bernstein, the "normative *force* of the idea of justice, its urgent claim" is based on, to quote Adorno, the "'persistence of suffering, fear, and threat' that remains in the world" but is wholly preventable (30; emphasis in original). The demand that Auschwitz not happen again is an example of "emphatic justice" that is attentive to and attuned to preventable corporeal and material bodily suffering and pain, in contrast to the more abstract, procedural, due process–oriented "liberal justice." Indeed, Bernstein argues that "Adorno's negative dialectics could just as well be thought of as a dialectics of injustice" (31). For Bernstein, "the priority of injustice over justice is the political face of the priority of the object over the subject, particular over universal, nonidentity over identity that structures Adorno's thought as a whole" (46). Bernstein concludes that Adorno offers "the microfoundations for this new negative politics and a model of the form of social criticism through which it can best be promoted" (51). For Bernstein, "the orienting theses of Adorno's thought" are as follows: "that moral universality has failed us, and failed us in tandem with the recognition of the way in which, generally, universality squanders particularity; that this pathology of reason requires a renewed attention to suppressed particulars; that suppressed particulars emerge into vision as cases of injustice; that social suffering is a manifestation of this injustice, and hence objective in itself; and hence to orient ethical and political action in relation to this sense of social suffering and injustice is to acknowledge a universality of the living premised upon our mutual dependency on one another as vulnerable creatures" (51).

    6. Espen Hammer's *Adorno & the Political* is perhaps the most thorough treatment to date of the political dimensions of Adorno's thought, of his views of theory and critique as praxis, and of his connections to current political philosophy. Hammer understands Adorno as a thinker concerned with critiquing structures of domination, encouraging resistance and subversion, and working toward radical social change: "The interest that consistently guided his research was emancipatory:

as opposed to simply interpreting the social phenomena within the relevant framework, it aimed at diagnosing the present with a view toward anticipating a more liberated, humane, and rational future" (1). Hammer argues, "While his vision of the conditions of democratic political activity is extremely bleak, the desire to resist and anticipate change remains a constant focus throughout his life" (11). Like Berman, Hammer also notes the ways that theory was itself deeply political for Adorno. His skepticism of direct action and mainstream participatory avenues of protest led him to propose theory itself as a praxis, indeed, as the only true form of praxis, given the alienating historical conditions of modernity. Hammer also emphasizes the political significance of art and aesthetics for Adorno, portraying these realms as necessary "placeholders" for politics, which Adorno thinks is no longer possible in the conventional sense (25). But Hammer also goes further in drawing out Adorno's value for democratic politics, in two ways. First, he valuably shows how the primary targets of Adorno's critiques (of the culture industry, of identity thinking, of idealism) are especially problematic because of the ways they undermine democratic ideals of autonomy. The culture industry of modernity not only manipulates people, but shapes them in fundamental ways, undermining the autonomy that liberal democracy assumes. Hammer notes, "While democracies require plurality as one of their essential conditions, according to Adorno, contemporary Western societies have been progressively evacuated of dissenting voices" (73). Hammer observes, "If Adorno is right, then liberal political theory, which holds rational agreement among free and equal agents to be the source of political legitimacy, is necessarily incapable of showing such legitimacy to be actualized" (81). Adorno's commitment to autonomy was a fundamental part of his thought: "Even in his most Marxist phases, he never repudiated his basic subscription to a liberal (or Kantian) concern for the autonomy of the individual" (12). Furthermore, his critiques are part and parcel of this larger political project of trying to recover a greater measure of autonomy: "The validity of Adorno's approach to politics cannot be separated from the 'success' of each of his critical interventions. If his social theory is bleak, indeed, the ethically informed, micro-interruptive operations that make up the bulk of his philosophical entries are models of responsible exercise of autonomy in the societies that today are called democratic" (8). In a second important advance, Hammer presents Adorno's work not only as critical, but also as a positive political theory that can offer valuable tools for negotiating daily life in liberal democratic mass societies, bringing Adorno into dialogue with Stanley Cavell to make a case for how both advance a kind of "ethical and political perfectionism" in which the self moves from conformity to greater self-reliance. As Hammer notes, Cavell, like Adorno, is interested in the problem of how the individual can maintain autonomy in a culture of conformism and recognizes "the existential and intellectual burden which a liberal order ideally places on individual citizens who seek to act rationally as social and political critics of their own society" (163). In Hammer's reading, for both Adorno and Cavell, "conformism and prejudice constitute the supreme threats to democracy," so the challenge becomes how to maintain a level of autonomy, self-authorization, and individual responsibility while existing in contexts and communities of conformism (165). Given these concerns, Hammer views Adorno's aloofness from conventional society, or his more elitist moments, as "strategic" ways of maintaining and protecting the individual, to whom Adorno assigns "extraordinary responsibility" for increasing the autonomy that is so vital to meaningful liberal democratic citizenship.

7. Shannon L. Mariotti and Joseph Lane, *A Political Companion to Marilynne Robinson* (Lexington: University Press of Kentucky, forthcoming).

8. Adorno, "The Meaning of Working through the Past," in *Critical Models,* 93.

9. "Appendix 1: Discussion of Professor Adorno's Lecture 'The Meaning of Working through the Past,'" in *Critical Models,* 296.

10. Adorno, "Critique," 281.

11. Ibid.

12. Ibid.

13. Hammer, *Adorno & the Political,* notes that if for Adorno the "wholly commodified culture industry thus signifies the reign of totalitarian myth—a world of repetition and sameness from which notions of otherness, heterogeneity, difference, the qualitative, and the new have been expulsed or liquidated," uncovering the nonidentical through the practice of critique is also a politics (75). Consequently, "politics (and practice) becomes the work of theory" (37).

14. "Appendix 1," 296.

15. Adorno, "The Meaning of Working through the Past," 98–99.

16. Adorno, *Minima Moralia,* 65.

17. Ibid., 59, 62.

18. Shannon Mariotti, "Damaged Life as Exuberant Vitality in America."

19. Adorno, *Negative Dialectics,* 6.

20. This is one key difference between Adorno and Foucault, though they share an interest in psychology and illness and have similar critiques of social normalization: the sense of loss and lament and the attempts at a recovery and recuperation that pervade Adorno's work are foreign to Foucault's understanding of subjectivity as always already being produced.

21. Adorno, *Minima Moralia,* 15.

22. Here Adorno echoes Marx's attempt, in the first chapter of *Capital,* to let the commodity "speak" and tell a different story from the conventional wisdom of political economy.

23. Adorno, *Minima Moralia,* 65.

24. Ibid.

25. Ibid.

26. Ibid., 65–66.

27. Ibid., 64.

28. Ibid., 230.

29. Ibid.

30. Ibid.

31. Ibid., 231.

32. Ibid., 61.

33. Ibid., 58.

34. Adorno sees this programming of the self as a loss, but he also notes that we cannot know what an unmutilated, whole, or complete subject would even look like, since our very understanding of subjectivity as well as of the biological and psychological makeup of the subject reflects the dominant mode of production in society. For Adorno, "there is no substratum beneath such 'deformations,' no ontic interior on which social mechanisms merely act externally: the deformation is not a sickness in men but in the society which begets its children with the 'hereditary taint' that biologism projects on to nature" (ibid., 229).

35. Ibid., 64.

36. Ibid., 63.

37. Ibid.

38. Ibid., 62.

39. Ibid., 62–63.

40. Ibid., 62.

41. Ibid., 59.

42. Ibid.

43. As Susan Buck-Morss writes in *The Origin of Negative Dialectics,* "The transitoriness of particulars was the promise of a different future, while their small size, their elusiveness to categorization implied a defiance of the very social structure they expressed" (76).

44. Adorno, "Resignation," 202.

45. Ibid.

46. Adorno, *Minima Moralia,* 63.

47. Marilynne Robinson, *When I Was a Child, I Read Books: Essays* (New York: Farrar, Straus and Giroux, 2012), xiv.

48. Marilynne Robinson, *The Death of Adam: Essays on Modern Thought* (1998; repr., New York: Picador, 2005), 12.

49. Ibid., 243.

50. Robinson, *When I Was a Child,* 7.

51. Robinson, *The Death of Adam,* 3.

52. Robinson, *When I Was a Child,* 7.

53. Robinson, *The Death of Adam,* 87.

54. Ibid., 171.

55. Marilynne Robinson, *Housekeeping* (New York: Farrar, Straus and Giroux, 1980); *Gilead* (New York: Farrar, Straus and Giroux, 2004); *Home* (New York: Farrar, Straus and Giroux, 2008).

56. David Foster Wallace, *This Is Water: Some Thoughts, Delivered on a Significant Occasion, about Living a Compassionate Life* (New York: Little, Brown, 2009).

57. Ibid., 8.
58. Ibid., 33.
59. Ibid., 60.
60. Ibid., 35–36.
61. Ibid., 50.
62. Ibid., 53–54; emphases in original.
63. Ibid., 76.
64. Ibid., 77; emphasis in original.
65. Ibid., 92.
66. Ibid., 117.
67. Ibid., 119.
68. Ibid., 120.
69. Ibid., 130–133.
70. Ibid., 56.

## 4. Democratic Leadership

The epigraph is from Adorno, "Democratic Leadership and Mass Manipulation," 420; emphasis in original.

1. Alvin W. Gouldner, preface to *Studies in Leadership,* xiii.
2. Gouldner, introduction to *Studies in Leadership,* 46.
3. Ibid.
4. Ibid.
5. Ibid., 49.
6. Ibid., 11.
7. Ibid., 13.
8. Ibid., 15.
9. Ibid.
10. Ibid., 16; emphasis in original.
11. Ibid., 18.
12. Ibid., 20.
13. Ibid.
14. Adorno, "Democratic Leadership and Mass Manipulation," 429.
15. Ibid.
16. Ibid.
17. Ibid., 419.
18. Ibid., 418.
19. Ibid., 419.
20. Ibid., 420.
21. Ibid., 432; emphasis in original.
22. Ibid., 418.
23. Ibid., 423.
24. Ibid., 420.

25. Ibid.

26. Ibid.

27. Ibid., 418.

28. Ibid., 421.

29. Ibid., 434.

30. Ibid., 429.

31. Ibid., 424–425.

32. Ibid., 427.

33. Ibid.

34. Ibid., 430.

35. Ibid., 432.

36. Ibid.

37. Ibid.

38. Ibid.

39. Ibid., 433.

40. Ibid., 434.

41. Ibid.

42. Ibid.

43. Ibid., 435.

44. Ibid.

45. Ibid.

46. Ibid.

47. Ibid.

48. Ibid.

49. Ibid., 431.

50. Ibid.

51. Theodor Adorno and Hellmut Becker, "Education for Maturity and Responsibility," trans. Robert French, Jem Thomas, and Dorothee Weymann, *History of the Human Sciences* 12, no. 3 (1999): 32.

52. Adorno, "Democratic Leadership and Mass Manipulation," 420.

53. Ibid., 421.

54. Ibid., 422.

55. Ibid.

56. Ibid., 423.

57. Ibid., 424.

58. Ibid.

59. Ibid.

60. Ibid., 431; emphasis in original.

## 5. Democratic Pedagogy

The epigraph is from Adorno and Becker, "Education for Maturity and Responsibility," 31.

1. See, for example, Adorno's essay "Philosophy and Teachers"; his radio lecture and essay "Taboos on the Teaching Vocation"; his radio lecture and essay "Education after Auschwitz"; Adorno and Becker, "Education for Maturity and Responsibility"; his essay "Concerning the Democratization of German Universities" ("Zur Demokratisierung der deutschen Universitäten"), in *Gesammelte Schriften*, 20:332; and his interview "Who's Afraid of the Ivory Tower? A Conversation with Theodor W. Adorno" (originally published in *Der Spiegel*, 5 May 1969 ("Keine Angst vor dem Elfenbeinturm"); this is an interview that Adorno gave to *Der Spiegel* after canceling his classes because of protests from students; it appears in English in Richter, *Language without Soil*, 227–238.

2. Adrian Wilder's "Pied Pipers and Polymaths: Adorno's Critique of Praxisism," in Holloway et al., *Negativity and Revolution*, represents a very different treatment of Adorno and education by analyzing his lectures to his own students in Frankfurt, which have recently been published. As Wilder notes, "The *doxa* on Adorno is that his philosophy was devoid of a politics and was proved hopelessly impotent in the face of real political praxis; worse, that he helped quench the fires of revolutionary enthusiasm" (35). But, in contrast to the conventional wisdom, Wilder finds that Adorno's lectures are deeply in dialogue with the political context that surrounded him every day as he taught, particularly with the student movement. Interestingly, Wilder employs Adorno's own method of reading Kant to read Adorno: "it may be more illuminating to read these lectures in their historical context rather than as the disembodied thoughts of a 'free-floating intellectual,' which it seems Adorno's student critics took him to be. . . . A useful way to read these lectures, though, might be not simply as philosophy or theory but also as an expression of the politically momentous times in which they were delivered. To read Adorno in a way which is consistent with his own avowed 'materialism' . . . to read Adorno, in other words, just as we will see Adorno read Kant's philosophy, not just as philosophy but as 'a kind of coded text from which the historical situation of spirit could be read, with the vague expectation that in doing so one could acquire something of truth itself'" (20). Wilder concludes that Adorno's lectures show him trying to avoid the "false alternative" of becoming a tool, an "intellectual figurehead," a "Pied Piper" for the student movements. Ultimately, Wilder sees Adorno as a deeply engaged, broadly interested "polymathic intellectual"—"neither crudely committed to every cause nor free-floating"—defending his critical role in "a specialised, instrumentalised world" (36). As Wilder says, "In a sense the very polymath quality of these lectures, the sheer scope of Adorno's attempt to make sense of the social whole and to pass on these insights to his students, is as important a legacy as their various reflections on the mediation of theory and practice" (34). In short, Wilder hopes his analysis of these lectures helps highlight the flawed and distorted nature of the *doxa* on Adorno and works against the vision of him as apolitical, insulated, and unengaged: "The above should have rendered such a charge more difficult to sustain. It is not borne out by a careful reading of these texts which do reveal the influence of the time in which they are written, and address them

in a philosophical language which does justice to their complexity and their mediatedness" (35). But this argument is made only through an analysis of Adorno's own pedagogical style, by analyzing his lectures for insights into how he taught.

3. In "Education after the Holocaust," in *Prismatic Thought*, Peter Uwe Hohendahl valuably explores many of Adorno's essays on pedagogy. He shows how Adorno suggests a "psychoanalytical model of enlightenment" that draws heavily from Freud and sees education as a way of fostering a more autonomous individual in ways not possible through more collective means (69). But Hohendahl resists seeing any kind of project or overall theory with respect to education in Adorno's work and thinks he only "commented on educational and pedagogical problems in occasional essays," saying these should be seen as "personal interventions" into problems that the "professional discourse tended to repress" (61).

4. For example, Jaimey Fisher's essay "Adorno's Lesson Plans?" analyzes the surprisingly optimistic and positive way that he writes about education in two of his most overtly political essays. Fisher shows how Adorno explored the need for democratization of educational culture, the progressive nature of his views on German higher education, and the need for the "inner democratization" of academic culture in terms of both students and professors (81). These writings on education "suggest a very different model of normativity and ethics than is typically the case in Adorno's writings" (97). But, as Fisher notes, Adorno's writings on education are "interwoven" with the other themes of his work, such as resistance to conformity, autonomy, and critical self-consciousness, though they ultimately advance "an argumentative line" that should be explored further for its "surprisingly optimistic declarations about its normative potential" (87). Fisher notes how this positive, productive, and optimistic tone seems to contradict the claim Adorno made later in life that he never said anything that was "immediately aimed at practical action." In his essay Fisher reads "The Meaning of Working through the Past" alongside a less well-known essay, "Concerning the Democratization of German Universities." The two essays were written around the same time. Fisher argues that Adorno offers a "positive, if skeptical, normativity" in these writings on education: "if one is ruminating on the status of normativity, one should also consider his lesson plans, as offered in this series of essays" (78). In "Adorno's Lesson Plans?" Fisher emphasizes Adorno's focus on Germans' "affective skepticism" about democracy and explores how he encourages teachers and psychologists to address the lack of commitment to democracy that is part of the German culture (89). All this clearly works to reconfigure our conventional image of Adorno. Fisher repeatedly emphasizes the "surprising optimism about the university and education" that characterizes these writings (84). But, again, the picture of Adorno that we get is shaped by where we look: "Part of what makes these odd turns surprising for readers familiar with Adorno's works like *Dialectic of Enlightenment*, *Negative Dialectics*, and *Aesthetic Theory* is their optimism about institutional engagement, which he generally assiduously critiques. Reading for education demonstrates how Adorno did allow for one realm of collective and institutional optimism, an area

that explicitly engages with, but also renders far more complex, the wider reeducation issues of the time" (93). Exploring the neglected areas of Adorno's corpus, such as his writings on education, shows us a different picture of this key critical theorist: "These contexts include areas that have been generally underemphasized in his Anglophone reception: his addressing, conceptually as well as directly, debates in the postwar German public sphere; his affirmation of Enlightenment ideals . . . as a cornerstone of his educational project; the latter subsequently representative of a clear engagement with remarkably optimistic normativity and praxis, signs of his unfolding a more normative ethics" (98).

5. In his essay "What Might Education Mean after Abu Ghraib," Henry Giroux explores how Adorno's "Education after Auschwitz" raises fundamental questions "about how acts of inhumanity are inextricably connected to the pedagogical practices that shape the conditions that bring them into being" in ways that might inform us today, in a new era of barbarism and brutality that was brought to light when the pictures of soldiers with prisoners at Abu Ghraib surfaced (12). Giroux argues that Adorno recognizes that education is vitally important in creating autonomous subjects who are "capable of refusing to participate in unspeakable injustices while actively working to eliminate the conditions that make such injustices possible" (13). Adorno can help us think through the process of how violence and torture become normalized and acceptable, how our "consent" to these forms of brutality become manufactured as an acceptable part of the "war on terror," and how the educational system is inextricably part of how we got to Abu Ghraib, as well as how we can move beyond it: "Adorno was insistent that education was crucial as a point of departure for imagining autonomy, recognizing the interdependency of human life, and stopping cycles of violence" (20).

6. Tyson Lewis's essay "From Aesthetics to Pedagogy and Back: Rethinking the Works of Theodor Adorno," *InterActions: UCLA Journal of Education and Information Studies* 2, no. 1 (2006): 1–17, argues that Adorno's writings on aesthetics set up a problem that his works on pedagogy and school reform attempt to address in more practical terms. Lewis argues that Adorno's education writings engage the politically dangerous figure of the philistine, defined as someone closed off to aesthetic experience, but also shut off to social suffering, receptivity to the other, social contradictions, and negativity. For Lewis, Adorno's democratic pedagogy should work against coldness and hardness and instead cultivate an openness to the new, but in so doing, the goals of education and aesthetics overlap: "If education is able to pierce the crusted hardness and coldness inherent in our commodified world of late capitalism, then it adequately produces the preconditions for aesthetic experience" (12). Pedagogy must work against fascist forms of subjectivity, whereby "education prepares us not only for democratic life but also for the experience of an openness to openness, which for Adorno remains the point where the promise of future happiness is reclaimed against the resentment of the philistine" (15).

7. In "Adorno on Education" K. Daniel Cho explores how Adorno's writings on

institutional and cultural education could help prevent future genocides. Focusing on "Education after Auschwitz," Cho argues that Adorno's "various names for philosophy—from 'critique,' through 'reflective' and 'intellectual' thought, to 'expansive concentration'—are thus unified in the single phrase 'critical self-reflection'" and concludes that "Adorno's aim is a critically self-reflexive school" that in turn helps create "a critically self-reflexive culture" (89). The ultimate goal is to overcome the reified consciousness, manifested as "the liquidation of individuality in favour of fashion trends and consumable goods" as well as a general "refusal to think deeply, a plugging up of one's ears and a shutting of one's eyes" (87). For Adorno, Cho argues, only critical self-reflection can work against reification, and, ultimately, "reified consciousness and reflective concentration will be the two antipodes which determine whether Auschwitz returns or not" (84). But while Cho sees Adorno's writings on education as a positive and productive supplement to what he sees as the more relentlessly negative and critical *Negative Dialectics,* he concludes that the writings on education are ultimately lacking in "utopian imagination": "The problem is that critical self-reflection, even as Adorno understands it, appears to be too defensive a posture. Critical self-reflection is a negative or diagnostic form of thought only. Its function is therefore to uncover and lay bare the wider social contradictions that constitute the self. And, to be sure, Adorno's focus is on preserving the right to negative thinking. However, preventing the next Auschwitz requires working towards a society in which its preconditions no longer exist. And, while this project requires negative thought to diagnose the ills of existing society, it goes beyond the scope of negativity. It requires actively resolving those ills. The forging of such resolutions is thought's positive movement. In other words, while Adorno does well to attend to the negative moment of critique, he neglects the positive moment of what Marcuse, in *Eros and Civilisation,* describes as the 'utopian imagination.' Education after Auschwitz must be unabashedly utopian" (93). But Cho's argument here fails to appreciate how, for Adorno, critique itself is both negative and positive, diagnostic and utopian, all in the same moment. For Adorno, critique *is* utopian, in that it works to highlight the nonidentical elements of the surrounding world that point toward possible alternatives. Adorno sees his practice of critique as containing a utopian desire, but critique is also a productive praxis for change from "wrong life" to a better alternative that the nonidentical points toward, in a way that does move beyond what is purely diagnostic and negative.

8. Volker Heins's "Saying Things That Hurt: Adorno as Educator" is the piece on Adorno that would seem most closely aligned with my own project. Heins promises to offer an "account of Adorno's concept and practice of a 'democratic pedagogy'" and argues, "Adorno's pedagogical interventions are not a footnote to his social theory, but a key to understanding his entire oeuvre" (68). Drawing from materials in the Adorno archive, Heins makes a strong argument against what he calls the "simplistic" and "almost cartoonish" cliché about Adorno's "political abstinence" (69). Heins argues that Adorno's "democratic pedagogy" aimed to make the younger generation of German citizens more "emotionally and intellectually sensitive," better able

to "absorb and communicate the traumatic rendering of the barbarous crimes of Nazi Germany" (71). The goal was to "instill a sense of mindfulness of the destructive potential of modern society and a habit of 'identification with the victims'" (72). Adorno emphasizes "subjective experiences and moral intuitions" and focuses not on democratic institutions but on the need to reeducate people in terms of their tastes, habits, and ideas (72). This is all accurate, but at no point does Heins explain what is particularly *democratic* about Adorno's pedagogical style. Indeed, in another part of the essay, Heins interprets Adorno's style in a way that is interesting but strikingly *un*democratic. Heins describes Adorno's "educational activism" as "prophetic," referring to the Hebrew prophets. Heins argues that Adorno "attempted to create awareness of the catastrophic state of the world and the need for radical moral change in order to avert (a repetition of) the worst" (78). Adorno crafted a "pedagogical and prophetic narrative" that worked in part by issuing paradoxical "wisdom statements" that people believed because they were emotionally satisfying. As Heins writes of Adorno's many quotable aphorisms and maxims, "they *sound* right" (79). Adorno would "strengthen his charismatic claims to authority" by issuing these wisdom statements, which would work to move his audience by appealing to extrarational emotions and intuitions. Indeed, Heins ends the essay by citing a fan letter one young female student wrote to Adorno after hearing him lecture, describing how she felt at once "enthused" and "profoundly shaken," emphasizing that his teachings would "have a transformative effect on my entire life" (79). The problem with this essay generally, as in the other secondary literature on Adorno and education, is that the theme of democratic pedagogy is not explored deeply enough or tied to Adorno's larger theory. Negative dialectics and the practice of critique do not figure in the essay and are not tied to this discussion of democratic pedagogy, beyond Heins's insistence that there is consistency between the different parts of his work and that there are not "two Adornos." But the nature of that connection is not explored. Another indication of how the concept of democratic pedagogy is not tied to Adorno's larger theory and practice of negative dialectics concerns a statement Heins makes about the surprisingly optimistic tone of these writings on education. Heins notes that Adorno's "pedagogy is predicated on the Enlightenment-era faith in the educability of the public" and its ability to develop autonomy (74). But Heins also notes that this positive tone seems to be in deep conflict with other of Adorno's writings that emphasize modern forces that push people to conform and adapt. Heins notes the conflict and says he will address this tension in the concluding section of the essay, but ultimately he gives only this brief statement: "Adorno never quite resolves the paradox of calling upon people to change their attitude while claiming that things can't really be changed"; he concludes that this kind of "contradictory message was part of his distinctly prophetic appeal" (79). But as *Adorno and Democracy* shows, the picture looks different when Adorno's writings on education are situated within the context of his larger theory and practice of negative dialectics. In fact, the possibility of change is always encapsulated within the nonidentical (another concept that does not appear in Heins's essay), and an understanding of Adorno's concept of critique as a fundamental human praxis also shows that he sees the ability to think and feel against the given as a capacity that is always available to humans if they can open themselves up to the nonidentical and experience the objects of the world around them in a different way.

9. As Richard Shaull notes in the foreword to Paulo Freire, *Pedagogy of the Oppressed* (New York: Continuum, 2000), "At first sight, Paulo Freire's method of teaching illiterates in Latin America seems to belong to a different world from that in which we find ourselves in this country. . . . But there are certain parallels in the two situations that should not be overlooked. Our advanced technological society is rapidly making objects of most of us and subtly programming us into conformity to the logic of its system. To the degree that this happens, we are also becoming submerged in a new 'culture of silence'" (33).

10. Freire, *Pedagogy of the Oppressed,* 48.

11. Ibid.

12. Ibid., 72.

13. Ibid., 71.

14. Ibid., 72.

15. Ibid., 71.

16. Ibid., 74.

17. Ibid., 88.

18. Ibid.

19. Ibid.

20. Ibid., 78.

21. Ibid., 65.

22. Ibid., 85.

23. Ibid., 48.

24. Ibid.; emphasis in original.

25. Ibid., 49.

26. Ibid., 39.

27. Ibid., 81.

28. Ibid., 61.

29. Ibid, 60–61; emphasis in original.

30. Ibid., 66.

31. Ibid., 128.

32. Ibid., 66.

33. Ibid., 91.

34. Ibid., 67.

35. Ibid., 68.

36. Adorno, "The Meaning of Working through the Past," 100.

37. Adorno, "Education after Auschwitz," in *Critical Models,* 203.

38. Ibid., 204.

39. Adorno, "The Meaning of Working through the Past," 100.

40. Ibid., 99.
41. "Appendix 1," 298.
42. Ibid.
43. This dialogue has also been translated as "Education for Autonomy"; see Theodor Adorno and Hellmut Becker, "Education for Autonomy," trans. David J. Parent, *Telos* 56 (Summer 1983): 102–118. Of the two translations that have appeared in English, I use the more recent, Adorno and Becker, "Education for Maturity and Responsibility."
44. Adorno, "Education for Maturity and Responsibility," 21.
45. Ibid.
46. Ibid., 30.
47. Ibid.
48. Ibid., 23.
49. Adorno, "Taboos on the Teaching Vocation," in *Critical Models,* 190.
50. Adorno, "Education after Auschwitz, 198.
51. Ibid.
52. Adorno, "Taboos on the Teaching Vocation," 189–190.
53. Adorno, "Education after Auschwitz," 191.
54. Ibid.
55. Ibid., 193.
56. Ibid.
57. Ibid., 195.
58. Adorno, "Taboos on the Teaching Vocation," 178.
59. Ibid., 189.
60. Adorno, "Education for Maturity and Responsibility," 31.
61. Ibid.
62. Ibid.
63. Ibid.
64. Adorno, "Education after Auschwitz," 196.
65. "Appendix 1," 300.
66. Adorno, "Education for Maturity and Responsibility," 31.
67. Freire, *Pedagogy of the Oppressed,* 61.
68. Adorno, "Education for Maturity and Responsibility," 32.

## 6. Seeing Small-Scale Resistance

The epigraph is from Adorno, *The Psychological Technique of Martin Luther Thomas' Radio Addresses,* 51.

1. Holloway et al., *Negativity and Revolution,* emphatically affirms the new approach scholars are taking toward Adorno's politics. These essays evolved from a permanent seminar titled "Subjectivity and Critical Theory" that is run at the Institute of Social Sciences and Humanities at the Autonomous University of Puebla in Mexico. The seminar participants decided to read Adorno's *Negative Dialectics* as

a way "to go deeper in [their] critique of modern capitalism," but also because of their collective frustration at how anticapitalist political practices were increasingly being conceived of in terms of poststructuralist philosophies that were alien to, even opposed to, any kind of dialectics, citing the work of Louis Althusser, Gilles Deleuze, Félix Guattari, Michel Foucault, Jacques Derrida, Pierre Macherey, and also more recently Michael Hardt, Antonio Negri, and Paolo Virno (41–42). The contributors want to show how Adorno's notion of negative dialectics overcomes some of the problems of dialectics in general that prompted these thinkers to turn toward poststructuralism. The volume focuses almost exclusively on *Negative Dialectics* and does not engage with the secondary literature on Adorno or the rest of his corpus, and the essays do not always analyze this text with an understanding of his writings as a whole. Indeed, the editors concede most of these points at the outset. As they note, "This is not a book about Adorno; nor is it written by specialists in Adorno or set out to give a full and active portrayal of Adorno and his work. It is written, rather, by a number of people who consider it important for the development of anti-capitalist thought to read Adorno and particularly to develop his idea of negative dialectics" (3). They see their volume as both "an argument and an exploration. It argues that it is theoretically and politically important to develop the notion of a negative dialectic. But the argument is a challenge and an exploration. The movement of negation is a movement that detonates concepts, detonates power, detonates identity, detonates all that is familiar to us. It opens up a frightening, vertiginous, exciting world in which we are forced to question everything around us. . . . We write in a context in which Zapatistas have made '*preguntando caminamos*' (asking we walk) a central principle of both political practice and scientific thought. That is the tone, then, of our argument and our exploration: *preguntando caminamos,* asking we walk" (11). But a volume like this marks how much our image of Adorno has changed in recent years, foregrounding a highly political understanding of the practice of negative dialectics and also fruitfully engaging Adorno not as a dead institution to be studied, but as a thinker who might help us solve some pressing contemporary problems.

    2. Holloway, in "Why Adorno?" in *Negativity and Revolution,* wants to align Adorno with Tronti, who wrote "Lenin in England" two years before *Negative Dialectics* was published and advanced the theory of *operaismo,* turning "orthodox Marxism on its head and put[ting] working-class struggle (and not capital) at the centre of their analysis" (14). In a similar way, "Adorno . . . turned orthodox Marxism on its head and put non-identity at the centre of [his] analysis" (14–15). Adorno and Tronti are similar "because the autonomist project puts working-class struggle (or anti-capitalist struggle) at the centre of our understanding of the world, as driving force and not as reaction, and because the project of critical theory also puts working-class struggle (as non-identity) at the centre of our understanding of the world, as driving force, not as reaction" (15). Holloway goes on to say, though, that this requires us to understand the nonidentical not as "just a philosophical concept" but as "the con-

ceptualisation of a social force" (13). Holloway asks: "Am I, then, saying that we can replace 'working-class struggle' for 'non-identity' . . . ? Yes, but obviously only if we understand class struggle as the movement of non-identity (a tautology, since non-identity can only be understood as movement)" (15–16). For Holloway, "*we* are non-identity. The force that does not fit, the force that contradicts all identification, the force that overflows its subjectivity, *we*. And who are *we*? We are the subject, uncontainable within any definition. We can say that we are the working class, but that makes sense only if we understand 'working class' as a concept that explodes against itself, a concept that bursts its own bounds" (13–14; emphases in original). Holloway finds a "non-identitarian class *we*" in class struggle, in the "contradictory *we* who live in-and-against capitalist society," a "disjointed, ill-fitting, creative we," an "antagonistic, self-antagonistic we" (14; emphases in original). Holloway admits that he may be going out on a limb here, perhaps even "doing violence" to Adorno's thought: "Does Adorno actually say that *we* are non-identity? Not as far as I know. Perhaps I am reading him in a non-identitarian way, against and beyond Adorno. But how else can we understand non-identity?" (14; emphasis in original). But he argues that it is "a creative violence" that may "take us forward in the struggle against capitalism, against the identity of a system built on death" (16). Adorno certainly does understand the nonidentical as a force at work in the material conditions of society, but it might be a stretch to say he understands it in terms of a specific group of people or in terms of the working class, especially when we consider his thoughts toward mass society, his thoughts on alienation, the culture industry, and "damaged life." The major weakness of this volume generally is that it reads *Negative Dialectics* in total isolation from, and without any reference to, Adorno's other works. But, despite these disagreements, my project is sympathetic with this desire to *use* Adorno's negative dialectics as a theory and practice to inform political practice today.

3. Applying Adorno's method of negative dialectics, Apostolidis, *Stations of the Cross,* grants preponderance to the cultural object of Christian right radio, exploring what this monad might tell us about the larger social whole, and considering how its energies might be mobilized in different directions. For Apostolidis (following Marx and Adorno), "a radical approach to religion does not merely dismiss it as a pack of capitalist lies, but tries to convert its protestative strength into different modes of historically concrete expression" (7). He concludes, "Adornian critical theory contributes something additional and distinctive to these endeavors by continuing to insist that thought's self-reflexivity depends also on moments in which it 'grants precedence' to a cultural object and then allows the criticism of cultural experience to reflect back on social theory. This is the meaning of negative dialectics, and it is what we have done in this study by devoting concentrated attention to our cultural object, *Focus on the Family,* and then letting its social physiognomy provoke new considerations about how political forces to transform post-Fordist conditions might be mobilized, and how critical theory itself might be communicated, constructed, and verified in the process of doing this by entering practical contexts of American Christianity" (219).

For another example of how Apostolidis uses Adorno's theory to inform the current condition, see Apostolidis, "Negative Dialectics and Inclusive Communication."

4. Adorno, "The Problem of a New Type of Human Being," 466.

5. Ibid., 467.

6. Adorno, "Radio Physiognomics," 95.

7. Ibid.

8. Ibid., 96.

9. Ibid., 97.

10. Ibid., 97, 98, 100.

11. Ibid., 102.

12. Ibid., 104.

13. Ibid.

14. Adorno, "A Social Critique of Radio Music," 140.

15. Ibid.

16. Ibid.

17. Ibid., 141.

18. Ibid.

19. Adorno, "Radio Physiognomics," 106.

20. Ibid., 107.

21. Ibid., 108.

22. Ibid., 109.

23. Ibid., 112.

24. Ibid., 113.

25. Ibid.

26. Ibid., 112.

27. Adorno, "On Popular Music," 317.

28. Ibid., 320.

29. Ibid., 322.

30. Ibid., 321.

31. Ibid., 322.

32. Ibid., 326.

33. Adorno, "Radio Physiognomics," 55.

34. Ibid.

35. Ibid., 63–64.

36. Ibid., 64.

37. Ibid., 129.

38. Ibid.

39. Ibid., 88.

40. Ibid., 90; emphasis in original.

41. Ibid., 91.

42. Robert Hullot-Kentor, "Second Salvage: Prolegomenon to a Reconstruction of *Current of Music*," in *Current of Music*, 21.

43. Ibid.

44. Adorno, *Psychological Technique of Martin Luther Thomas' Radio Addresses,* 51.

45. Ibid.

46. Ibid.

47. Ibid., 52.

48. Ibid., 34.

49. Ibid., 66.

50. Marx, "Contribution to the Critique of Hegel's Philosophy of Right: Introduction," in *The Marx-Engels Reader,* ed. Mark C. Tucker, 2nd ed. (New York: W. W. Norton, 1978), 54; emphases in original.

51. Ibid.

52. Indeed, in "On the Jewish Question," in *The Marx-Engels Reader,* Marx is critical of those who focus solely on the political emancipation of the Jews, when the aim should be more universally the complete emancipation of all humans. As Marx says, "Human emancipation will only be complete when the real, individual man has absorbed into himself the abstract citizen, when as an individual man, in his everyday life, in his work, and in his relationships, he has become a species-being" (46).

53. Stephen Crook, the editor of *The Stars Down to Earth,* observes in his introduction, "Adorno and Irrational Authoritarianism": "For Adorno the prejudice, aggression and conformism of fascism could not be dismissed as a heteronomous intrusion into the otherwise civilized order of modern society. On the contrary, fascism is at home in capitalist modernity. . . . It was because he saw fascism as a possibility built into the very fabric of modern capitalism that Adorno was muted in his celebration of the defeat of its Italian and German manifestations. To state the case crudely, Adorno saw the commodified American culture of mass-consumption, movies, jazz and radio serials as putting into play the same basic psychodynamic principles that formed the basis of fascism: psychological dependency and social conformism" (13). Crook also remarks: "For Adorno there is a fundamental symmetry between mass-culture and fascism, both of which feed-off and reproduce immature character structures with high, almost child-like, dependency needs. Radio soap operas, newspaper astrology columns and fascist propaganda share the characteristic that they operate by at once meeting and manipulating the dependency needs of the pseudo-individual" (10–11).

54. Adorno, *The Stars Down to Earth,* 153.

55. Ibid., 155.

56. Ibid., 155–156.

57. Ibid., 156.

58. Ibid.

59. Ibid., 158.

60. Ibid., 131.

61. Ibid., 70.

62. Ibid., 71.

63. Ibid.

64. Ibid., 89.

65. Ibid., 105.

66. Ibid., 82.

67. Ibid., 128.

68. Ibid., 154.

69. See Adorno, "'What a Music Appreciation Hour Should Be': Exposé, Radio Programmes on WNYC and Draft," in *Current of Music*, 216–270.

70. Adorno, "Analytical Study of the *NBC Music Appreciation Hour*," in *Current of Music*, 165.

71. Ibid., 166.

72. Ibid., 167, 191.

73. Ibid., 183.

74. Ibid., 191.

75. Ibid.

76. Ibid., 199.

77. Ibid., 197.

78. Ibid., 173.

79. Ibid., 191.

80. Ibid., 210.

81. Adorno, "'What a Music Appreciation Hour Should Be,'" 218.

82. Ibid., 220, 221.

83. Ibid., 222.

84. Ibid.

85. Ibid., 219.

86. Ibid., 222.

87. Ibid., 219; emphasis in original.

88. Ibid.

## Conclusion

1. J. K. Gibson-Graham, *A Postcapitalist Politics* (Minneapolis: University of Minnesota Press, 2006).

2. Ibid., 71.

3. Ibid., xxxiv.

4. Ibid., xxxv, xxxvi.

5. Ibid., xxxvi.

6. Ibid., 131.

7. Ibid., 133.

8. Ibid., 152.

9. Ibid., 25.

10. Ibid., 51.

11. Ibid., 135.

12. Ibid., 137.

13. Ibid., 24.

14. Ibid.

15. Ibid., 152.

16. Ibid., 127.

17. Ibid., 128.

18. Ibid., 135.

19. Ibid., 136.

20. Ibid., 145.

21. Ibid., 137.

22. Ibid.

23. Ibid., 154.

24. Ibid., 162.

25. Ibid.

26. Eve Kosofsky Sedgwick, "Paranoid Reading and Reparative Reading, or, You're So Paranoid, You Probably Think This Essay Is about You," in *Touching Feeling: Affect, Pedagogy, Performativity* (Durham: Duke University Press, 2003), 123–152.

27. Gibson-Graham, *A Postcapitalist Politics,* 4; emphasis in original.

28. Ibid.

29. Ibid., 7.

30. Ibid., 54, 60.

31. Hannah Arendt, *Between Past and Future: Eight Exercises in Political Thought* (New York: Penguin Books, 1968), 115.

32. John Dryzek, Bonnie Honig, and Anne Phillips, eds., *The Oxford Handbook of Political Theory* (New York: Oxford University Press, 2006), 5.

33. Ibid., 4.

34. Sheldon Wolin, *The Presence of the Past: Essays on the State and the Constitution* (Baltimore: Johns Hopkins University Press, 1989), 1.

35. Jane Bennett, "From the Editor," *Political Theory* 41, no. 1 (2013): 3–4; emphasis in original.

36. Wendy Brown, "At the Edge," *Political Theory* 30, no. 4 (2002): 573–574.

37. Ibid., 574.

# Bibliography

Adorno, Theodor. "Analytical Study of the *NBC Music Appreciation Hour*." In *Current of Music: Elements of a Radio Theory*. Malden, Mass.: Polity, 2009.

———. "Anti-Semitism and Fascist Propaganda." In *The Stars Down to Earth and Other Essays on the Irrational in Culture*. Edited by Stephen Crook. 1994. Reprint, New York: Routledge, 2001.

———. "Anti-Semitism and Fascist Propaganda." In *Gesammelte Schriften*, vol. 8. Edited by Rolf Tiedemann et al. Frankfurt am Main: Suhrkamp, 1972.

———. "Appendix 1: Discussion to Professor Adorno's Lecture 'The Meaning of Working through the Past.'" In *Critical Models: Interventions and Catchwords*. Translated by Henry Pickford. New York: Columbia University Press, 2005.

———. "Concerning the Democratization of German Universities" ("Zur Demokratisierung der deutschen Universitäten"). In *Gesammelte Schriften*, vol. 20. Edited by Rolf Tiedemann et al. Frankfurt am Main: Suhrkamp, 1983.

———. *Critical Models: Interventions and Catchwords*. Translated by Henry Pickford. 1998. Reprint, New York: Columbia University Press, 2005.

———. *Current of Music: Elements of a Radio Theory*. Edited by Robert Hullot-Kentor. Malden, Mass.: Polity, 2009.

———. "Democratic Leadership and Mass Manipulation," in *Studies in Leadership: Leadership and Democratic Action*. Edited by Alvin Gouldner. 1950. Reprint, New York: Russell and Russell, 1965.

———. "Democratic Leadership and Mass Manipulation." In *Gesammelte Schriften*, vol. 20. Edited by Rolf Tiedemann et al. Frankfurt am Main: Suhrkamp, 1986.

———. "Education after Auschwitz." In *Critical Models: Interventions and Catchwords*. Translated by Henry Pickford. New York: Columbia University Press, 2005.

———. *Essays on Music*. Edited by Richard Leppert. Translated by Susan H. Gillespie. Berkeley: University of California Press, 2002.

———. "Freudian Theory and the Pattern of Fascist Propaganda." In *Gesammelte Schriften*, vol. 8. Edited by Rolf Tiedemann et al. Frankfurt am Main: Suhrkamp, 1972.

———. *Kant's "Critique of Pure Reason (1959)."* Translated by Rodney Livingstone. Stanford: Stanford University Press, 2001.

———. "Keine Angst vor dem Elfenbeinturm." *Der Spiegel*, 5 May 1969.

———. "The Meaning of Working through the Past." In *Critical Models: Interventions and Catchwords*. Translated by Henry Pickford. New York: Columbia University Press, 2005.

———. *Minima Moralia: Reflections from Damaged Life*. Translated by E. F. N. Jephcott. London: Verso, 1974.

———. *Minima Moralia: Reflexionen aus dem beschädigten Leben*. In *Gesammelte Schriften*, vol. 4. Edited by Rolf Tiedemann et al. Frankfurt am Main: Suhrkamp, 1951.

———. *Negative Dialectics*. Translated by E. B. Ashton. New York: Continuum, 1973.

———. *Negative Dialektik*. In *Gesammelte Schriften*, vol. 6. Edited by Rolf Tiedemann et al. Frankfurt am Main: Suhrkamp, 1970.

———. "On Popular Music." In *Current of Music: Elements of a Radio Theory*. Malden, Mass.: Polity, 2009.

———. *The Psychological Technique of Martin Luther Thomas' Radio Addresses*. Stanford: Stanford University Press, 2000.

———. *The Psychological Technique of Martin Luther Thomas' Radio Addresses*. In *Gesammelte Schriften*, vol. 9. Edited by Rolf Tiedemann et al. Frankfurt am Main: Suhrkamp, 1975.

———. "Radio Physiognomics." In *Current of Music: Elements of a Radio Theory*. Malden, Mass.: Polity, 2009.

———. "A Social Critique of Radio Music." In *Current of Music: Elements of a Radio Theory*. Malden, Mass.: Polity, 2009.

———. *The Stars Down to Earth and Other Essays on the Irrational in Culture*. Edited by Stephen Crook. 1994. Reprint, New York: Routledge, 2001.

———. *The Stars Down to Earth: The* Los Angeles Times *Astrology Column. Gesammelte Schriften*, vol. 9. Edited by Rolf Tiedemann et al. Frankfurt am Main: Suhrkamp, 1975.

———. *Studies in the Authoritarian Personality*. In *Gesammelte Schriften*, vol. 9. Edited by Rolf Tiedemann et al. Frankfurt am Main: Suhrkamp, 1975.

———. "Taboos on the Teaching Vocation." In *Critical Models: Interventions and Catchwords*. Translated by Henry Pickford. New York: Columbia University Press, 2005.

———. "'What a Music Appreciation Hour Should Be': Exposé, Radio Programmes on WNYC and Draft." In *Current of Music: Elements of a Radio Theory*. Malden, Mass.: Polity, 2009.

———. "Who's Afraid of the Ivory Tower? A Conversation with Theodor W. Adorno." Edited and translated by Gerhard Richter. In *Language without Soil: Adorno and Late Philosophical Modernity*. Edited by Gerhard Richter. New York: Fordham University Press, 2010, 227–238.

Adorno, Theodor, and Hellmut Becker. "Education for Autonomy." Translated by David J. Parent. *Telos* 56 (Summer 1983): 102–118.

———. "Education for Maturity and Responsibility." Translated by Robert French,

Jem Thomas, and Dorothee Weymann. *History of the Human Sciences* 12, no. 3 (1999): 21–34.

Adorno, Theodor, and Hanns Eisler. *Composing for the Films.* 1947. Reprint, New York: Continuum, 2007.

Adorno, Theodor, Else Frenkel-Brunswik, Daniel Levinson, and Nevitt Sanford. *The Authoritarian Personality.* 1950. Reprint, New York: W. W. Norton, 1993.

Adorno, Theodor, and Max Horkheimer. *Towards a New Manifesto.* Translated by Rodney Livingstone. New York: Verso, 2011.

Agamben, Giorgio, Alain Badiou, Daniel Bensaïd, Wendy Brown, Jean-Luc Nancy, Jacques Rancière, Kristin Ross, and Slavoj Žižek. Translated by William McCuaig. *Democracy in What State?* New York: Columbia University Press, 2011.

Ahmed, Sara. *The Promise of Happiness.* Durham: Duke University Press, 2010.

Apostolidis, Paul. "Negative Dialectics and Inclusive Communication." In *Feminist Interpretations of Theodor Adorno.* Edited by Renée Heberle. University Park: Pennsylvania State University Press, 2006, 233–256.

———. *Stations of the Cross: Adorno and Christian Right Radio.* Durham: Duke University Press, 2000.

Arendt, Hannah. *Between Past and Future: Eight Exercises in Political Thought.* New York: Penguin Books, 1968.

Balk, Alfred. *The Rise of Radio: From Marconi through the Golden Age.* Jefferson, N.C.: McFarland, 2006.

Bennett, Jane. "From the Editor," *Political Theory* 41, no. 1 (2013): 3–4.

Berlant, Lauren. *Cruel Optimism.* Durham: Duke University Press, 2011.

———. *The Queen of America Goes to Washington City: Essays on Sex and Citizenship.* Durham: Duke University Press, 1997.

Berman, Russell. "Adorno's Politics." In *Adorno: A Critical Reader.* Edited by Nigel Gibson and Andrew Rubin. Malden, Mass.: Blackwell, 2002.

Berman, Russell, Ulrich Plass, and Joshua Rayman, eds. Special issue, "Adorno and America," *Telos* 149 (Winter 2009).

Bernstein, J. M. *Adorno: Disenchantment and Ethics.* New York: Cambridge University Press, 2001.

———. "Intact and Fragmented Bodies: Versions of Ethics 'after Auschwitz.'" *New German Critique* 97 (2006): 31–52.

———. "Negative Dialectics as Fate." In *Cambridge Companion to Adorno.* Edited by Tom Huhn. New York: Cambridge University Press, 2004.

———. "Political Modernism: The New, Revolution, and Civil Disobedience in Arendt and Adorno." In *Arendt and Adorno: Political and Philosophical Investigations.* Edited by Lars Rensmann and Samir Gandesha. Stanford: Stanford University Press, 2012.

———. "Suffering Injustice: Misrecognition as Moral Injury in Critical Theory." In *Language without Soil: Adorno and Late Philosophical Modernity.* Edited by Gerhard Richter. New York: Fordham University Press, 2010.

Brennan, Teresa. *The Transmission of Affect*. Ithaca: Cornell University Press, 2004.

Brown, Wendy. "American Nightmare: Neoliberalism, Neoconservatism, and De-Democratization." *Political Theory* 34, no. 6 (2006): 690–714.

———. "At the Edge." *Political Theory* 30, no. 4 (2002): 556–576.

———. "Neoliberalism and the End of Liberal Democracy." In Brown, *Edgework: Critical Essays on Knowledge and Politics*. Princeton: Princeton University Press, 2005, 37–59.

———. "We Are All Democrats Now . . . ," in *Democracy in What State?* By Giorgio Agamben et al. Translated by William McCuaig. New York: Columbia University Press, 2011, 44–57.

Buck-Morss, Susan. *The Origin of Negative Dialectics*. New York: Free Press, 1977.

Cho, K. Daniel. "Adorno on Education; or, Can Critical Self-Reflection Prevent the Next Auschwitz?" *Historical Materialism* 17, no. 1 (2009): 74–97.

Claussen, Detlev. "Intellectual Transfer: Theodor W. Adorno's American Experience." *New German Critique* 97 (Winter 2006): 5–14.

———. *Theodor W. Adorno: One Last Genius*. Cambridge: Belknap Press of Harvard University Press, 2008.

Cook, Deborah, ed. *Adorno: Key Concepts*. Stocksfield, U.K.: Acumen, 2008.

Crook, Stephen. "Adorno and Irrational Authoritarianism." In *The Stars Down to Earth*. Edited by Stephen Crook. 1994. Reprint, New York: Routledge, 2001.

Cvetkovich, Ann. *Depression: A Public Feeling*. Durham: Duke University Press, 2012.

Douglas, Andrew. "Democratic Darkness and Adorno's Redemptive Criticism." *Philosophy and Social Criticism* 36, no. 7 (2010): 819–836.

Douglas, Susan J. *Listening In: Radio and the American Imagination*. Minneapolis: University of Minnesota Press, 2004.

Dryzek, John, Bonnie Honig, and Anne Phillips, eds. *The Oxford Handbook of Political Theory*. New York: Oxford University Press, 2006.

Fisher, Jaimey. "Adorno's Lesson Plans? The Ethics of (Re)Education in 'The Meaning of "Working through the Past."'" In *Language without Soil: Adorno and Late Philosophical Modernity*. Edited by Gerhard Richter. New York: Fordham University Press, 2010.

Foster, Roger. *Adorno: The Recovery of Experience*. Albany: State University of New York Press, 2007.

Freire, Paulo. *Pedagogy of the Oppressed*. New York: Continuum, 2000.

Gerhardt, Christina, ed. Special issue, "Adorno and Ethics." *New German Critique* 97, no. 1 (2006).

Gibson-Graham, J. K. *A Postcapitalist Politics*. Minneapolis: University of Minnesota Press, 2006.

Giroux, Henry. "What Might Education Mean after Abu Ghraib: Revisiting Adorno's Politics of Education." *Comparative Studies of South Asia, Africa and the Middle East* 24, no. 1 (2004): 3–22.

Gouldner, Alvin W. "Introduction." In *Studies in Leadership: Leadership and Democratic Action.* Edited by Alvin W. Gouldner. 1950. Reprint, New York: Russell and Russell, 1965.

Gregg, Melissa, and Gregory J. Seigworth. "Introduction: An Inventory of Shimmers." In *The Affect Theory Reader.* Edited by Melissa Gregg and Gregory J. Seigworth. Durham: Duke University Press, 2010.

Hammer, Espen. *Adorno & the Political.* New York: Routledge, 2006.

Hardt, Michael. "Foreword: What Affects Are Good For." In *The Affective Turn: Theorizing the Social.* Edited by Patricia Ticineto Clough with Jean O'Malley Halley. Durham: Duke University Press, 2007.

Heins, Volker. "Saying Things That Hurt: Adorno as Educator." *Thesis Eleven* 110, no. 1 (2012): 69–82.

Hilmes, Michele. *Radio Voices: American Broadcasting, 1922–1952.* Minneapolis: University of Minnesota Press, 1997.

Hohendahl, Peter Uwe. *The Fleeting Promise of Art: Adorno's Aesthetic Theory Revisited.* Ithaca: Cornell University Press, 2013.

———. *Prismatic Thought: Theodor W. Adorno.* Lincoln: University of Nebraska Press, 1995.

Holloway, John. "Why Adorno?" In *Negativity and Revolution: Adorno and Political Activism.* Edited by John Holloway, Fernando Matamoros, and Sergio Tischler. London: Pluto Press, 2009.

Holloway, John, Fernando Matamoros, and Sergio Tischler, eds. *Negativity and Revolution: Adorno and Political Activism.* London: Pluto Press, 2009.

Huhn, Tom, ed. *Cambridge Companion to Adorno.* New York: Cambridge University Press, 2004.

Hullot-Kentor, Robert. "Second Salvage: Prolegomenon to a Reconstruction of *Current of Music.*" In *Current of Music: Elements of a Radio Theory.* Malden, Mass.: Polity, 2009.

Jäger, Lorenz. *Adorno: A Political Biography.* Translated by Stewart Spencer. New Haven: Yale University Press, 2004.

Jay, Martin. "Adorno in America." In *Permanent Exile: Essays on the Intellectual Migration from Germany to America.* New York: Columbia University Press, 1986.

Jenemann, David. *Adorno in America.* Minneapolis: University of Minnesota Press, 2007.

Lewis, Tyson. "From Aesthetics to Pedagogy and Back: Rethinking the Works of Theodor Adorno." *InterActions: UCLA Journal of Education and Information Studies* 2, no. 1 (2006): 1–17.

Lowenthal, Leo. "The Utopian Motif in Suspension: A Conversation with Leo Lowenthal." Interview by W. Martin Lüdke. Translated by Ted R. Weeks. In *An Unmastered Past: The Autobiographical Reflections of Leo Lowenthal.* Edited by Martin Jay. Berkeley: University of California Press, 1987.

Lukács, Georg. *The Theory of the Novel.* Cambridge: MIT Press, 1994.

Marasco, Robyn. *The Highway of Despair: Critical Theory after Hegel.* New York: Columbia University Press, 2015.

Marcuse, Herbert. *One-Dimensional Man: Studies in the Ideology of Advanced Industrial Society.* 2nd ed. Boston: Beacon Press, 1991.

Mariotti, Shannon. "Adorno on the Radio: Democratic Leadership as Democratic Pedagogy." *Political Theory* 42, no. 4 (2014): 415–442.

———. "Communicating to the Demos." *Review of Politics* 72 (Summer 2010): 561–563.

———. "Critique from the Margins: Adorno and the Politics of Withdrawal." *Political Theory* 36, no. 3 (2008): 456–465.

———. "Damaged Life as Exuberant Vitality in America: Adorno, Alienation, and the Psychic Economy." *Telos* 149 (Winter 2009): 169–190.

———. *Thoreau's Democratic Withdrawal: Alienation, Participation, and Modernity.* Madison: University of Wisconsin Press, 2010.

Mariotti, Shannon L., and Joseph Lane. *A Political Companion to Marilynne Robinson.* Lexington: University Press of Kentucky, forthcoming.

Marx, Karl. *Capital,* vol. 1, *A Critique of Political Economy.* New York: Penguin, 1992.

———. "Contribution to the Critique of Hegel's Philosophy of Right: Introduction." In *The Marx-Engels Reader.* Edited by Mark C. Tucker. 2nd ed. New York: W. W. Norton, 1978.

———. "On the Jewish Question." In *The Marx-Engels Reader.* Edited by Mark C. Tucker. 2nd ed. New York: W. W. Norton, 1978.

Morris, Martin. *Rethinking the Communicative Turn: Adorno, Habermas, and the Problem of Communicative Freedom.* Albany: State University of New York Press, 2001.

Müller-Doohm, Stefan. *Adorno: A Biography.* Translated by Rodney Livingstone. Malden, Mass.: Polity Press, 2005.

O'Connor, Brian. *Adorno's Negative Dialectic: Philosophy and the Possibility of Critical Rationality.* Cambridge: MIT Press, 2004.

Offe, Claus. "Theodor W. Adorno: 'Culture Industry' and Other Views of the 'American Century.'" In *Reflections on America: Tocqueville, Weber, and Adorno in the United States.* Malden, Mass.: Polity, 2005, 69–92.

Rayman, Joshua. "Adorno's American Reception." *Telos* 149 (Winter 2009): 6–29.

Rensmann, Lars, and Samir Gandesha. "Understanding Political Modernity: Rereading Arendt and Adorno in Comparative Perspective." In *Arendt and Adorno: Political and Philosophical Investigations.* Edited by Lars Rensmann and Samir Gandesha. Stanford: Stanford University Press, 2012.

Robinson, Marilynne. *The Death of Adam: Essays on Modern Thought.* 1998. Reprint, New York: Picador, 2005.

———. *Gilead.* New York: Farrar, Straus and Giroux, 2004.

———. *Home.* New York: Farrar, Straus and Giroux, 2008.

———. *Housekeeping.* New York: Farrar, Straus and Giroux, 1980.

———. *When I Was a Child, I Read Books: Essays.* New York: Farrar, Straus and Giroux, 2012.

Schweppenhäuser, Gerhard. *Theodor W. Adorno: An Introduction.* Durham: Duke University Press, 2009.

Sedgwick, Eve Kosofsky. "Paranoid Reading and Reparative Reading, or, You're So Paranoid, You Probably Think This Essay Is about You." In *Touching Feeling: Affect, Pedagogy, Performativity.* Durham: Duke University Press, 2003, 123–152.

Tettlebaum, Marianne. "Political Philosophy." In *Adorno: Key Concepts.* Edited by Deborah Cook. Stocksfield, U.K.: Acumen, 2008.

Villa, Dana. "From the Critique of Identity to Plurality in Politics: Reconsidering Adorno and Arendt." In *Arendt and Adorno: Political and Philosophical Investigations.* Edited by Lars Rensmann and Samir Gandesha. Stanford: Stanford University Press, 2012.

Wallace, David Foster. *This Is Water: Some Thoughts, Delivered on a Significant Occasion, about Living a Compassionate Life.* New York: Little, Brown, 2009.

Wheatland, Thomas. *The Frankfurt School in Exile.* Minneapolis: University of Minnesota Press, 2009.

Wiggershaus, Rolf. *The Frankfurt School: Its History, Theories, and Political Significance.* Translated by Michael Robertson. 1993. Reprint, Cambridge: MIT Press, 1995.

Wilder, Adrian. "Pied Pipers and Polymaths: Adorno's Critique of Praxisism." In *Negativity and Revolution: Adorno and Political Activism.* Edited by John Holloway, Fernando Matamoros, and Sergio Tischler. London: Pluto Press, 2009.

Wolin, Richard. *The Frankfurt School Revisited, and Other Essays on Politics and Society.* New York: Routledge, 2006.

Wolin, Sheldon. *The Presence of the Past: Essays on the State and the Constitution.* Baltimore: Johns Hopkins University Press, 1989.

.

# Index

abstract exchange, 48–52
action: thinking as, 47
Adorno, Theodor: current political value of the works on democratic theory and practice, 18–19; democratic nature of the writings on education, 17–18; focus on and use of radio, 3–4; "message in a bottle" metaphor and, 1–3; modern studies of the political thought of, 67–68; "navigating difficult waters" metaphor and, 2, 3; paranoid and reparative modes of theorizing and, 153–55; place of America in the theorizing of, 15; political significance of the thoughts on experience, 17; political theory and world building, 12–13, 155–57; presence and importance of negative dialects within all the works of, 4, 10, 12–13, 16–17, 69; reassessment of the negativity and despair associated with, 20–23; a revised narrative of his relationship to the political, 13–14, 123–24
*Adorno: Disenchantment and Ethics* (Bernstein), 180–81n5
"Adorno in America" (Jay), 169–70n2
*Adorno in America* (Jenemann), 164–65n12, 164n11, 169n1
"Adorno on Education" (Cho), 189–90n7

"Adorno's Lesson Plans?" (Fisher), 188–89n4
*Adorno's Negative Dialectic* (O'Connor), 173–74n6
"Adorno's Politics" (Berman), 179–80n3
*Adorno & the Political* (Hammer), 181–83n6
affect: Adorno and, 61–65; concept of, 59–61; recent popularity of interdisciplinary work on, 58. *See also* affect theory
affective hope, 63–64
affective responses: nonidentical countertendencies as, 61, 62
affect theory: Adorno and, 47, 58–59, 61–65; affective hope, 63–64; connection between autonomy and receptivity, 45–46, 47; new materialism and, 64–65; overview, 59–61; queer theory and, 63; recent popularity of interdisciplinary work on the affects, 58
Ahmed, Sara, 61, 62, 177n49, 177–78n58
alienation: a case study in negative dialectics, 74–81; from democracy, Adorno's democratic pedagogy and, 116–17; from democracy as self-alienation, 70; as a determined cheerful normality in *Minima Moralia,* 30; Freire's analysis of *Pedagogy of the Oppressed,* 106–12;

209

nonidentical elements/qualities *(cont.)*
47, 74; community-research action
projects and a postcapitalist politics,
149–51; concept and discussion of,
54–56; countertendencies and, 97;
negative dialectics and, 55; political
stakes of experiencing, case study
from *Minima Moralia,* 74–81; the
promise of confrontations with,
63–64; the works of Marilynne
Robinson and, 82–83
nonidentical countertendencies: as
affective responses, 61, 62; as
feelings and emotions with political
significance, 62–63
"not living": Adorno's notion of, 76
noumenal, 52

O'Connor, Brian, 173–74n6
Offe, Claus, 15, 25–26, 171n5
Operation Boomerang: as
Adorno's project of democratic
enlightenment, 94, 95–98 (*see
also* democratic enlightenment);
community-action research projects
and, 148–49; countertendencies
and their transformative reversals,
125–34
oppression: Freire's analysis of in
*Pedagogy of the Oppressed,* 106–12
optimism: Berlant's notion of, 64

paranoid style of theorizing: Adorno
seen as a practitioner of, 154–55;
description of, 153–54
*Pedagogy of the Oppressed* (Freire), 106–12
personal interviews, 100
personalism: the physiognomy of
radio and, 33–34; used by the radio
demagogue Martin Luther Thomas,
38–39
phenomenal, 52

physiognomy of radio, 31–35
"Pied Pipers and Polymaths: Adorno's
Critique of Praxisism" (Wilder),
187–88n2
Pioneer Valley Rethinking Economy
project, 147–48
*Political Companion to Marilynne
Robinson, A* (Mariotti & Lane), 69
political problems: feelings and
emotions as indicators of, 62–63
political theory: Adorno and world
building, 12–13, 155–57
positivism: in Adorno's analysis of
the *Los Angeles Times*'s astrology
column, 42–43; the physiognomy
of radio and, 33–34; in the radio
speeches of Martin Luther Thomas,
39–40
postcapitalist politics, 145–53
*Postcapitalist Politics, A* (Gibson-
Graham), 145–53
praxis of critique: Adorno's concept of
democratic leadership and, 92–93;
"banking" concept of education
and, 109–10; democracy and
(*see* democracy and the praxis of
critique); to recover the essential
qualities of commodity, 49, 51–52;
as resistance, 51–52, 56–58. *See also*
critical consciousness; critique
prescribed happiness: a case study in
negative dialectics, 74–81
privacy: in Adorno's critique of radio,
34–35
"problem-posing method" of education,
110–12
*Promise of Happiness, The* (Ahmed), 61,
177–78n58, 177n49
propaganda, 103
protest: Adorno's rethinking of civic
education for, 118–19
pseudo-democracy: Adorno's analysis

www.ingramcontent.com/pod-product-compliance
Lightning Source LLC
Chambersburg PA
CBHW031546260326
41914CB00002B/299